THE LIGHT THAT UNITES

The Light That Unites

RABBI AARON GOLDSCHEIDER

ARTWORK BY
Aitana Perlmutter

OU PRESS

The Light That Unites

Revised Edition

Published by
OU PRESS
an imprint of the Orthodox Union
11 Broadway
New York, NY 10004
oupress.org
oupress@ou.org

First Edition published by Renana Publishers

ISBN: 978-1-61465-473-5
ARTWORK: Aitana Perlmutter
JACKET, BOOK DESIGN & ILLUSTRATION: Natalie Friedemann-Weinberg
TYPESETTING: Raphaël Freeman, Renana Typesetting

THE BERNARD AND RITA PITKOFF EDITION
OF THE LIGHT THAT UNITES

With gratitude to Hashem for the countless blessings in our lives, we dedicate
this book in honor of our parents, Bernard & Rita Pitkoff. Words cannot express
our appreciation and love for you both. You dedicated your lives to your children
and grandchildren and set us on a path of knowledge, faith, and Torah. You filled
our home with a love of family and heritage and a deep and abiding love of Israel.
You are the example of everything we hope our children will grow up to be.

Just as our parents taught us, we are commanded to teach our children and
pass on our traditions *mi'dor l'dor.* And so, we also dedicate this book to
our children, Joshua, Danielle, and Andrew, who make us so very proud
to be their parents each and every day. May Hashem continue to bless you
with honor, strength, courage, and joy. For you have been our blessing.

May this book, written by our rabbi and dear friend, Rabbi Aaron
Goldscheider, help illuminate the meaning and sanctify the celebration
of Chanukah as we gather together as Am Yisroel to light our menorahs
and thank Hashem for his bountiful blessings and for the miracles
he performed for our forefathers in their days at this time.

Dedicated by David & Cindy Pitkoff

EIGHT FLAMES OF WARMTH AND KINDNESS

First Night

Dedicated to our founding principal and guiding soul, Mr. Walter Schuchatowitz

The students of Bi-Cultural Day School, Stamford, CT

Second Night

In honor of my father, Jacques Siboni *z"l*, who, like the Maccabees before him, ignited the flame in the Israeli war of Independence in 1948, and kept it lit for his children, grandchildren and great grandchildren.

Dedicated by David and Myriam Siboni Leibowitz

Third Night

In loving memory of Michael Lazar Matz *z"l*

Dedicated by Dov and Beth Matz

Fourth Night

In loving memory of Fannie and Paul Gurman *z"l* and Alvin Boltax *z"l*

Dedicated by Ron and Nancy Gurman

Fifth Night

In loving memory of Esther Alix Bilski *z"l*

Sixth Night

In loving memory of Teddy Miller *z"l*

Seventh Night

In loving memory of Toby and Larry Levy *z"l*

Eighth Night

In gratitude to Hashem for the blessings of our children and grandchildren and in honor of our teachers, Rabbi Aaron and Karen Goldscheider.

Dedicated by Mitchell and Ricki Lubart.

CONTENTS

PREFACE

THE MITZVAH OF KINDLING THE CHANUKAH CANDLES IS FORMULATED IN AN odd manner in the Gemara (*Shabbat* 21b). The basic mitzvah is stated as *"ner ish u'beito,"* one candle is kindled for the entire household each night of Chanukah. The performance of the mitzvah is thus expressed as the obligation of the household, rather than in the customary form of an individual obligation.

One could ask why the Gemara formulated the mitzvah as a household obligation rather than an individual obligation. The answer is that our Sages wanted to emphasize a fundamental aspect of the Chanukah holiday – that, at its core, it celebrates the sanctity of the Jewish home and the Jewish family. They wanted to stress the importance of the Jewish household, and to teach us that Chanukah was not only about the battle to defend the Beit Hamikdash but also a battle to defend the Jewish family. There is an external Beit Hamikdash, but there is also an internal Beit Hamikdash, the Jewish home. As the Torah tells us, when the Almighty pronounced His commandment for the Jewish people to construct the Mishkan, the tabernacle in the desert, He said, "Let them make Me a Mikdash, and I will dwell among them." The *Shechina*, God's presence, dwells among the Jewish people in their homes, and each Jewish home is imbued with the qualities of the Beit Hamikdash. While the Greeks defiled the external Beit Hamikdash with pagan worship, they also viciously sought to desecrate the internal Beit Hamikdash, the Jewish family.

Maimonides, in recounting the historical background that led up to Chanukah, states (*Hilkhot Chanukah* 3:1), "…the Greek authorities imposed evil decrees on the Jews, and prohibited their religion, and did not permit them to study Torah or perform mitzvot, and took hold of their wealth and their daughters, and entered the Beit Hamikdash and defiled it…." Maimonides' reference to the Greeks' taking hold of the Jewish daughters is an allusion to the infamous practice that a bride was first subjected to rape by the governing official before being permitted to unite with her husband. The Greeks, perceiving the significance of the Jewish home and realizing that as long as its sanctity was intact they could never defeat the Jews, waged war against the Jewish home as vigorously as they tried to vanquish the Beit Hamikdash. Chanukah celebrates the Jewish victory in both theaters of that war.

Indeed, the Jewish family and the Jewish home have been viewed by our tradition as a microcosm of the Beit Hamikdash. Just as the Beit Hamikdash served as the beacon of Torah and Jewish identity on the national level, the Jewish home has served, on a more intimate level, as the bulwark of Torah values and means of transmitting the *mesorah*, our tradition, from generation to generation. Our Sages clearly perceived the critical role played by the Jewish home and its innate similarity to the Beit Hamikdash. They saw, for example, that the homes of the Matriarchs and Patriarchs partook of the same qualities as the Beit Hamikdash. Rashi, in his commentary on Chumash (Bereishit 24:67), quotes the Midrash that the tent of Sarah our Matriarch was endowed with three wondrous qualities: the Shabbat candles miraculously remained lit from one Shabbat to the next; the challah she prepared expanded far out of proportion to the ingredients she used; and clouds of glory continuously hovered over the tent. These wondrous qualities of Sarah's tent, the home she shared with Abraham our forefather, mirrored the sanctity of the Mishkan, the tabernacle in the desert that was the forerunner of the Beit Hamikdash: the flames of the Menorah remained lit continuously; the *lechem hapanim* — the loaves of show bread used in the service — stayed warm long after they would been expected to cool; and the Divine Presence, in the form of a protective cloud, constantly rested above.

The identity of the Jewish home with the Beit Hamikdash is the reason our Sages insisted on expressing the mitzvah lighting the Chanukah candles in its basic, most elemental form of observance — *ner ish u'beito* — as a household obligation. We must always remember the dimension of Chanukah which celebrates the victory of the Jewish home, its sanctity, unity, and everlasting vitality.

OU Press is proud to present *The Light That Unites* to the Jewish community. Rabbi Goldscheider has assembled an outstanding collection of material that will surely enhance the nightly experience of lighting Chanukah candles, and *The Light That Unites* will thereby further strengthen and enrich the Jewish home, a central theme of the Chanukah celebration.

Menachem Dov Genack
General Editor
OU Press

INTRODUCTION

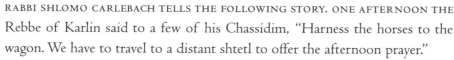

RABBI SHLOMO CARLEBACH TELLS THE FOLLOWING STORY. ONE AFTERNOON THE Rebbe of Karlin said to a few of his Chassidim, "Harness the horses to the wagon. We have to travel to a distant shtetl to offer the afternoon prayer."

They looked at each other in amazement, for they knew that the time was rapidly approaching when it would be too late for the afternoon prayer.

They traveled long past dark.

The Rebbe pointed in the direction they were traveling and said, "See that little inn on the top of the hill, at the edge of the shtetl? One of the few Jews in this shtetl lives in that inn. That's where we will pray."

The wagon stopped at the inn. The Rebbe and his Chassidim walked up the path and knocked on the door. A very old man responded to their knock. He stood in the doorway, startled.

The Chassidim addressed the old man: "We have arrived with our Rebbe from far away. We need to pray the afternoon service. May we come in?"

The old man moved away from the doorway, and the Rebbe and his Chassidim entered one by one. They knew that there must be a special reason for their Rebbe to have brought them to this place, though it was not apparent to them. Nevertheless, they began to pray very loudly, as this was their custom.

A few peasants who were on the street heard the loud noise and came to see. They were moved by the heartfelt prayers and the chance to be in this setting. After the service the peasants wanted to show how grateful they were for having been allowed to share in the holy prayer, so they ran home and returned with apples, grapes, and oranges.

Together they made a wonderful feast, and sang and danced and studied with the Rebbe until very late. The Rebbe blessed each of them and then told them that he needed to return home.

The Chassidim piled into the wagon. The Rebbe was the last to take a seat, and, as he boarded the wagon, he called the old man to come out of the inn. He said to him, "Nu, tell me already!"

The old man said hesitatingly, "I want you to know that my grandfather lived in this inn. Exactly one hundred years ago, when I was a lad of seven, the Baal Shem Tov (c. 1700–1760) was here. I remember the occasion so clearly. It was exactly like tonight. He arrived late with a group of his followers. He asked my grandfather if he could daven Minchah in this inn.

"When the peasants heard the prayers they came to join him. They made a feast and danced together. Afterwards the Baal Shem Tov blessed each of them.

"Before he left, the Baal Shem Tov put his hands on my head and said, 'My dear little boy, remember what I am telling you. I want you to know that one hundred years from now, someone will come here. He will do the same thing I did. Tell him I was here. Tell him I was here.'"

The Jew has lovingly lit the Chanukah menorah for close to two thousand years. We gather with family and friends to celebrate these inspiring days, commemorating ancient events that still speak with relevance and meaning to our own lives. For generations Jews have lit the menorah, and will continue to light and celebrate these eight wondrous days for the rest of time.

The sacred days of Chanukah are a time when we open our hearts to the light of God.

The Jewish soul is drawn to Chanukah. These sacred days rekindle hope in the heart of every Jew. The Jewish soul is drawn to the flames of the menorah, to the amazing miracles, to the bravery and heroism of our ancestors. Our souls expand to feel an even deeper longing for holiness.

The Light That Unites

What is it that draws each of us to the light of Chanukah?

Jews across the world feel a unique bond on Chanukah, not easily matched by any other time in the Jewish calendar. Not only does lighting the menorah unite families, bringing grandparents, parents, and children closer to one another, but also we recognize that what we are doing in our homes is being reenacted in Jewish homes around the world. We feel part of a much larger, unifying ritual.

During these sacred days, entire Jewish communities come together to light the menorah and to offer praise and gratitude to God. The Chanukah light unites us all.

On a deeper level, the holiday of Chanukah does not just connect us with those around us, but also unites us with those who preceded us and those who will follow. Our act of lighting the menorah connects us with the first Menorah lighting, which took place three thousand years ago.

Aaron, the high priest, lit the Menorah each day that the Israelites traveled through the wilderness. So important was this act that, according to our Sages, God revealed to Aaron that even after the Temple's destruction, amazingly, the lighting of the Menorah would be passed on from generation to generation.

God tells Aaron: In the future, heroic defenders of our faith, the Maccabees, will reclaim the Holy Temple in Jerusalem and will light the Menorah. Hundreds of years after the era of the Maccabees, sadly, the Temple will again be destroyed and the Jewish people will be dispersed. But the Menorah will not be forgotten (Ramban, Numbers 8:2).

Jewish families all over the world, for generations to come, will continue to light the menorah. The menorah lives on.

When each of us lights the menorah, there is another aspect of *uniting* we should be aware of. Namely, Judaism teaches that each person is endowed with a divine spark, an inner light, which God implanted in each one of us. As it says in the Torah verse, "this light is good" (Genesis 1:4) — there is hidden potential within the heart of each person. Chanukah reminds us of our inner light, our God-given talents, and our uniqueness that we strive to reveal to the world.

Chanukah unites us with our very essence.

Transforming Your Menorah Lighting

> "It is fitting to recite many joyous songs and poems during the half hour after the candles are lit. It is fitting to recount and tell one's children and family members the miracles and wonders that God performed for us."
>
> (Rabbi Alexander Ziskind, *Yesod V'Shoresh Ha'avodah, sha'ar 12, ch. 1*)

For those who wish to deepen the experience of lighting the menorah, this book is meant to help you accomplish this goal.

When we light the Chanukah candles, there is, of course, the mechanical act of lighting. This, however, is merely a physical act. Rabbi Joseph Soloveitchik (1903–1993) taught that if this is all we do, then our lighting lacks the fullest expression of the mitzvah.

What does one need to do in order to celebrate Chanukah fully?

Above all we must internalize the feeling of gratitude. This is the genuine fulfillment of the commandment: thanking and extolling God for the miracle and for our ability to perform the mitzvah. Ideally, we do so with profound appreciation for God's protection, His care, His concern, and the miracles that God provided in days past and in our day.

The custom of remaining present and rejoicing in front of the Chanukah candles perfectly reenacts the way the miracle first occurred. At the time of the first Chanukah, when the Menorah was lit in the newly rededicated Temple, the Jews gazed in wonder at the flames that were not burning out. This is another reason that we stress the importance of gazing at the candles and joyously celebrate following their kindling.

Our Chanukah lighting should also be engaging, replete with words of wisdom and inspiring thoughts that awaken our souls and lift our hearts.

The Kotzker Rebbe (1787–1859) uniquely explained the Torah verse "You shall keep My decrees and My laws that a person does, and *live by them*" (Leviticus 18:15). He teaches that we should perform the commandments with vitality and fervor, not out of habit, not by rote. We need to bring life to the performance of the mitzvot.

Our Chassidic tradition places special emphasis on the moments following the lighting. For example, the beloved Chassidic Rebbe Levi Yitzchak of Berditchev (c. 1740–1810) teaches that Chanukah is a holiday that celebrates the Torah. The Syrian Greeks sought to eradicate the Jewish people's unique devotion to Torah and its study. God brought about miracles to ensure its preservation. Therefore, it is most fitting that Chanukah should be filled with words of Torah, as we demonstrate our love and appreciation for the Torah and for its salvation.

Rabbi Joseph Soloveitchik taught that the greatness of Chanukah consists not so much in the importance of the miracles that occurred *ba'yamim hahem*, "in days of yore," more than two thousand years ago, but most importantly *ba'zman hazeh*, "in our times." The greatness is in the meaning of the ancient miracles in the here and now.

Every year we need to rediscover the miracle of Chanukah; to reexperience and relive it for ourselves. The more one is inspired by the lighting, the greater the mitzvah one performs.

How Best to Use This Book: A Chanukah Companion

Think of this book as a companion for your lighting ritual, in effect a "Haggadah for Chanukah." The traditional blessings and prayers are included, as well as appropriate Psalms with commentary.

Rabbi Joseph Soloveitchik once commented that Chanukah has yet to be mined for its multifaceted insights and relevant lessons. This volume is a humble attempt to address that need, to fill that void. In that spirit, eight major themes of Chanukah are illuminated:

1) PEACE   5) MIRACLES

2) LOVE   6) HOPE

3) FAMILY   7) UNITY

4) HEROISM   8) HOLINESS

These themes capture some of the holiday's most engaging and relevant motifs.

Each night of Chanukah, a new theme is illuminated together with relevant Torah teachings and inspirational stories, corresponding to the number of candles that are lit that particular night (one teaching for night one, two teachings for night two, etc.).

The Torah teachers in this volume span the generations. The insights of the ancient giants, such as the Rambam (Maimonides, 1135–1204) and Ibn Ezra (1089–1167), are interspersed alongside contemporary sages, such as the Chafetz Chaim (1839–1933), Rabbi Abraham Isaac Kook (1865–1935), and the Lubavitcher Rebbe (1902–1994).

There are thirty-six candles that are lit during Chanukah (1 + 2 + 3 + 4 + 5 + 6 + 7 + 8 = 36), not including the *shamash* candle, which is used only to facilitate the lighting. This book therefore contains thirty-six teachings – one teaching per candle. While the candles are burning, try reading some of the thoughts connected with that night, or, even better, share them aloud.

The Birkat Hamazon, Grace after Meals, is also included in this volume with a variety of comments on the Al Hanisim prayer, with the hope that your celebration with friends and family will also include a festive and enriching Chanukah meal.

Turning Our Children into Great Lights

On Chanukah, when Jewish consciousness yearns for our great and meaningful future, it is no wonder that our attention turns to our children. Children represent the future.

When a child first comes into the world, we pray that he or she will become a great light.

Immediately following the circumcision at a *brit milah*, we name the baby boy with the recital of *kriat hashem*, literally "calling the name," announcing the baby's name for the first time. The recital concludes with the wish on behalf of all those present, *Zeh hakatan gadol yihyeh*, "May this little one become great."

This is certainly not merely a wish for the tiny child to get bigger.

Rabbi Joseph Soloveitchik suggested that the key to understanding the words *gadol* and *katan*, "great" and "little," is to study these words where they first appear in the Torah. The words appear for the very first time, and in the same verse, in reference to the sun and the moon, "And God made two great lights, a great light to rule the day and a little light to rule the night…" (Genesis 1:16). The *gadol*, "the great light," refers to the sun and the *katan*, "the little one," refers to the moon. The moon is not itself a light source; it gets its light from the sun. A *katan* receives and reflects, while the *gadol*, the great one, gives.

This is precisely what we intend to convey when we bless a new baby. The child is now a *katan*; he is a receiver of light. We pray that the child will learn from his parents and teachers and will emulate and reflect their ways, absorbing their noble qualities.

More importantly, though, we pray that the child grow and develop into a *gadol*, who, like the sun, will be a great source of light, providing illumination to the world. Strengthened by the Torah and living a committed life, the growing child will hopefully mature into a shining example to others, providing warmth and wisdom.

In the candles of the menorah we envision the illumination to which we aspire for our children: that they blossom into lights, becoming models of inspiration to others.

Chanukah: A Framework for Our Future

In the epic story of the Akeidah or the Binding of Isaac, Abraham and Isaac walk toward Mount Moriah to fulfill the command of God. Two servants also accompany them on this journey. As Abraham prepares to ascend the mountain, he turns to his two servants and says: *Shvu lachem poh…v'ani v'hana'ar nelcha ad koh* (שְׁבוּ לָכֶם פֹּה...וַאֲנִי וְהַנַּעַר, נֵלְכָה עַד־כֹּה), "You stay here…and I and the lad will go there" (Genesis 22:5).

Rabbi Joseph Soloveitchik asks: What was Abraham implying with these words?

For all of mankind the here and now is of utmost importance. This is the meaning of Abraham stating you are *poh*, "here." You are here; as members of the nations of the world, you give your attention to where you are now and where you have come from. The worldview of the servants covers the past and present only, not making them fit to join in the unique destiny of the Jewish people.

The Jewish people, on the other hand, strive to reach a grand and exalted future. This is the meaning of Abraham's term *koh*, "there." The Jew lives in the present with a covenantal promise of a future messianic day. The heart of the Jew is alive with a yearning for wholeness and peace. We work to bring that day closer. Rabbi Soloveitchik said that for the Jew, "the future is responsible for the present."

A novel Chassidic teaching boldly suggests that there is an allusion to Chanukah in this verse and that the festival of Chanukah embodies the Jewish expectation of the coming of the Messiah.

Chanukah is hinted at with the word *koh* (כֹּה). These letters represent the date of the festival (25 = כה) and make up the second half of the word *Chanukah*: *chaf-heh* (חנו-כה).

Embedded within the theme of Chanukah is an allusion to our unique destiny. Chanukah is the only holiday whose underlying events happened in Israel. It is the only holiday that centers around the Temple. Chanukah awakens the Jew's mind and heart to the grand vision of the future. The golden Menorah will once again offer its illumination *b'chatzrot kodshecha*, "in the holy courtyard" of Jerusalem in all of its glory.

The spiritual master the Sfat Emet, the great Gerrer Rebbe (1847–1905), once remarked that we have the custom to light the menorah at the doorway because Chanukah signals the ultimate salvation and the rededication of the entire world. Lighting the menorah at the doorway demonstrates how the days of Chanukah are symbolically the "door" or "entranceway," the beginning of the ultimate redemption.

In essence, Chanukah is the story of our unique destiny. It is one of those great moments of mystery and triumph, in which a great but threatened people are almost overcome and destroyed by a menacing and muscular culture with completely antithetical values and morality.

Suddenly, indeed miraculously, with great inner strength, that people – the Jewish people – triumph and rise to even greater heights.

Chanukah thus becomes an important milestone in the dramatic story of Jewish survival and our inexplicable ability to thrive against all odds. We celebrate God's guiding hand, once again redeeming our people from despair and replacing the darkness with a world of light and hope.

The Menorah Will Be Lit Again: A Prayer

Chanukah fills us with blessing and light. We pray that we will be transformed and uplifted, discovering our faith in God and love for our fellow person. We pray that the light of Chanukah will light our way within the darkness, and that we will be redeemed.

The following was the heartfelt prayer offered by the great lover of the Jewish people, the Chassidic master Rabbi Levi Yitzchak of Berditchev:

Master of the World, what does it take to rebuild the Holy Temple in Jerusalem? Some iron, some stones, and some water.
Well, we have plenty of that.

Iron?
Look at the ironclad resilience of your people. We have been tested time and time again, and we have remained steadfast and strong like iron. So many have tried to force us to bend our ways and we have not bent one iota.

Stone?
Father in heaven, You know that there have been those of us who have not

been able to withstand the suffering, and their hearts have turned to stone. They have tried, but the challenges have been too great; their soft and sensitive hearts have been transformed into stone.

Water?

*Oy...*dear God, how many tears have been shed throughout our long and bitter exile? How many broken hearts have cried rivers and oceans of tears? How many tears have been spilled over the tragedies of our brothers and sisters?

So You see, You have everything You need.
Then what are You waiting for?

✳   ✳   ✳

I humbly thank God for the gift of writing a work of Torah teachings in the holy city of Jerusalem. It is a dream come true to produce this book in the place where our prophets, thousands of years ago, prophesied: *Ki mi'tzion tetzei Torah, u'dvar Hashem mi'rushalayim* (כִּי מִצִּיּוֹן תֵּצֵא תוֹרָה, וּדְבַר־יְהֹוָה מִירוּשָׁלָם), "From Zion shall go forth the teachings of Torah and the word of God from Jerusalem" (Micah 4:2, Isaiah 2:3). May this work be a small contribution in bringing about the final redemption.

תם ונשלם בעז"ה ית' וית'
תושלב"ע

Aaron Goldscheider
Jerusalem, Israel
Chanukah 5778

Lighting the Menorah

PREPARING TO LIGHT

Eight Tips to Enhance Your Chanukah Celebration

Lighting the menorah is one of those special moments; we want it to be lasting and memorable. Our Sages advise not to rush through this precious mitzvah. Slow down. Be wholeheartedly in the moment.

Pious Jews have been known to recite the entire book of Psalms while sitting by the menorah. Some have had the custom of reflecting and meditating while gazing at the candles.

These customs are meant to deepen the experience of kindling the Chanukah candles. They may be best captured in an old Chassidic saying: "Sit by the candles and listen to the story that they tell."

The following are eight tried-and-true ways to make your Chanukah celebration more engaging.

1. GATHER THE FAMILY TOGETHER. When it is time to light the menorah, make sure everyone is present. There are some sources that suggest that the age-old custom of playing dreidel was originally intended to ensure that the children would be present for the lighting and would stay for a while thereafter. Simply gathering the family for the lighting already transforms this moment into a happening. Each person lighting a menorah makes the experience even more engaging.

2. TURN OFF THE LIGHTS. There are those who have the tradition of turning off the lights in the room before lighting, thereby giving center stage to the real star of the show: the menorah. Make sure everyone has a menorah to light — especially the children. It is a thrill for children to light the menorah and to watch it flicker and burn.

3. GATHER CHAIRS FACING THE MENORAH. Following the lighting, sit down

together. Share a relevant thought, the Chanukah story, or a story of a modern-day Jewish hero that highlights the themes of the day. Or share your own memory of Chanukahs past. Those who are blessed to have grandparents present, sit and listen to their stories as they share their own Chanukah memories. How beautiful it is to experience the passing of tradition from one generation to another before our very eyes.

4. NO WORK, PLEASE. According to Jewish custom, no work should be done in the house while the flames remain lit. Put aside the phone calls, electronics, and answering your e-mails. Instead, give your total attention to the beauty of the night and of your family. It is the "holiday of the home," says the Talmud. Let nothing interfere with letting the beautiful light of Chanukah fill your home.

5. DANCE TOGETHER. Once the candles are lit, play some joyous music. Take your children, your family, and your friends by the hand — and dance. The days of Chanukah are meant to fill us with happiness. Dancing is one of the best ways to feel the joy of the moment. There is something about holding hands and lifting one's feet that brings a smile to everyone's face.

6. OFFER A PRIVATE PRAYER. The beloved Chassidic master Rebbe Nachman of Breslov taught that the time during which the candles are lit is a sacred moment for prayer. After all, in the eyes of the mystics, these aren't just any candles. These are flames that connect us to both the miraculous and the eternal.

Do you have a friend who, unfortunately, is ill? Is there a family member or friend who is going through hard times? Pray for those in need at this time. Choose a prayer from the book of Psalms or offer personal words. In the presence of the holy flames, we can open ourselves to heartfelt prayers.

7. INVITE FRIENDS AND FAMILY TO SHARE THE LIGHTING WITH YOU. A great rabbi once said, "If you want your holiday to be meaningful, give it to somebody else." The more we share the holiday with others, the greater the experience will be for ourselves and for our families.

8. ENJOY A CELEBRATORY DINNER. What a beautiful custom to celebrate Chanukah with a meal that honors the holiday! While the menorah is still lit, sit around the dinner table and enjoy delicious holiday foods. For some it's fried potato latkes, for others jelly donuts; still others have the custom of serving dairy delights. Whatever you choose, these delicious foods give us a real taste of the miracle.

Winter, when the daylight hours are the shortest, is the darkest time of the year. We all need the Chanukah light. Our souls yearn for it.

The eight nights of Chanukah offer many precious gifts. They fill us with hope, provide us with encouragement, and offer us a renewal that will carry us through the weeks and months to come.

Incorporating the hints above will enrich and personalize the beauty of Chanukah. Each of us can enjoy our best Chanukah ever.

Instructions for Lighting

The candles are added to the menorah each night from right to left, but are kindled from left to right. This means that facing the menorah, the rightmost candle is the first candle to be kindled on the first night. Each subsequent night, a candle is added to the left.

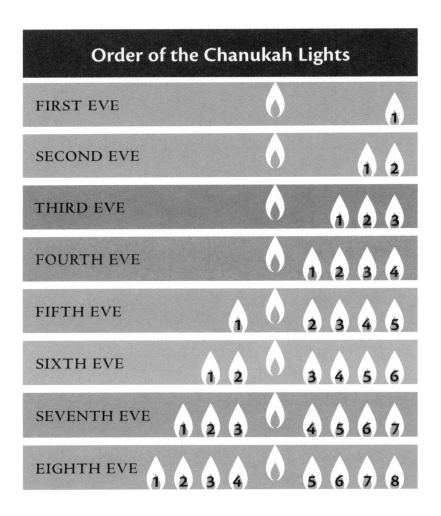

Prayers before Lighting

Before the lighting of the menorah, the entire household should gather for the kindling, in order to publicize the miracle.

Some have the custom of reciting preliminary prayers before lighting, which are intended to encourage the meaningful fulfillment of the mitzvah. These prayers should inspire great joy and a heightened awareness of the special meaning of the menorah lighting.

The text of two of these prayers is presented below. They were composed by *tzaddikim*, righteous rabbis, to help us focus on the deeper meaning of this unique mitzvah.

A Prayer by Rebbe Tzvi Elimelech of Dinov, author of the Bnei Yissaschar

The Chassidic master the Dinover Rebbe (1783–1841) is widely considered the "Rebbe of Chanukah" because of his passionate emphasis in his writings on the themes of this precious holiday. He penned the following meditation as a prayer to be recited before lighting. The Rebbe has us focus on kindling with great enthusiasm and love, capturing in our hearts the spirit of our forefathers who witnessed first hand the miracle of Chanukah.

לְשֵׁם יִחוּד קוּדְשָׁא בְּרִיךְ הוּא וּשְׁכִינְתֵּהּ, בִּדְחִילוּ וּרְחִימוּ, וּרְחִימוּ וּדְחִילוּ, לְיַחֵד שֵׁם י״ה בּו״ה בְּיִחוּדָא שְׁלִים, בְּשֵׁם כָּל יִשְׂרָאֵל. הִנְנִי מְכַוֵּן בְּהַדְלָקַת נֵר חֲנֻכָּה לְקַיֵּם מִצְוַת בּוֹרְאִי כַּאֲשֶׁר צִוּוּנִי חֲכָמֵינוּ זִכְרוֹנָם לִבְרָכָה, לְתַקֵּן אֶת שׁוֹרְשָׁהּ בִּמְקוֹם עֶלְיוֹן.

וּבְכֵן, יְהִי רָצוֹן מִלְּפָנֶיךָ יְיָ אֱלֹהֵינוּ וֵאלֹהֵי אֲבוֹתֵינוּ, שֶׁתְּהֵא חֲשׁוּבָה וּמְקֻבֶּלֶת וּמְרֻצָּה לְפָנֶיךָ מִצְוַת הַדְלָקַת נֵר חֲנֻכָּה, כְּאִלּוּ כִּוַּנְתִּי כָּל הַכַּוָּנוֹת שֶׁכִּוְּנוּ הַכֹּהֲנִים מְשָׁרְתֵי הַשֵּׁם בְּעֵת אֲשֶׁר הֶעֱרוּ לַמָּוֶת נַפְשָׁם בִּשְׁבִיל כְּבוֹד שִׁמְךָ הַגָּדוֹל הַגִּבּוֹר וְהַנּוֹרָא. וְאַתָּה בְּרַחֲמֶיךָ הָרַבִּים עוֹרַדְתָּ נִצְחֲךָ עֲלֵיהֶם לְנַצֵּחַ אֶת אוֹיְבֵיהֶם וּלְנַצֵּחַ עַל מְלֶאכֶת בֵּית יְיָ. וְהִנְנִי עוֹשֶׂה עַל דַּעְתָּם וְעַל כַּוָּנָתָם וְעַל דַּעַת כָּל הַצַּדִּיקִים וְהַחֲסִידִים שֶׁהָיוּ בְּאוֹתוֹ הַדּוֹר שֶׁהֻשְׁפְּעָה לָהֶם נִסָּיךְ וְזָכוּ לְאוֹר בְּאוֹר הַחַיִּים, וְעַל דַּעַת כָּל הַצַּדִּיקִים וְהַחֲסִידִים שֶׁבְּדוֹרוֹתֵינוּ, וּפִי כְּפִיהֶם וַעֲשִׂיתִי כַּעֲשִׂיתָם. וּבִזְכוּת הַמִּצְוָה הַזֹּאת תְּזַכֵּנוּ לְנַצֵּחַ אֶת אוֹיְבֵינוּ וּלְנַצֵּחַ עַל מְלֶאכֶת בֵּית יְיָ, וְגַלֵּה כְּבוֹד מַלְכוּתְךָ עָלֵינוּ מְהֵרָה וְלֹא יָמוּשׁ הַתּוֹרָה מִפִּינוּ וּמִפִּי זַרְעֵינוּ וּמִפִּי זֶרַע זַרְעֵינוּ מֵעַתָּה וְעַד עוֹלָם, וְנִזְכֶּה לְבָנִים תַּלְמִידֵי חֲכָמִים. אָמֵן, כֵּן יְהִי רָצוֹן. קַדְּשֵׁנוּ בְּמִצְוֹתֶיךָ וְתֵן חֶלְקֵנוּ בְּתוֹרָתֶךָ, שַׂבְּעֵנוּ מִטּוּבֶךָ וְשַׂמַּח נַפְשֵׁנוּ בִּישׁוּעָתֶךָ, וְטַהֵר לִבֵּנוּ לְעָבְדְּךָ בֶּאֱמֶת. מְלֹךְ עַל

כָּל הָעוֹלָם כֻּלּוֹ בִּכְבוֹדֶךָ, וְהִנָּשֵׂא עַל כָּל הָאָרֶץ בִּיקָרֶךָ, וְהוֹפַע בַּהֲדַר גְּאוֹן עֻזֶּךָ עַל כָּל יוֹשְׁבֵי תֵבֵל אַרְצֶךָ, וְיֵדַע כָּל פָּעוּל כִּי אַתָּה פְעַלְתּוֹ וְיָבִין כָּל יָצוּר כִּי אַתָּה יְצַרְתּוֹ, וְיֹאמַר כֹּל אֲשֶׁר נְשָׁמָה בְאַפּ״וֹ (בגי׳ חנוכ״ה) יְהֹו״ה אֱלֹהֵ״י יִשְׂרָאֵ״ל מֶלֶ״ךְ וּמַלְכוּתוֹ בַּכֹּ״ל מָשָׁלָ״ה (בגי׳ כ״ו פעמים חנ״ה אותיות חנוכ״ה, ובגי׳ מתתיה״ו ב״ן יוחנ״ן כה״ן גדו״ל חשמונ״אי ובני״ו), אָמֵן נֶצַח סֶלָה וָעֶד.

For the sake of the unification of the Holy One, blessed be He, and His Divine Presence, in fear and in love, and in love and in fear, to unify the name Yud-Kei with Vav-Kei in perfect unity, in the name of all Israel. Behold, in kindling the Chanukah light, I intend to fulfill the commandment of my Creator, as our Sages, of blessed memory, have commanded me, to perfect its root on high.

And so, may it be Your will, Lord, our God and God of our forefathers, that this mitzvah of (my) kindling the Chanukah light be considered as worthy, acceptable, and favorable before You as if I had in mind all the intentions (intended for this mitzvah) that the *kohanim*, the ministers of Hashem, had in mind, when they put their lives on the line for the sake of the honor of Your great, mighty, and awesome name, You in Your great mercy awakened victory for them, to defeat their enemies, and to oversee the work of the Temple of Hashem. And behold, I am acting according to their thought and their intention, and according to the intention of all the righteous and pious ones of that same generation (of Chanukah), for whom You (Hashem) bestowed Your miracle though which they merited to bask in the light of the living, and (I am acting) according to the intention of all the righteous and pious in our generation — may my mouth be as their mouths, and may my actions be as their actions (with respect to my performance of the mitzvah of lighting the Chanukah lights). And in the merit of this mitzvah, may we merit to defeat our enemies, and oversee the work of the Temple of Hashem, and reveal the glory of Your kingship upon us speedily, and may the Torah not depart from our mouths, nor from the mouths of our offspring's offspring, from this and forever, and may we merit children who are Torah scholars. Amen, so may it be Your will. Sanctify us with Your commandments and grant us our share in Your Torah, satisfy us from Your goodness and gladden us with Your salvation, and purify our hearts to serve You in truth (sincerely). Reign over the entire universe in Your glory, be exalted over all the world in Your splendor, and reveal Yourself in the majestic grandeur of Your strength over all the dwellers of Your inhabited world. And let everything that has been made know that You are its Maker, and let everything that has been molded understand that You are its Molder, and let everything with a life's breath in its nostrils proclaim: "Hashem, God of Israel, is King, and His kingship rules over everything." Amen, selah! Forever and all eternity!

Prayer of Rebbe Nosson

The following prayer was composed by the Chassidic master Rabbi Nosson of Breslov (1780–1844). This prayer is found in his classic collection of original prayers, *Likutei Tefilot*. The prayer gives voice to our feelings and aspirations that are awakened when kindling the holy lights of Chanukah.

וְעׇזְרֵנוּ בְּרַחֲמֶיךָ הָרַבִּים, שֶׁנִּזְכֶּה לְקַיֵּם מִצְוַת הַדְלָקַת נֵר חֲנֻכָּה בִּזְמַנּוֹ בִּשְׁלֵמוּת כָּרָאוּי בִּקְדֻשָּׁה וּבְטׇהֳרָה וּבְכַוָּנָה גְדוֹלָה וַעֲצוּמָה כָּרָאוּי. וְנִזְכֶּה לְתַקֵּן כָּל הַתִּקּוּנִים הָאֵלֶּה שֶׁהִזְכַּרְנוּ לְפָנֶיךָ עַל־יְדֵי מִצְוַת נֵר חֲנֻכָּה. וְיֵחָשֵׁב לְפָנֶיךָ קִיּוּם מִצְוָתֵנוּ כְּאִלּוּ קִיַּמְנוּהָ בְּכָל פְּרָטֶיהָ וְדִקְדּוּקֶיהָ וְכַוָּנוֹתֶיהָ וְתַרְיַ"ג מִצְוֹת הַתְּלוּיִם בָּהּ. וְיָאִירוּ לְפָנֶיךָ אוֹר קְדֻשַּׁת מִצְוָתֵנוּ בְּכָל הָעוֹלָמוֹת כֻּלָּם. וְנִזְכֶּה לְתַקֵּן כָּל הָעוֹלָמוֹת כֻּלָּם, עַל־יְדֵי קִיּוּם מִצְוָה זוֹ. וְעַל־יְדֵי קִיּוּם כָּל הַמִּצְוֹת דְּאוֹרַיְתָא וּדְרַבָּנָן שֶׁתְּזַכֵּנוּ בְּרַחֲמֶיךָ לְקַיֵּם כֻּלָּם בְּאַהֲבָה וּבְיִרְאָה בְּאַהֲבָה וּבְשִׂמְחָה גְדוֹלָה וּבִשְׁלֵמוּת גְּדוֹלָה, עַד שֶׁנִּזְכֶּה לְהַמְשִׁיךְ שָׁלוֹם מֵאִתְּךָ בְּכָל הָעוֹלָמוֹת כֻּלָּם. וִיקֻיַּם מִקְרָא שֶׁכָּתוּב: "יְיָ עֹז לְעַמּוֹ יִתֵּן יְיָ יְבָרֵךְ אֶת עַמּוֹ בַשָּׁלוֹם".

"עֹשֶׂה שָׁלוֹם בִּמְרוֹמָיו הוּא בְּרַחֲמָיו יַעֲשֶׂה שָׁלוֹם עָלֵינוּ וְעַל כָּל יִשְׂרָאֵל וְאִמְרוּ אָמֵן".

Help me to carry out the mitzvah of kindling the Chanukah lamp in its season in the best possible way, in holiness and purity and with great devotion. Through the mitzvah of the Chanukah lights, let me rectify everything I have mentioned in my prayer. Consider my fulfilment of the mitzvah as if I had carried it out in all its details and fine points and intentions, together with all the six hundred thirteen mitzvot that are bound up with it. Let the light of the holiness of our mitzvot shine before You in all the worlds. Let us repair all the worlds through fulfilling this mitzvah, together with all the commandments laid down in the Torah and by the rabbis. Help us carry out all of them perfectly, in love, awe, and great joy, until we draw Godly peace into all the worlds, and "Hashem will give power to His people, Hashem will bless His people with peace."

He Who makes peace in His high places will lovingly make peace for us and for all Israel, and say, Amen.

THE MENORAH LIGHTING

Adding a Candle Each Night

Rabbi Abraham Isaac Kook, known for his immense love for every Jew no matter their level of observance, was once asked, "Who is on a greater spiritual level, a person on a low rung or on a high rung of the spiritual ladder? Rabbi Kook answered: It depends which direction the person is moving. If the person on the low rung is climbing and growing day by day, he/she is spiritually alive and engaged. Conversely, if a person on a high rung is moving downward, he/she has lost spiritual elan and may continue to sink."

We generally do not have a mitzvah in which the quality of "ascending" is built into the performance of the mitzvah itself. One exception is the mitzvah of the Chanukah lights. The Talmudic sage Hillel holds that we light an additional candle each night of Chanukah because we need to "ascend in holiness."

An essential aspect to this mitzvah is that each night we add a new light. The source for adding a new light is the law that we should always strive to be *ma'alin b'kodesh*, to increase and intensify sanctity (Talmud, *Shabbat* 21b). The menorah is a powerful symbol of our spiritual strivings, ascending the ladder in our devotion and commitment, step by step, night after night.

Lighting the Candles Left to Right: A Deeper Meaning

If we are adding candles from right to left, why then do we light the candles from left to right? When performing rituals we generally say that the right side takes precedence: for example, we hold the Kiddush cup in the right hand. The Rebbe of Strikov suggested that the lighting of the menorah should parallel our hearts. We light on the left, which parallels a person's heart, which is also on the left. We thereby exemplify the teaching of the Rambam in which he calls the menorah lighting a *mitzvah chavivah ad meod*, "a most beloved mitzvah."

The Procedure and Blessings for Lighting

On all nights, the first two blessings are recited before the kindling. On the first night, the third blessing, *shehecheyanu*, is also recited.

בָּרוּךְ אַתָּה יְהֹוָה אֱלֹהֵינוּ מֶלֶךְ הָעוֹלָם, אֲשֶׁר קִדְּשָׁנוּ בְּמִצְוֹתָיו, וְצִוָּנוּ לְהַדְלִיק נֵר שֶׁל חֲנֻכָּה.

Baruch Atah Adonai Eloheinu Melech ha'olam, asher kiddeshanu b'mitzvotav v'tzivanu l'hadlik ner shel Chanukah.

Blessed are You, Lord our God, King of the universe, Who has sanctified us with His commandments, and has commanded us to kindle the light of Chanukah.

בָּרוּךְ אַתָּה יְהֹוָה אֱלֹהֵינוּ מֶלֶךְ הָעוֹלָם, שֶׁעָשָׂה נִסִּים לַאֲבוֹתֵינוּ בַּיָּמִים הָהֵם בַּזְּמַן הַזֶּה.

Baruch Atah Adonai Eloheinu Melech ha'olam, She'asah nisim la'avoteinu ba'yamim hahem ba'zman hazeh.

Blessed are You, Lord our God, King of the universe, Who wrought miracles for our forefathers, in those days at this time.

בָּרוּךְ אַתָּה יְהֹוָה אֱלֹהֵינוּ מֶלֶךְ הָעוֹלָם, שֶׁהֶחֱיָנוּ וְקִיְּמָנוּ וְהִגִּיעָנוּ לַזְּמַן הַזֶּה.

Baruch Atah Adonai Eloheinu Melech ha'olam, shehecheyanu v'kiyemanu v'higianu la'zman hazeh.

Blessed are You, Lord our God, King of the universe, Who has kept us alive, sustained us, and caused us to reach this time.

בָּרוּךְ – *Baruch* The word *baruch* is generally translated as "bless." It is the opening word of every blessing.

Rabbi Chaim of Volozhin (1749–1821) taught that the word *baruch* means "increase." Thus we find, for example, the verse says: "God will bless [*berach*] your bread" (Exodus 23:25). This does not mean that God will praise our bread. It means that He will bring an *increase* to our harvest.

When we make a blessing, we ask for an increase of Godliness in our lives; in other words, we endeavor to become more aware of God. We attempt to increase His presence in the world. The more aware we are of God, the more we invite His presence in our lives.

בָּרוּךְ אַתָּה – *Baruch Atah* Rabbi Joseph Soloveitchik explains that blessings are addressed to God in the second person, "Blessed are *You*," rather than in the third person, "Blessed is He," in order to affirm God's very presence before us. It is as if one says, "Where are you, God? You are right here with me." Through the use of the second person singular, we reveal the Divine Presence directly in front of us. A Jew is thus a partner in the revelation of God every time he recites a blessing.

אֲדֹנָי – *Ado-nai* "O, Lord," the significance of the appellation *Ado-nai*, from the root *adon*, owner, is discussed in the Talmud (*Berachot* 7b), where it states that from the time of the creation of the world, no one ever called God *Ado-nai* until Abraham did so (Genesis 15:8). Rabbi Joseph Soloveitchik explains that Abraham's most significant spiritual discovery was the understanding that the Master of the universe runs the world. The importance of the name *Ado-nai* connects God as an abstract concept to His relationship with the world on a practical level. God is not only the Creator of the world; *Ado-nai* signifies that He owns and manages it.

מֶלֶךְ הָעוֹלָם – *Melech ha'olam* As Creator of the world, God is the master of everything. God owns His creations – the infinite universe, from our small earth to the outer fringes of the cosmos. Rabbi Joseph Soloveitchik explains that God has partnered with man, appointing him the precious guardian of His worldly works. However, whatever man earns and enjoys, or clings to, none of it is his, but God's. When we beseech God as *Melech ha'olam*, King of the universe, we are acknowledging God's absolute mastery over the world.

הָעוֹלָם – *ha'olam* The Hebrew word for "world," *ha'olam* (הָעוֹלָם), is related to *he'elem* (הֶעְלֵם), which translates into English as "concealment." The world is a place that conceals the sublime sacred light. But certain portions of the Hebrew calendar draw back the veil and allow unique aspects of the hidden lights to enter our lives. This is especially true for the lights of Chanukah, which help us see the world as the miracle it truly is.

לְהַדְלִיק נֵר שֶׁל חֲנֻכָּה – *l'hadlik ner shel Chanukah* Rabbi Levi Yitzchak of Berditchev suggested that when we say the blessing thanking God for the mitzvah of lighting the candles of Chanukah, we refer not only to the act of lighting, but also we are expressing gratitude for renewing our own inner light, our inner essence that now flickers even more brightly. At the precious moment of the menorah lighting, we feel spiritually uplifted and inspired.

לְהַדְלִיק נֵר שֶׁל חֲנֻכָּה – *l'hadlik ner shel Chanukah* Reb Shlomo Carlebach (1926–1994) said: "The blessing that we say over the light is *l'hadlik ner shel Chanukah* – 'to kindle the light of Chanukah.' We don't say, …*b'Chanukah* – 'to kindle the light *on* Chanukah.'

"We kindle the light *of* Chanukah! That means that the light is already there. We have only to kindle it. The light that we are seeing now is the light of the *kohanim*, the priests in the Holy Temple. It is the same light that burned from the bit of oil that lasted eight days. It is the *same* light. That light is waiting in heaven all year long to be brought down through the kindling of our Chanukah menorahs."

לְהַדְלִיק נֵר שֶׁל חֲנֻכָּה – *l'hadlik ner shel Chanukah* Rabbi Abraham Isaac Kook, in his *Siddur Olat Rayah*, wonders why the blessing recited over the Chanukah candles is phrased "to kindle the Chanukah *light*" rather than "to kindle the Chanukah *lights*." The saintly rabbi explains that the branches of the menorah symbolize the different forms of light that must shine within the nation. Many lights are needed, such as Torah, prophecy, wisdom, justice, heroism, joy, and love. These diverse ideals are often seen to be at odds with one another and may lead to fragmentation and strife between their adherents.

The multiple ideals and values appear to us to be separate. But that separateness will not last forever. In the future there will be a clear awareness that all the lights, with all their particulars, are really one light.

Although we light more than one candle, we must focus on the unity that the candles represent. The blessing over the Chanukah candles does not refer to "lights"; this blessing, which raises our consciousness to the ideal vision, refers to a single "light" of Chanukah.

שֶׁעָשָׂה נִסִּים לַאֲבוֹתֵינוּ – *She'asah nisim la'avoteinu* Rabbi Joseph Soloveitchik explains the unusual practice of reciting not one, but two blessings each night of Chanukah. He suggests that the second blessing of *She'asah nisim*, whereby we thank God for the miracle of Chanukah, points to the critical importance of articulating the meaning of the lighting.

Apparently, reciting the first blessing on the mitzvah is not sufficient; one needs to elucidate, to understand, and to appreciate the reasons we are celebrating. We learn from the second Chanukah blessing the importance of delving into and articulating the meaning and relevance of the lighting.

שֶׁהֶחֱיָנוּ – *shehecheyanu* Rebbe Nachman of Breslov (1772–1811) instructed his students to focus on the present: "We have nothing in this world except for the very day and hour in which we stand, for the world tomorrow is a different place altogether" (*Likutei Moharan* 272). We must relate to the present with meaning, lest it pass by unnoticed. The beloved blessing of *shehecheyanu* directs us to dwell in the present. The blessing awakens us to the hour and encourages us to experience closeness with God.

After the first candle is kindled, Hanerot Halalu (next page) is recited, and the remaining candles are kindled during its recitation. Some wait until after completing the kindling of all the lights to recite it.

It is praiseworthy to remain by the candles for the first half hour after their lighting.

After the kindling and reciting Hanerot Halalu, many have the custom of reciting various prayers and chapters of Tehillim (Psalms). Most widely recited is the beloved poem of Maoz Tzur.

The most commonly recited prayers and Psalms are presented here. The Chassidic tradition teaches that the moments after lighting are considered auspicious for prayer and personal supplication.

AFTER THE KINDLING

Hanerot Halalu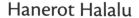

The text of Hanerot Halalu is of ancient origin and is found in the Talmudic tractate *Soferim* (20:6). These words we chant following the lighting have been lovingly recited for two thousand years. This prayer, according to some texts, contains precisely thirty-six words to parallel the thirty-six candles that are lit over Chanukah. The first two words "these candles" are not part of the count of thirty-six and therefore can be understood to mean, "*Hanerot halalu* — these candles — are thirty-six."

We generally perform mitzvot without the need for an accompanying recitation. The purpose of reciting the prayer Hanerot Halalu is to enhance the mitzvah by publicizing and giving verbal expression to the Chanukah miracle.

הַנֵּרוֹת הַלָּלוּ אֲנַחְנוּ מַדְלִיקִין עַל הַנִּסִּים וְעַל הַנִּפְלָאוֹת וְעַל
הַתְּשׁוּעוֹת וְעַל הַמִּלְחָמוֹת, שֶׁעָשִׂיתָ לַאֲבוֹתֵינוּ בַּיָּמִים הָהֵם
בַּזְּמַן הַזֶּה, עַל יְדֵי כֹּהֲנֶיךָ הַקְּדוֹשִׁים. וְכָל שְׁמוֹנַת יְמֵי חֲנֻכָּה,
הַנֵּרוֹת הַלָּלוּ קֹדֶשׁ הֵם, וְאֵין לָנוּ רְשׁוּת לְהִשְׁתַּמֵּשׁ בָּהֶם, אֶלָּא
לִרְאוֹתָם בִּלְבַד, כְּדֵי לְהוֹדוֹת וּלְהַלֵּל לְשִׁמְךָ הַגָּדוֹל עַל נִסֶּיךָ
וְעַל נִפְלְאוֹתֶיךָ וְעַל יְשׁוּעָתֶךָ.

These lights we kindle for the miracles and for the wonders, and for the salvations and for the battles that You performed for our forefathers in those days at this time, through the hand of Your holy *kohanim*. And on all eight days of Chanukah these lights are holy. And we do not have permission to make [ordinary] use of them, only to gaze at them, in order to give thanks and to offer praise to Your great name, for Your miracles and for Your wonders and Your salvations.

הַנֵּרוֹת הַלָּלוּ – *Hanerot halalu, "These lights"* The Chassidic master Rabbi Levi Yitzchak of Berditchev asks how we can say "these candles" in the plural on the first night, since on the first night of Chanukah the mitzvah is to light only a single candle!

The Rebbe answers: With every candle that one lights here, a candle is lit above in heaven.

His answer suggests the idea that every mitzvah has a ripple effect. When we bring light in one place, it impacts beyond one's immediate surrounding. Light spreads all around.

The Baal Shem Tov, the founder of the Chassidic movement, had a special love for Chanukah, greater than all the other holidays of the year. This is because Chanukah candles represent the innate gift of the Jewish soul to spread light and illuminate worlds.

קֹדֶשׁ הֵם – *kodesh hem, "[they] are holy"* Rabbi Abraham Isaac Kook saw great symbolism in the miracle of the oil.

Even after all the assimilation and oppression of Judaism brought about by Greek rule, one jug of pure oil remained unaffected; God did not allow and never will allow for the Jewish people to be obliterated.

No matter how far any individual Jew or the nation as a whole strays from God, there will always remain a small inextinguishable core.

Similarly, while the Syrian Greek army broke through the walls of the Temple and contaminated its purity, spreading many negative influences, the pure jug of oil could not be contaminated.

Like that jug of oil found with the seal of the *kohen gadol*, "high priest," all Jews have within them a spark, a likeness to the high priest, that longs for holiness and service to the Lord. The inner essence of every Jew remains pure and good.

The miracle of the oil represents God's assurance that the Jewish people and any individual Jew has the ability to always come closer to God.

אֶלָּא לִרְאוֹתָם בִּלְבָד – *Ela lirotam bilvad, "[We are permitted] only to gaze at [the lights]"* Our Sages prohibited benefit from the Chanukah candles, ruling that "we are not permitted to make use of the Chanukah lights." In doing so they sought to mirror the laws of the Menorah of the Temple.

Rabbi Joseph Soloveitchik taught that when celebrating the Jewish holidays, we do not merely commemorate the past; rather, we are to *reexperience* the event as if we were actually there. A classic example of this is the way we observe Passover by tasting the matzah and eating the bitter herbs, the actual food and tastes experienced by our forefathers in Egypt. On Chanukah, by kindling the lights of the menorah we *reenact* the miraculous lighting that Chanukah commemorates.

Maoz Tzur

מָעוֹז צוּר

Maoz Tzur is a *piyut*, a liturgical poem, praising God for all the miracles and wonders that He has performed for us, not just on Chanukah, but throughout history. It recalls the various exiles, such as the Egyptian, Babylonian, Persian, and Greek. We were able to endure these painful times with God's help, and we thank Him for redeeming us from each of them. The concluding paragraph contains a heartfelt plea for the final redemption. The essence of the Chanukah story is told in the twenty-four Hebrew words that form the fifth stanza of the Maoz Tzur.

The poem was composed by a poet named Mordechai who, according to many opinions, lived in the thirteenth century CE in Germany. His name is contained within the poem, written in an acrostic: *Mordechai chazak* (מָרְדְּכַי חָזָק), "[May] Mordechai [be] strong." The initial letters of each of the first five stanzas spell *Mordechai*, and the initial letters of the first three words of the sixth stanza spell *chazak*. It is debated whether the last stanza was part of the original composition or added later. The custom of chanting this poem after the kindling of the menorah was adopted by Jews many hundreds of years ago.

Mark Twain, one of America's greatest writers, and no philo-Semite, nevertheless captured the essence of Maoz Tzur:

In 1899 he wrote:

The Egyptian, the Babylonian, and the Persian rose, filled the planet with sound and splendor, then faded to dream-stuff and passed away; the Greek and the Roman followed, and made a vast noise, and they are gone; other peoples have sprung up and held their torch high for a time, but it burned out, and they sit in twilight now, or have vanished. The Jew saw them all, beat them all, and is now what he always was, exhibiting no decadence, no infirmities of age, no weakening of his parts, no slowing of his energies, no dulling of his alert and aggressive mind. All things are mortal but the Jew; all other forces pass, but he remains.

Mighty Rock of my salvation [i.e., God],

מָעוֹז צוּר יְשׁוּעָתִי

You, God, are comparable to a mighty rock, and You save me, as it says (Psalms 31:3): הֱיֵה לִי מָעוֹז...לְהוֹשִׁיעֵנִי – *Be for me a Mighty Rock...to save me.*

it is a delight to praise You.

לְךָ נָאֶה לְשַׁבֵּחַ,

It is befitting to praise You, the mighty Rock of My salvation, and to offer thanksgiving for all Your salvations.

Restore my House of Prayer [the Temple],

תִּכּוֹן בֵּית תְּפִלָּתִי

Rebuild the Temple, which is called the Beit Tefillah (House of Prayer), as it says (Isaiah 56:7): כִּי בֵיתִי בֵּית תְּפִלָּה יִקָּרֵא לְכָל הָעַמִּים – *For My House shall be called a House of Prayer for all the nations.*

and there I will bring a thanksgiving offering.

וְשָׁם תּוֹדָה נְזַבֵּחַ,

And then, in the rebuilt Temple, we will bring thanksgiving offerings to You, for Your deliverance during the time of the final redemption.

When You [God] will have prepared the slaughter for the barking foe,

לְעֵת תָּכִין מַטְבֵּחַ
מִצָּר הַמְנַבֵּחַ,

When You (at the final redemption) will have destroyed the enemies of Israel, who are compared to barking dogs (see *Bereshit Rabbah* 45:9 and *Pesikta d'Rav Kahana*, Parashat Zachor; see also Isaiah 56:10), as it says (Isaiah 34:6): כִּי זֶבַח לַה' בְּבָצְרָה וְטֶבַח גָּדוֹל בְּאֶרֶץ אֱדוֹם – *For there is an offering for God in Botzrah, and a great slaughter in the land of Edom.*

then I shall conclude with a song of praise, the dedication of the Altar.

אָז אֶגְמֹר בְּשִׁיר מִזְמוֹר
חֲנֻכַּת הַמִּזְבֵּחַ.

Then I shall conclude all my singing with a song of praise for the building and dedication of the Altar and Temple. (The *Mechilta* [Beshalach, *Shirah* 1] explains that there are ten *shirot* [songs]. Throughout history, Israel sang nine *shirot*, including Shirat Hayam, the Song by the Sea. The final tenth *shirah* will be sung at the final redemption, and it is the tenth song that this phrase is referring to.)

THE EGYPTIAN EXILE
*Praising and thanking God for the redemption from
the bondage of Egypt with overt miracles*

Troubles have sated my soul,

רָעוֹת שָׂבְעָה נַפְשִׁי

The countless sufferings endured in Egypt filled the Jewish people's souls to the saturation point.

from my anguish my
strength dissolved.

בְּיָגוֹן כֹּחִי כָלָה,

As a result of the anguish, the physical and emotional strength of the Jews ebbed, such that they were on the brink of being unable to endure any further suffering.

They embittered my
life with hardship,

חַיַּי מֵרְרוּ בְקֹשִׁי

The Egyptians embittered their lives with hard work, as it says (Exodus 1:14): וַיְמָרְרוּ אֶת חַיֵּיהֶם בַּעֲבוֹדָה קָשָׁה – *They embittered their lives with hard work.*

in the subjugation of the
calf-like kingdom [Egypt].

בְּשִׁעְבּוּד מַלְכוּת עֶגְלָה,

This occurred in the subjugation imposed upon them by the kingdom of Egypt, which is called עֶגְלָה, a calf, as it says (Jeremiah 46:20): עֶגְלָה יְפֵה־פִיָּה מִצְרַיִם – *Egypt [is beautiful] like a very fair calf.*

But with [the power of]
His [God's] great hand, He
took out the treasured
[nation, i.e., the Jews].

וּבְיָדוֹ הַגְּדוֹלָה
הוֹצִיא אֶת הַסְּגֻלָּה,

With His strong hand, God removed from Egypt His treasured nation – the Jewish people, who are as dear to Him as the most valuable treasure, as it says (Exodus 19:5): וִהְיִיתֶם לִי סְגֻלָּה מִכָּל הָעַמִּים – *You [Israel] shall be to Me the most beloved treasure from amongst all the nations.*

Pharaoh's army and all his offspring sank like a stone into the deep [the sea].

חֵיל פַּרְעֹה וְכָל זַרְעוֹ יָרְדוּ כְּאֶבֶן בִּמְצוּלָה.

In the process of God's taking the Jews out of Egypt, Pharaoh's entire army and all his subjects, including his children, drowned in the Sea of Reeds, as the waters came crashing down upon them when they chased the Jews into the sea that had miraculously split, as it says (Exodus 15:5): יָרְדוּ בִמְצוֹלֹת כְּמוֹ אֶבֶן – *They [the Egyptians] descended into the depths like a stone.*

THE BABYLONIAN EXILE

Praising and thanking God for the redemption from the Babylonian exile and the subsequent building of the Second Temple

To the Holy of Holies of His Temple, He [God] brought me,

דְּבִיר קָדְשׁוֹ הֱבִיאָנִי

After God established the Jewish people securely in the Land of Israel for the first time (i.e., after the Exodus). He brought us to the First Temple, to the Holy of Holies, which is known as the דְּבִיר (see I Kings 6:5).

but there too I did not find [peace and] quiet,

וְגַם שָׁם לֹא שָׁקַטְתִּי,

However, even when dwelling in the Land of Israel and in possession of the Temple, the Jewish people nonetheless did not find rest from their suffering for long.

[for] an oppressor came and exiled me,

וּבָא נוֹגֵשׂ וְהִגְלַנִי

A new suffering soon came from Nevuchadnetzar, king of Babylon, who is called a נוֹגֵשׂ, *an oppressor* (see Isaiah 14:4), as he exiled us to Babylon after conquering Eretz Israel and destroying the First Temple.

because I served strange [gods],

כִּי זָרִים עָבַדְתִּי,

The suffering of the Babylonian exile came upon us as a punishment [from God] for serving idolatry.

and I drank benumbing wine
[i.e., the bitterness of the exile],

וְיֵין רַעַל מְסַכְתִּי

Wine deadens sensitivity and emotions and seals them off from external
stimuli. Thus, the phrase וְיֵין רַעַל מְסַכְתִּי means that we drank the wine of
suffering, to the extent that we had become so paralyzed by the pain that
our senses became numb and our hearts deadened, as it says (Psalms 60:5):
הִשְׁקִיתָנוּ יַיִן תַּרְעֵלָה – *You made us drink benumbing wine* (see Rashi there;
see also *Shabbat* 13b).

[yet] when I had only barely
departed [from the Land
of Israel, and only been
in the Babylonian exile a
relatively short time],

כִּמְעַט שֶׁעָבַרְתִּי,

Although our future looked dismal as we endured our exile in Babylon and
we began to sink both physically and spiritually, such that it appeared there
was no hope, it was not so long after we had been exiled that…

the end came to [the empire] of
Babylon, [and] Zerubavel [led
us back to the Land of Israel] –

קֵץ בָּבֶל, זְרֻבָּבֶל

God brought the Babylonian Empire to an end, and, under the leadership of
Zerubavel, He led us back to the Land of Israel to build the Second Temple.

at the end of seventy [years of
the Babylonian exile], I was saved.

לְקֵץ שִׁבְעִים נוֹשַׁעְתִּי.

In total, the Babylonian exile lasted only seventy years, and thereafter we
were redeemed and once again merited to live in the Land of Israel and
serve God in the new Temple.

THE PERSIAN-MEDIAN EXILE/MIRACLE OF PURIM
*Praising and thanking God for the redemption from
the Persian-Median exile via the fall of Haman and the
uplifting of Mordechai in the miracle of Purim*

To cut down the towering cypress
[Mordechai] sought the Aggagite,
son of Hammedata [Haman].

כְּרֹת קוֹמַת בְּרוֹשׁ בִּקֵּשׁ
אֲגָגִי בֶּן הַמְּדָתָא,

During the time of Purim, Haman, known as the Aggagite, son of Hammedata (see Esther 3:1), sought to cut down and destroy Mordechai, who is called בְּרוֹשׁ, *a cypress [tree]* (see *Megillah* 10b).

But it [Haman's evil plan] became a trap and a stumbling block for him [instead]

וַנִּהְיְתָה לּוֹ לְפַח וּלְמוֹקֵשׁ

Haman's evil plans recoiled on his own head, as it says (Esther 7:10): אֶת וַיִּתְלוּ הָמָן עַל הָעֵץ אֲשֶׁר הֵכִין לְמָרְדְּכַי – *And they hanged Haman on the gallows that he [Haman] had prepared for Mordechai.*

and his arrogance was stilled [as a result].

וְגַאֲוָתוֹ נִשְׁבָּתָה,

As a result of the miraculous turnabout of his plans, Haman's arrogance was silenced.

[And] the head of the Benjaminite [Mordechai] You [God] raised up,

רֹאשׁ יְמִינִי נִשֵּׂאתָ

At the same time, God exalted the honor of Mordechai, who is known as יְמִינִי, the *Benjaminite* (because he descended from the tribe of Binyamin: see Esther 2:5), to be viceroy to the king.

and [regarding] the enemy [Haman], his name You blotted out.

וְאוֹיֵב שְׁמוֹ מָחִיתָ,

And regarding the enemy Haman, You caused his name to be obliterated from the earth, just as it says regarding the mitzvah of destroying the memory of Amalek (the evil nation of which Haman was a member): תִּמְחֶה אֶת זֵכֶר עֲמָלֵק מִתַּחַת הַשָּׁמָיִם – *You shall wipe out the memory of Amalek from under the Heaven* (Deuteronomy 25:19).

His [Haman's] many sons, and possessions, You hanged on the gallows.

רֹב בָּנָיו וְקִנְיָנָיו עַל הָעֵץ תָּלִיתָ.

The glory Haman had from his many sons and possessions, and about which he boasted greatly (see Esther 5:11), came to a sudden end when God caused Haman and his sons to be hanged on the gallows.

THE GREEK EXILE/MIRACLE OF CHANUKAH
Praising and thanking God for Israel's salvation through the Chashmonaim during the reign of the evil Syrian-Greek Empire in the Land of Israel, for the resulting miracle of the oil, and for the establishment of Chanukah as an annual eight-day holiday

Greeks gathered against me in the days of the Chashmonaim.

יְוָנִים נִקְבְּצוּ עָלַי אֲזַי בִּימֵי חַשְׁמַנִּים,

The Syrian-Greeks gathered to make war upon the Jews during the days of the Chashmonaim.

And they breached the walls of my towers [the Temple],

וּפָרְצוּ חוֹמוֹת מִגְדָּלַי

They made thirteen breaches in the Soreg wall surrounding the Temple (see *Middot* 2:3; see also 4:29–31). Since the Sanctuary building of the Temple was quite tall, and since the Mizbe'ach, Altar, in the Temple had a wide base, narrower top, and tall corners, as do many fortified towers, the Temple was called a *migdal*, tower (see *Song of Songs Rabbah* 4:4:9; see also *Sukkah* 49a and Rashi there).

and defiled all the oils.

וְטִמְּאוּ כָּל הַשְּׁמָנִים,

They deliberately sought out all of the oils that had been prepared for use in the daily kindling of the Menorah in the Temple and defiled them all (see *Shabbat* 21b).

Yet from the one remnant of the flasks [the one flask of pure oil that was found], a miracle was performed for the roses [i.e., for the Jewish people].

וּמִנּוֹתַר קַנְקַנִּים נַעֲשָׂה נֵס לַשּׁוֹשַׁנִּים,

Amongst all the defiled flasks of oil, the Chashmonaim found only one that had not been defiled, and from that one remnant flask, a miracle occurred for the Jews, who are called שׁוֹשַׁנִּים, roses (see Rashi, Psalms 80:1; see also 3:35), such that even though there was only one day's worth of oil in the flask, they kindled from that oil for eight days (see *Shabbat* 21b).

[Then] men of understanding [the Sages] established eight days [of Chanukah] for song and jubilation.

בְּנֵי בִינָה יְמֵי שְׁמוֹנָה קָבְעוּ שִׁיר וּרְנָנִים.

Therefore, in commemoration of the great miracle, the wise Torah sages and leaders of that generation established that these eight days, beginning on the 25th of Kislev, would be days of singing and jubilation, on which the Jewish people would sing and rejoice with *hallel* (praise) and *hoda'ah* (thanksgiving) to God for the miracles He performed for them (see *Shabbat* 21b).

THE (CURRENT) ROMAN EXILE

Prayer to hasten the final redemption from the Roman exile, and the plea to topple the evil kingdom of Edom (i.e. Rome), which, even though may not exist as it once did, persists through its physical and spiritual successors, in both hidden and overt ways.

Bare Your holy arm [God],

חֲשׂף זְרוֹעַ קָדְשֶׁךָ

God, reveal Your great power to us and to the entire world, as it says (Isaiah 52:10): חָשַׂף ה' אֶת זְרוֹעַ קָדְשׁוֹ לְעֵינֵי כָּל הַגּוֹיִם וְרָאוּ כָל־אַפְסֵי אָרֶץ אֵת יְשׁוּעַת אֱלֹקֵינוּ – *God has bared His holy arm in the sight of all the nations, and all the ends of the Earth shall see the salvation of our God.*

and hasten the time of the salvation.

וְקָרֵב קֵץ הַיְשׁוּעָה,

God, please hasten the coming of the final redemption.

Avenge the spilled blood of Your servants [the Jews] from the wicked nation.

נְקֹם נִקְמַת דַּם עֲבָדֶיךָ מֵאֻמָּה הָרְשָׁעָה,

God, avenge the blood of Israel, Your servants, that has been spilled throughout the millennia by the evil kingdom of Edom (i.e., Rome and all of its physical and spiritual successors), as well as by all the other evil regimes that have persecuted and continue to persecute our people, and spill our blood like water.

For the salvation has been delayed for us too long

כִּי אָרְכָה לָּנוּ הַיְשׁוּעָה

The time until our salvation has been overly extended. The duration of our exile has been longer than that of any of our previous exiles, and we barely have the strength to wait any longer.

and there is no end to the days of evil.

וְאֵין קֵץ לִימֵי הָרָעָה,

Moreover, our suffering in this exile has been more extensive than in all previous exiles. We continue to suffer and experience hard times, and it seems unending.

Drive away the Red One [Eisav's descendants who oppress us] into the shadowy darkness,

דְּחֵה אַדְמוֹן בְּצֵל צַלְמוֹן

God, topple the evil nations descended from Eisav, who is the father of Edom (see Genesis 36:1), and who is called אַדְמוֹנִי, the Red One (see Genesis 25:25), letting them descend into the darkness of Gehinnom (purgatory), which is called צַלְמוֹן, the shadow (see *Berachot* 15b).

and establish for us the seven shepherds [who will conquer our oppressors].

הָקֵם לָנוּ רוֹעִים שִׁבְעָה.

God, quickly bring us the seven leaders referred to as the "seven shepherds," who will conquer our oppressors and lead us toward the promised final redemption, as it says (Micah 5:4): וַהֲקֵמֹנוּ עָלָיו שִׁבְעָה רֹעִים – *Seven shepherds shall be set against them (our enemies).* The Talmud (*Sukkah* 52b) indicates that these seven shepherds are David, Adam, Seth, Methuselah, Abraham, Jacob, and Moses.

מָעוֹז צוּר יְשׁוּעָתִי – *Maoz Tzur yeshuati,* "O mighty Rock of my salvation" God is frequently referred to in Scripture as a "Rock." The term connotes strength and dependability. The Talmud (*Berachot* 10a) interprets the word *tzur* in another sense, as similar to the word *tzayar,* "a molder." Only God can fashion all materials and circumstances to correspond to His will. Accordingly, in the opening of this poem this term is used to hint that God has fashioned every circumstance as a means toward the Jewish people's salvation.

וּפָרְצוּ חוֹמוֹת מִגְדָּלַי – *u'fartzu chomot migdalai,* "[the Greeks] breached the walls of my towers" The Temple is generally not referred to in our literature as a "tower." What does this phrase allude to? Perhaps, the Jewish home, the "tower" or fortress of the Jewish people. The Greeks were determined to undermine the value system of the Jewish family.

Rabbi Abraham Isaac Kook suggested that the essence of the Chanukah story was the victory of the Jewish home heroically fending off a spiritual war waged against its wholesomeness. This is why the ritual of the menorah lighting is celebrated specifically in the home, the centerpiece of purity and modesty. As the Talmud says, the ritual is to be observed *ner ish u'veito* (נֵר אִישׁ וּבֵיתוֹ), "a candle lit in each home."

וּמִנּוֹתַר קַנְקַנִּים – *u'minotar kankanim,* "from the one remnant of the flasks" We say in Maoz Tzur that "the miracle of Chanukah was done with one remaining jar of oil." The question is: Why did the Greeks *not* find that jar of oil?

Reb Shlomo Carlebach answered: "The truth is that the Greeks saw the jar, but you know what they thought? It's so small, why bother with it? The Greeks and the rest of the world cannot understand that something so exalted can come out of something so small. The holiness of the Jew is that with one drop of leftover oil, we can bring light to the whole world."

לַשּׁוֹשַׁנִּים – *la'shoshanim,* "for the roses [i.e., for the Jewish people]" Why are the Jewish people symbolized by *shoshanim,* "roses"?

The verse in *Song of Songs* (2:2) compares the Jewish people to a "rose among the thorns." Rashi (1040–1104) comments that the Jew often lives in hostile settings. The gentle rose is in danger of being pierced by the thorns that surround her. This homily captures the essence of the Chanukah story. The onslaught of painful decrees threatened our spiritual survival. In the face of hostility, the Jews heroically maintained their pristine beauty and delicate inner beauty.

רוֹעִים שִׁבְעָה – *ro'im shivah*, "seven shepherds" The poem of Maoz Tzur concludes with a prayer for the "seven shepherds" who will lead us to the final redemption. The Sages identify them as Adam, Seth, and Methuselah, representing mankind as a whole, and Abraham, Jacob, and Moses, representing Israel. David, who represents the messianic dynasty, will stand at the center (Talmud, *Sukkah* 52b). This description of the redemption highlights the Jewish vision for Messianic times that will bring peace and harmony to *all* people and to the entire world.

Psalms   תְּהִלִּים

Customs vary regarding the recitation of further Psalms and prayers. The order presented here follows that of the classic *Siddur Beit Yaakov* compiled by Rabbi Yaakov Emden in the mid-1700s. This is the order also found in the classic *Siddur Otzar Hatefilot*.

✿ PSALM 90:17 AND PSALM 91

This psalm contains layers of extraordinary meaning. When Moses completed the building of the Mishkan or Tabernacle, he prayed that God's presence would fill the newly constructed space. Moses recited the words that later would be adopted in Psalm 90: "May the pleasantness of the Lord our God be upon us; let the work of our hands be established," (Rashi, Exodus 39:43).

The psalm that follows is known as the psalm of blessing. These words are also recited as a prayer as we conclude Shabbat. On the nights of Chanukah, we offer these words asking God to send His blessings to assist us in our effort to bring God's light into the world.

Our tradition teaches that these were the very words of blessing that Moses gave to those who assisted in building the Mishkan (Rashi, Exodus 39:43). These words are most appropriate as we light the menorah, which is reminiscent of the golden Menorah first fashioned that stood in the wilderness in the Tabernacle.

When the Maccabees gathered for war, they recited this psalm. Appropriately, we recite the same psalm that the Maccabees said when they prepared for battle, so many years ago (*Magen Avraham*, commentary on the *Shulchan Aruch, Orach Chaim, siman* 295).

Praying for protection and asking God for courage and resolve are meaningful motifs to meditate on following the lighting of the menorah.

וִיהִי ׀ נֹעַם אֲדֹנָי אֱלֹהֵינוּ עָלֵינוּ וּמַעֲשֵׂה יָדֵינוּ כּוֹנְנָה עָלֵינוּ וּמַעֲשֵׂה יָדֵינוּ כּוֹנְנֵהוּ:

יֹשֵׁב בְּסֵתֶר עֶלְיוֹן בְּצֵל שַׁדַּי יִתְלוֹנָן: אֹמַר לַיהוָה מַחְסִי וּמְצוּדָתִי אֱלֹהַי אֶבְטַח־בּוֹ: כִּי הוּא יַצִּילְךָ מִפַּח יָקוּשׁ מִדֶּבֶר הַוּוֹת: בְּאֶבְרָתוֹ ׀ יָסֶךְ לָךְ וְתַחַת־כְּנָפָיו תֶּחְסֶה צִנָּה וְסֹחֵרָה אֲמִתּוֹ: לֹא־תִירָא מִפַּחַד לָיְלָה מֵחֵץ יָעוּף יוֹמָם: מִדֶּבֶר בָּאֹפֶל יַהֲלֹךְ מִקֶּטֶב יָשׁוּד צָהֳרָיִם: יִפֹּל מִצִּדְּךָ ׀ אֶלֶף וּרְבָבָה מִימִינֶךָ אֵלֶיךָ לֹא יִגָּשׁ: רַק בְּעֵינֶיךָ תַבִּיט וְשִׁלֻּמַת רְשָׁעִים תִּרְאֶה: כִּי־אַתָּה יְהוָה מַחְסִי עֶלְיוֹן שַׂמְתָּ מְעוֹנֶךָ: לֹא־תְאֻנֶּה אֵלֶיךָ רָעָה וְנֶגַע לֹא־יִקְרַב בְּאָהֳלֶךָ: כִּי מַלְאָכָיו יְצַוֶּה־לָּךְ לִשְׁמָרְךָ בְּכָל־דְּרָכֶיךָ: עַל־כַּפַּיִם יִשָּׂאוּנְךָ פֶּן־תִּגֹּף בָּאֶבֶן רַגְלֶךָ: עַל־שַׁחַל וָפֶתֶן תִּדְרֹךְ תִּרְמֹס כְּפִיר וְתַנִּין: כִּי בִי חָשַׁק וַאֲפַלְּטֵהוּ אֲשַׂגְּבֵהוּ כִּי־יָדַע שְׁמִי: יִקְרָאֵנִי ׀ וְאֶעֱנֵהוּ עִמּוֹ־אָנֹכִי בְצָרָה אֲחַלְּצֵהוּ וַאֲכַבְּדֵהוּ: אֹרֶךְ יָמִים אַשְׂבִּיעֵהוּ וְאַרְאֵהוּ בִּישׁוּעָתִי:

May the pleasantness of the Lord our God be upon us; let the work of our hands be established, O establish the work of our hands!

O you who dwell in the shelter of the Most High and abide in the protection of Shaddai — I say of the Lord, my refuge and stronghold, my God in whom I trust, that He will save you from the fowler's trap, from the destructive plague. He will cover you with His pinions; you will find refuge under His wings; His fidelity is an encircling shield. You need not fear the terror by night, or the arrow that flies by day, the plague that stalks in the darkness, or the scourge that ravages at noon.

A thousand may fall at your left side, ten thousand at your right, but it shall not reach you. You will see it with your eyes, you will witness the punishment of the wicked. Because you took the LORD – my refuge, the Most High – as your haven, no harm will befall you, no disease touch your tent. For He will order His angels to guard you wherever you go. They will carry you in their hands lest you hurt your foot on a stone. You will tread on cubs and vipers; you will trample lions and asps. "Because he is devoted to Me I will deliver him; I will keep him safe, for he knows My name. When he calls on Me, I will answer him; I will be with him in distress; I will rescue him and make him honored; I will let him live to a ripe old age, and show him My salvation."

וִיהִי נֹעַם – *Vihi noam,* "May the pleasantness [of the Lord...establish the work of our hands]" Rabbi Isaac Jacob Reines (1839–1915), a great religious Zionist leader, explains why this prayer was chosen for the Chanukah lighting. When other miracles happened for the Jewish people in our history, they took place without great effort by the Jews.

The miracle of Chanukah, however, came about through the heroic deeds of the Hasmoneans and the self-sacrifice of those who participated in the struggle against the Greeks. Therefore we recite, "...establish the work of our hands." This emphasizes that we did not rely entirely on miracles; rather, we performed our part and God blessed our initiative and dedication.

❧ PSALM 67

The text of this psalm, according to an ancient tradition, was revealed to both Moses and David in a unique vision – they saw the words in the form of a seven-branched menorah. Each word of the psalm appeared etched on its branches (see illustration). The seven verses in the psalm allude to the seven-branched Menorah that stood in the Holy Temple. This is why this psalm has special significance on Chanukah. The psalm also speaks of the light of God, which is especially meaningful as we gaze at the light of the menorah.

An eighteenth- or nineteenth-century shiviti *(depiction of Psalm 67 in the shape of a Menorah), author unknown. Royal Library, Denmark, Department of Oriental and Judaica Collections, Cod. Heb. 46:5.*

Psalm 67 is a prayer for the ultimate redemption when all the nations of the world will recognize the greatness of God.

The mystics teach that the seven sentences parallel the seven branches of the Temple Menorah. The psalm contains precisely forty-nine words, to parallel the total number of cups, flowers, knobs, and flames found on the Menorah that stood in the Temple.

לַמְנַצֵּחַ בִּנְגִינֹת מִזְמוֹר שִׁיר: אֱלֹהִים יְחָנֵּנוּ וִיבָרְכֵנוּ יָאֵר פָּנָיו אִתָּנוּ סֶלָה:
לָדַעַת בָּאָרֶץ דַּרְכֶּךָ בְּכָל־גּוֹיִם יְשׁוּעָתֶךָ: יוֹדוּךָ עַמִּים ׀ אֱלֹהִים יוֹדוּךָ עַמִּים
כֻּלָּם: יִשְׂמְחוּ וִירַנְּנוּ לְאֻמִּים כִּי־תִשְׁפֹּט עַמִּים מִישׁוֹר וּלְאֻמִּים ׀ בָּאָרֶץ
תַּנְחֵם סֶלָה: יוֹדוּךָ עַמִּים ׀ אֱלֹהִים יוֹדוּךָ עַמִּים כֻּלָּם: אֶרֶץ נָתְנָה יְבוּלָהּ
יְבָרְכֵנוּ אֱלֹהִים אֱלֹהֵינוּ: יְבָרְכֵנוּ אֱלֹהִים וְיִירְאוּ אֹתוֹ כָּל־אַפְסֵי־אָרֶץ:

For the leader; with instrumental music. A psalm. A song. May God be gracious to us and bless us; may He show us favor, selah. That Your way be known on earth, Your deliverance among all nations. Peoples will praise You, O God; all peoples will praise You. Nations will exult and shout for joy, for You rule the peoples with equity, You guide the nations of the earth. Selah. The peoples will praise You, O God; all peoples will praise You. May the earth yield its produce; may God, our God, bless us. May God bless us, and be revered to the ends of the earth.

🎵 ANA B'CHOACH

אב״ג ית״ץ	אָנָּא בְּכֹחַ גְּדֻלַּת יְמִינְךָ תַּתִּיר צְרוּרָה
קר״ע שׂט״ן	קַבֵּל רִנַּת עַמְּךָ שַׂגְּבֵנוּ טַהֲרֵנוּ נוֹרָא
נג״ד יכ״ש	נָא גִבּוֹר דּוֹרְשֵׁי יְחוּדְךָ כְּבָבַת שָׁמְרֵם
בט״ר צת״ג	בָּרְכֵם טַהֲרֵם רַחֲמֵם צִדְקָתְךָ תָּמִיד גָּמְלֵם
חק״ב טנ״ע	חֲסִין קָדוֹשׁ בְּרֹב טוּבְךָ נַהֵל עֲדָתֶךָ
יג״ל פז״ק	יָחִיד גֵּאֶה לְעַמְּךָ פְּנֵה זוֹכְרֵי קְדֻשָּׁתֶךָ
שק״ו צי״ת	שַׁוְעָתֵנוּ קַבֵּל וּשְׁמַע צַעֲקָתֵנוּ יוֹדֵעַ תַּעֲלוּמוֹת

בָּרוּךְ שֵׁם כְּבוֹד מַלְכוּתוֹ לְעוֹלָם וָעֶד

We beg you! With the strength of Your right hand's greatness, unite the bundled sins.

Accept the prayer of Your nation;

strengthen us, purify us, Oh Awesome One.

Please, Oh Strong One – those who foster Your

Oneness, guard them like the apple of an eye.

Bless them, purify them, show them pity,

may Your righteousness always reward them.

Powerful Holy One, with Your abundant

goodness guide Your congregation.

One and only Exalted One, turn to Your nation,

which proclaims Your holiness.

Accept our entreaty and hear our cry, Oh Knower of mysteries.

Blessed be the name of His glorious kingdom forever and ever.

אָנָּא בְּכֹחַ – *Ana b'choach,* **"We beg You! With [Your] strength"** This ancient mystical prayer is attributed to the Talmudic sage Rabbi Nechunyah ben Hakanah. In these deeply spiritual passages, the number eight plays a significant role. Seven phrases are followed by a final verse. In this final phrase we recite the same words said during the prayer of the Shema. Originally the words *Baruch shem kevod malchuto l'olam va'ed* (בָּרוּךְ שֵׁם כְּבוֹד מַלְכוּתוֹ לְעוֹלָם וָעֶד), "Blessed be the name of His glorious kingdom for ever and ever," were uttered by our patriarch Jacob before he passed away, surrounded by his sons, after he was assured of their total commitment and unified dedication to God.

❧ PSALM 30

מִזְמוֹר שִׁיר־חֲנֻכַּת הַבַּיִת לְדָוִד: אֲרוֹמִמְךָ יְהֹוָה כִּי דִלִּיתָנִי וְלֹא־שִׂמַּחְתָּ
אֹיְבַי לִי: יְהֹוָה אֱלֹהָי שִׁוַּעְתִּי אֵלֶיךָ וַתִּרְפָּאֵנִי: יְהֹוָה הֶעֱלִיתָ מִן־שְׁאוֹל
נַפְשִׁי חִיִּיתַנִי מִיּוֹרְדִי־[מִיָּרְדִי־] בוֹר: זַמְּרוּ לַיהֹוָה חֲסִידָיו וְהוֹדוּ לְזֵכֶר
קָדְשׁוֹ: כִּי רֶגַע ׀ בְּאַפּוֹ חַיִּים בִּרְצוֹנוֹ בָּעֶרֶב יָלִין בֶּכִי וְלַבֹּקֶר רִנָּה: וַאֲנִי
אָמַרְתִּי בְשַׁלְוִי בַּל־אֶמּוֹט לְעוֹלָם: יְהֹוָה בִּרְצוֹנְךָ הֶעֱמַדְתָּה לְהַרְרִי עֹז

הַסְתַּרְתָּ פָנֶיךָ הָיִיתִי נִבְהָל: אֵלֶיךָ יְהוָה אֶקְרָא וְאֶל־אֲדֹנָי אֶתְחַנָּן: מַה־
בֶּצַע בְּדָמִי בְּרִדְתִּי אֶל־שָׁחַת הֲיוֹדְךָ עָפָר הֲיַגִּיד אֲמִתֶּךָ: שְׁמַע־יְהוָה
וְחָנֵּנִי יְהוָה הֱיֵה־עֹזֵר לִי: הָפַכְתָּ מִסְפְּדִי לְמָחוֹל לִי פִּתַּחְתָּ שַׂקִּי וַתְּאַזְּרֵנִי
שִׂמְחָה: לְמַעַן ׀ יְזַמֶּרְךָ כָבוֹד וְלֹא יִדֹּם יְהוָה אֱלֹהַי לְעוֹלָם אוֹדֶךָ:

A melody, a song of David for the dedication of the House. I extol
You, O Lord, for You have lifted me up and not let my enemies rejoice
over me. O Lord, my God, I cried out to You, and You healed me. O
Lord, You brought me up from Sheol, preserved me from going down
into the Pit. O you faithful of the Lord, sing to Him, and praise His
holy name. For He is angry but a moment, and when He is pleased
there is life. One may lie down weeping at nightfall; but at dawn there
are shouts of joy. When I was untroubled, I thought, "I shall never be
shaken," for You, O Lord, when You were pleased, made [me] firm as a
mighty mountain. When You hid Your face, I was terrified. I called to
You, O Lord; to my Lord I made appeal, "What is to be gained from my
death, from my descent into the pit? Can dust praise You? Can it declare
Your faithfulness? Hear, O Lord, and have mercy on me; O Lord, be
my help!" You turned my lament into dancing, you undid my sackcloth
and girded me with joy, that [my] whole being might sing hymns to You
endlessly; O Lord my God, I will praise You forever.

מִזְמוֹר שִׁיר – *Mizmor shir,* "A melody, a song" The first two words seem to be redun-
dant. *Mizmor* is often translated as "melody'" and *shir* as "song." Are they not the
same? Rabbi Abraham Isaac Kook contrasts the two terms: *mizmor* relates to our
emotions and our soulful yearnings. *Shir,* on the other hand, represents that which
is orderly and thought out; the term *shir* reflects a rational or intellectual approach.

When we engage with both emotions and intellect when serving God, there is a
fusion of logic and feeling. The synthesis of the heart and mind results in the ideal
service of the Almighty.

שִׁיר הַמַּעֲלוֹת לְדָוִד הִנֵּה מַה־טּוֹב וּמַה־נָּעִים שֶׁבֶת אַחִים גַּם־יָחַד: כְּשֶׁמֶן הַטּוֹב עַל־הָרֹאשׁ יֹרֵד עַל־הַזָּקָן זְקַן־אַהֲרֹן שֶׁיֹּרֵד עַל־פִּי מִדּוֹתָיו: כְּטַל־חֶרְמוֹן שֶׁיֹּרֵד עַל־הַרְרֵי צִיּוֹן כִּי שָׁם ׀ צִוָּה יְהוָה אֶת־הַבְּרָכָה חַיִּים עַד־הָעוֹלָם:

A song of ascents. Of David. Behold, how good and how pleasant to dwell together as brothers. It is like fine oil on the head running down onto the beard, the beard of Aaron, that comes down over the collar of his robe; like the dew of Hermon that falls upon the mountains of Zion. There the LORD ordained blessing, everlasting life.

הִנֵּה מַה־טּוֹב, וּמַה־נָּעִים – *Hineh mah tov u'mah na'im*, "Behold, how good and how pleasant" Moses and Aaron are the paradigm of brotherly love par excellence. Though different in nature and action, Moses and Aaron complemented one another, and together they formed a perfectly balanced leadership for the Jewish people.

The psalm opens with the well-known phrase *Hineh mah tov u'mah na'im shevet achim gam yachad*, "Behold, how good and how pleasant to dwell together as brothers." This chapter of Psalms is perfectly suited for Chanukah because it alludes to the "secret" of our salvation, namely, that our redemption will be achieved through *ahavat chinam*, "boundless love" for one another. One of Rabbi Kook's most beloved teachings stated: "If the Temple was destroyed due to baseless hate, it will be rebuilt with boundless love."

The following psalm shares with Chanukah the pervasive themes of praise, gratitude, and the recognition of God's power and kindness. The Rambam taught us that the festival of Chanukah is dedicated to *hallel v'hoda'ah*, "praise and thanks" to the Holy One. This uplifting psalm offers us an expression of heartfelt gratitude for our salvation.

רַנְּנוּ צַדִּיקִים בַּיהוָה לַיְשָׁרִים נָאוָה תְהִלָּה: הוֹדוּ לַיהוָה בְּכִנּוֹר בְּנֵבֶל
עָשׂוֹר זַמְּרוּ־לוֹ: שִׁירוּ־לוֹ שִׁיר חָדָשׁ הֵיטִיבוּ נַגֵּן בִּתְרוּעָה: כִּי־יָשָׁר דְּבַר־
יְהוָה וְכָל־מַעֲשֵׂהוּ בֶּאֱמוּנָה: אֹהֵב צְדָקָה וּמִשְׁפָּט חֶסֶד יְהוָה מָלְאָה
הָאָרֶץ: בִּדְבַר יְהוָה שָׁמַיִם נַעֲשׂוּ וּבְרוּחַ פִּיו כָּל־צְבָאָם: כֹּנֵס כַּנֵּד מֵי הַיָּם
נֹתֵן בְּאֹצָרוֹת תְּהוֹמוֹת: יִירְאוּ מֵיהוָה כָּל־הָאָרֶץ מִמֶּנּוּ יָגוּרוּ כָּל־יֹשְׁבֵי
תֵבֵל: כִּי הוּא אָמַר וַיֶּהִי הוּא־צִוָּה וַיַּעֲמֹד: יְהוָה הֵפִיר עֲצַת־גּוֹיִם הֵנִיא
מַחְשְׁבוֹת עַמִּים: עֲצַת יְהוָה לְעוֹלָם תַּעֲמֹד מַחְשְׁבוֹת לִבּוֹ לְדֹר וָדֹר:
אַשְׁרֵי הַגּוֹי אֲשֶׁר־יְהוָה אֱלֹהָיו הָעָם ׀ בָּחַר לְנַחֲלָה לוֹ: מִשָּׁמַיִם הִבִּיט
יְהוָה רָאָה אֶת־כָּל־בְּנֵי הָאָדָם: מִמְּכוֹן־שִׁבְתּוֹ הִשְׁגִּיחַ אֶל כָּל־יֹשְׁבֵי
הָאָרֶץ: הַיֹּצֵר יַחַד לִבָּם הַמֵּבִין אֶל־כָּל־מַעֲשֵׂיהֶם: אֵין־הַמֶּלֶךְ נוֹשָׁע
בְּרָב־חָיִל גִּבּוֹר לֹא־יִנָּצֵל בְּרָב־כֹּחַ: שֶׁקֶר הַסּוּס לִתְשׁוּעָה וּבְרֹב חֵילוֹ לֹא
יְמַלֵּט: הִנֵּה עֵין יְהוָה אֶל־יְרֵאָיו לַמְיַחֲלִים לְחַסְדּוֹ: לְהַצִּיל מִמָּוֶת נַפְשָׁם
וּלְחַיּוֹתָם בָּרָעָב: נַפְשֵׁנוּ חִכְּתָה לַיהוָה עֶזְרֵנוּ וּמָגִנֵּנוּ הוּא: כִּי־בוֹ יִשְׂמַח
לִבֵּנוּ כִּי בְשֵׁם קָדְשׁוֹ בָטָחְנוּ: יְהִי־חַסְדְּךָ יְהוָה עָלֵינוּ כַּאֲשֶׁר יִחַלְנוּ לָךְ:

Sing forth, O you righteous, to the LORD; it is fit that the upright acclaim Him. Praise the LORD with the lyre; with the ten-stringed harp sing to Him; sing Him a new song; play sweetly with shouts of joy. For the word of the LORD is right; His every deed is faithful. He loves what is right and just; the earth is full of the LORD's faithful care. By the word of the LORD the heavens were made, by the breath of His mouth, all their host. He heaps up the ocean waters like a mound, stores the deep in vaults. Let all the earth fear the LORD; let all the inhabitants of the world dread Him. For He spoke, and it was; He commanded, and it endured. The LORD frustrates the plans of nations, brings to naught the designs of peoples. What the LORD plans endures forever, what He designs, for ages on end. Happy the nation whose God is the LORD, the people He has chosen to be His own. The LORD looks down from heaven; He sees all mankind. From His dwelling-place He gazes on all the inhabitants of the earth – He who fashions the hearts of them all, who discerns all their doings. Kings are not delivered by a large force; warriors are not saved by great strength; horses are a false hope for deliverance; for all their great power they provide no escape. Truly the eye of the LORD is on those who fear Him, who wait for His faithful care to save them from death, to sustain them in famine. We set our hope on the LORD, He is our help and shield; in Him our hearts rejoice, for in His holy name we trust. May we enjoy, O LORD, Your faithful care, as we have put our hope in You.

THE DEEPER MEANING

Eight Meditations When Lighting from Rabbi Shlomo Carlebach

We kindle the lights by the door or the window of the house because on Chanukah all the doors and windows of our hearts are open to one another.

Do you know what is so special about the lights of Chanukah? You see them, yet you know that they are not just ordinary candles burning. The lights are full of secrets, full of mystery, full of depth. When I see Chanukah candles lit, I am aware that there is something deeper, something beyond this world.

Do you know what is so special about the lights of Chanukah? You see them, yet you know that they are not just ordinary candles burning. The lights are full of secrets, full of mystery, full of depth. When I see Chanukah candles lit, I am aware that there is something deeper, something beyond this world.

The Baal Shem Tov teaches that whatever heights a Jew reaches on Yom Kippur, which is a very high place, this cannot compare to where a Jew reaches on the nights of Chanukah.

On Chanukah we want to wipe out pagan worship in the same way that the Maccabees once did during the days of Chanukah. In Hebrew, pagan worship is called *avodah zarah* — literally, "strange worship," worship that you are a stranger to. You might be serving God, but you are serving God like a stranger, serving Him without your heart. So every year on Chanukah we are meant to wipe away strange worship. To do this, our worship has to flow from the deepest part of our hearts.

Kindling the Chanukah lights is a lesson in Jewish history. Knowing the past is vital, but living it and reliving it is the obligation of every Jew.

§

Can you imagine how much the *kohanim*, the holy priests, were crying the first night of Chanukah? They were praying so hard that this light should last forever. Because they kindled the light with so many tears, this is why this light is still shining.

§

The whole world says, "Live up to your potential." I say, "Go beyond your potential." This is the miracle of Chanukah — one light that surpassed everyone's expectations.

§

Chanukah is a time when God is visiting us in our homes. It is a very beautiful thing to be invited by the king to visit him in his palace. But when the King of kings takes time out to visit you in *your* house, *gevalt*...it means He loves you so much.

Why Do We Light with Olive Oil?

There are several ways that one may fulfill the mitzvah of lighting the Chanukah menorah. While one may certainly use wax candles, beeswax candles, paraffin, and an assortment of oils, the most preferred way of lighting the menorah is with olive oil.

Why olive oil? Importantly, this is the oil that the Jewish people used to light the Menorah in the Holy Temple, and it was with olive oil that the miracle occurred. Today, when we light our menorahs using olive oil, we closely mirror the way the *kohanim* lit the Menorah in Jerusalem.

Yet, there are other reasons why olive oil is significant and contains special symbolism, especially on Chanukah.

For the Greeks, everything that was *externally beautiful was good*; to the Jew, everything that is *inwardly good is beautiful*.

The victory of Chanukah was the victory of an inner essence over external appearance, of light over darkness. The olive is an appropriate symbol of this victory, for the light of the Menorah comes from the oil of the olive. Although the olive seems to be just a small and undistinguished fruit, its outer appearance is misleading. There is actually so much more to the olive than meets the eye. Inside this tiny fruit is the oil that can light an entire room.

While the olive appears to be just a small and simple food, when transformed into oil, this simple fruit turns out to have contained light. Seeing the light that emanates from the olive's oil, we are awakened to the possibilities of light hidden in other places, light packed into the simplest of physical things — waiting to be revealed through our usage and understanding. We are also reminded that if we look beyond the superficialities of this world, beyond the mask of darkness, we can perceive light.

At Chanukah time the olives on the trees are late in their season and have been darkening from green to black. It is the black olives that contain the most oil. The blacker the olive, the more light it contains. Sometimes we need to wait, to bide our time, in order to have greater understanding.

The lighting of the menorah by the Maccabees was the victory of this patient understanding that there is so much more to the world than meets the eye.

Chassidic tradition teaches that the word *hashemen* (הַשֶּׁמֶן), "the oil," has the same letters as *neshamah* (נְשָׁמָה), "soul." The oil is the hidden essence of the olive; the soul is the hidden essence of man.

The first mention of an olive in the Torah is when the olive branch is brought by the dove to Noah as a fitting symbol for light and hope. The prophet Jeremiah refers to the Jewish people being as beautiful as the olive tree – abundant in vitality and oil (Jeremiah 11:1).

The Sages in the Midrash elaborate on this comparison (*Exodus Rabbah* 36:1):

- Just as the leaves of the olive tree do not fall, neither in the summer nor the winter, so too the Jewish people's existence will never wither away.

- Just as olive oil does not mix with any other liquid and always rises to the top, so too the Jewish people will always remain distinct and serve as a model to the world.

- Just as olive oil brings light to the world, so too the Jewish people are a light and an inspiration to all mankind.

The olive tree has been a source of inspiration for Jews in modern times as well. Many Israelis have marveled at the tenacity of the olive tree during hazardous times.

For example, during the Second Lebanon War of 2006, many olive trees were burned badly by rocket fire. Unlike most trees, however, the olive tree did not catch on fire in the conventional sense. Instead it burned from within. The symbolism of the tree that was burned but seemed not to be consumed reminded many Israelis of the burning bush that Moses encountered.

In addition, even when olive trees were burned and seemingly destroyed, they were not dead. Amazingly, they sprouted new growth surrounding the burned-away trunk, with the new growth creating a ring around the spot where the original trunk stood. Again, there was a powerful message of comfort: that renewal can follow on the heels of significant adversity.

A Kabbalistic Perspective on the Thirty-Six Candles of Chanukah

Did you know that the thirty-six candles we light correspond to the thirty-six hours that Adam and Eve lived in the Garden of Eden?

So says Rabbi Tzvi Elimelech of Dinov (1783–1841) in his classic work *Bnei Yissaschar*. Drawing on Kabbalistic sources, the Rebbe makes the equation between the total of the thirty-six candles that are lit on Chanukah and the thirty-six hours of pure divine light that Adam and Eve experienced in the Garden of Eden, at the very beginning of time.

Jewish tradition teaches us that Adam and Eve were created on the last day of creation, on a Friday. The world they lived in consisted not only of the physical light but also a spiritual light that graced the universe.

God's first words, "Let there be light" (Genesis 1:3), did not refer to the light of the sun or the moon. Rather, the first light created by God was a spiritual light that filled the world with truth and clarity. This unique light was with Adam and Eve for thirty-six hours while they were in the Garden of Eden.

When the original man and woman deviated from the path of goodness, that unique light ended. It was left behind in Paradise when they were ordered to leave the Garden, after Shabbat.

The Rebbe of Dinov teaches that the lights we kindle in our homes on

Chanukah are reminiscent of the first light that God gave man. From our own small candles, we envision a spark of the divine light. This is a spiritual light that is meant to reveal both holiness in the world and the inner goodness found in all of creation.

It is no coincidence then that both the light of Chanukah and the pure light that was created at the beginning of time share the same number.

The lights of Chanukah remind us that the spiritual light that once adorned mankind can be lit up again. We actually pray for this light each day in our daily morning prayers: *Ohr chadash al Tzion ta'ir* (אוֹר חָדָשׁ עַל צִיּוֹן תָּאִיר), "May You shine a new light on Zion."

When Rabbi Shlomo Carlebach shared this teaching from the Dinover Rebbe, he would add the following:

> When we stand in front of the holy candles we are reminded that our world can be perfected. We are awakened to dream of a world reminiscent of the Garden of Eden: a place of peace and serenity, a place of kindness and of love.
>
> Do you know what the saddest thing in the world is? When we stop longing for a perfect world.
>
> Chanukah teaches us not be satisfied with *a little bit* of light, *a little bit* of good, *a little bit* of peace…but to passionately desire the most perfect light. We can never allow ourselves to lose sight of a great and lofty vision of what this world could look like. The light of Chanukah reveals to us a light of pure goodness that once filled this world…a light that will surely be revealed again.

In the glow of the menorah we see a glimmer of the original light of creation. This light radiates the signs of the final victory over evil.

We live in a world of hidden light, and it is up to us to repair the world, by righting injustice, by treating everyone and everything with loving compassion, by discerning the divine light at the core of every dark shell.

In the introduction to his biblical commentary, the Ramban (Nachmanides, 1194–1270) states that everything is to be found within the Torah, either in open or hidden fashion. As an example, he points out that Rabbi Akiva learned thousands of ideas even from the *tagin*, the crowns that adorn the tops of the letters in a Torah scroll (Talmud, *Menachot* 29b).

Bearing this in mind, the *Bnei Yissaschar* indicates that in the phrase "And God saw the light, that it was good" (Genesis 1:4), one finds a hint to the mitzvah of lighting the Chanukah candles.

Carefully look at the word *tov*, "good," and take note specifically of the *tagin*, the crown of the letter *tet* (ט). Usually, this letter, the first letter of the word *tov*, contains only three *tagin*, but here it contains four.

הָאוֹר כִּי טוֹב

The reason for this, he explains, is that the letter *tet* (ט) has the *gematria* or numerical equivalent of nine. And nine times four equals thirty-six — alluding to the thirty-six lights that are kindled during Chanukah.

This allusion appears in the verse that says that "God saw the light, that it was good," which indicates God's approval of the establishment of the lights of Chanukah and His love of our performance of the mitzvah of lighting the menorah for all time.

A Teaching for Each Candle

PEACE

"Just as the Temple was destroyed by senseless hatred,
so it will be rebuilt by the exact opposite: senseless love."

Rabbi Abraham Isaac Hakohen Kook

FIRE OR LIGHT?
The Great Chanukah Debate

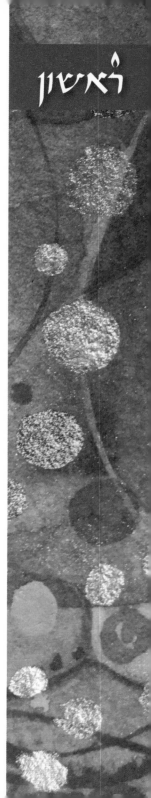

THE GREAT TALMUDIC SAGE SHAMMAI WAS OF THE OPINION THAT ONE lights the menorah with eight candles on the first night and subtracts one on each succeeding night.

His beloved opponent Hillel taught otherwise: that we light one candle the first night and add one additional candle on each of the following nights.

If Hillel's opinion feels right to us, it is perhaps because, after all, this is the custom the Jewish people have adopted since Talmudic times, when the lighting of the menorah was first instituted.

How do we understand their debate? Was it just a difference in style, or is there something deeper behind the differing approaches of these two giants?

The great Jerusalem sage Rabbi Shlomo Yosef Zevin (1888–1978) offered the following beautiful clarifying insight. He said that the debate revolves around an important distinction: whether Chanukah is a time to celebrate our ability to defeat evil, or whether it is about our ability to demonstrate how even a little bit of light can chase away a great deal of darkness.

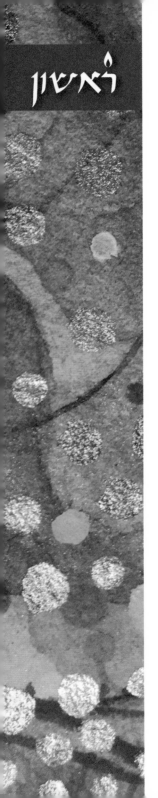

Stated otherwise, do we view the Chanukah candles as *fire* or as *light*?

Shammai indicates that our celebration is one of fire. It demonstrates our capacity to powerfully burn and consume the foe until there is nothing left. We begin with eight candles and symbolically show the tenacious power of our fire to wipe out our aggressors and subdue evil.

Hillel, on the other hand, teaches that we light one additional candle each night, demonstrating the power of the light to grow and expand. In the words of the Talmud (*Shabbat* 21b), *mosif v'holech*, "add and move forward." We choose to live with kindness, wisdom, and spreading the light of the Torah.

Adding a new Chanukah candle every night tells us that we must endeavor to increase our light and spread it throughout the world. Thus we begin with one light on the first night and add holiness each day, elevating the spiritual level each time.

We have chosen the path of Hillel. We prefer to choose light and to ever increase it; our way is the way of pleasantness that promotes healing and wholeness to the world.

There is a beautiful children's song that highlights these ideas:

We have come to chase away darkness;	באנו חושך לגרש
In our hands are *light* and *fire*.	בידינו אור ואש
Each one is a small light;	כל אחד הוא אור קטן
But together, we are a mighty light.	וכולנו אור איתן
Go away darkness, move aside night;	סורה חושך הלאה שחור
Go away because of the light.	סורה מפני האור

A teacher who was close with the Lubavitcher Rebbe, Rabbi Menachem Mendel Schneerson (1902–1994), once came to him for advice. His deep emotional pain as a Holocaust survivor was preventing him from fulfilling his teaching responsibilities. "There are no words to console you," the Rebbe said, "but you cannot allow the Holocaust to continue in your life." He counseled the man with words he had learned from his father-in-law, the previous Rebbe: "We are day workers, and our task is to shed light. We need not expend our energies in battling darkness. We need only to create day, and night will fade away."

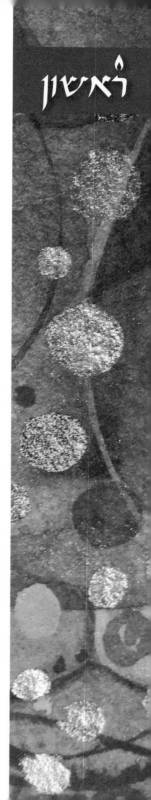

LOVE

"If God had given me two hearts, I could use one for hating and the other one for love. But since I was given only one heart, I have only room for love."

RABBI SHLOMO CARLEBACH

BE A LAMPLIGHTER

THE REVERED LUBAVITCHER REBBE, RABBI MENACHEM MENDEL SCHNEER-son, shared the following teaching, which offers an invaluable insight into the deeper meaning of Chanukah.

A student asked the Rebbe, "How does one become a pious Jew?"

The Rebbe replied, "To be a Jew is to be like a lamplighter. In the olden days, there was a person in every town who would light the gas streetlamps with a fire that he carried at the end of a long stick. On the street corner the lamps were there, ready to be lit. The lamplighter knows that the fire is not his own personal fire to keep for himself. He goes from lamp to lamp to set them alight."

The student asked his Rebbe, "But what if the lamp is far off in the wilderness?"

"This too one must light," answered the Rebbe.

Asked the student, "But what if the lamp is on an island in the midst of the sea?"

"Then one must take off one's clothes, jump into the water, and light it there!"

Asked the student, "Is this the Jew's mission?"

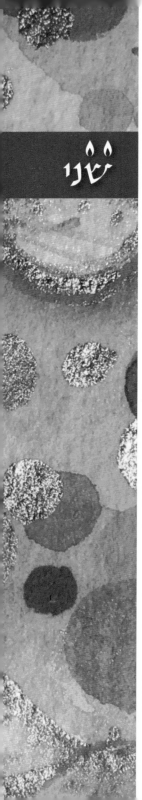

The Rebbe thought for a moment and then said, "Yes, that is a Jew's calling."

The student then said, "But Rebbe, I see no lamps!"

The Rebbe answered, "That is because you are not yet a lamplighter."

The student asked, "So how does one become a lamplighter?"

The Rebbe replied, "One must begin with oneself. Cleanse yourself and you will become more refined. Only then does one see that others are also a source of light, just waiting to be ignited. When, heaven forbid, one is crude, then one sees crudeness; but when one is noble, one sees nobility."

Today, there are so many lamps just waiting to be lit.

"It is written," said the Rebbe, "'The soul of the human is a lamp of God' (Proverbs 20:27). A pious Jew is one who puts personal affairs aside and goes around lighting up the souls of others with Torah and with mitzvot. Jewish souls are ready to be lit…it is simply a matter of uncovering the spark that is hidden within.

"Sometimes that person who is to be ignited is just around the corner. Sometimes he or she is to be found far away in the wilderness or across the sea.

"But no matter where they may be found, there must be someone who disregards personal comforts and convenience, and with self-sacrifice goes out to light these lamps and to ignite these souls.

"When you reach out with the essence of your soul, then the essence of your soul bonds with the essence of your friend's soul.

"When you reach out with love, the Godliness within your soul unites with the Godliness in your friend's soul. In this way the lamp is lit.

"This is the true calling of a Jew, to be a lamplighter. Your mission is to light up souls."

The act of taking the *shamash* candle in our hands and placing its flame to the wicks of the candles helps us to become God's lamplighter. Lighting the Chanukah candles each night puts us in this mode and spirit to take the next step and light up all those whom we can possibly reach.

"What do you do?" the Lubavitcher Rebbe asked a young man who came to meet with him.

"I'm a student at university," he responded. "I'm studying for a master's degree in education."

"That's special," the Rebbe said. "I, too, attended university some years ago."

Somewhat surprised, the young man asked, "And what did you study, theology?"

"No, I studied electrical engineering," the Rebbe responded with a smile. "But I prefer to turn the lights on in people's souls."

The Rebbe explained: "You see, every human being has a soul, a divine spark that burns inside them. Sometimes a person moves away from their inner light – it might even seem that the light of their soul has been snuffed out. But the soul is like a pilot light – it never goes out completely. All it needs is for someone to fan the embers with love, until their spiritual fire burns bright again."

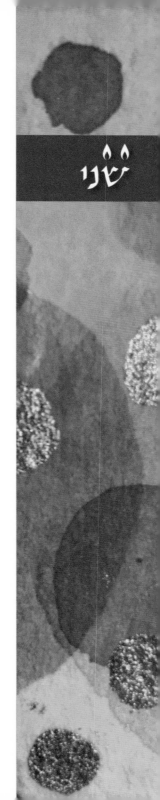

TURNING SPEARS
INTO PLOUGHSHARES

IT MAY BE THE MOST UNUSUAL MENORAH IN THE WORLD. SOME WOULD argue that it is the most authentic representation of the menorah that was lit by the Chashmonaim (Hasmoneans) during the first Chanukah. It can be found on a rooftop in the town of Sderot, Israel. It is indeed a unique menorah.

The town of Sderot sits in striking range of Gaza. Ten thousand rockets have been fired into Sderot and the Western Negev since 2001. The Kassam Rocket Menorah sits on top of the Sderot Yeshiva, where hundreds of young men study Torah and also serve in the Israeli army.

When Rabbi Yisrael Meir Lau, then chief rabbi of Israel, visited this rooftop menorah, he taught that the menorah that was lit at the time of Chanukah was not the golden Menorah in the Temple. The golden Menorah had been removed from the Temple. When the Maccabees returned to the Temple, the Menorah was not there.

The Menorah that was lit was a makeshift menorah made of bars of iron, presumably from the iron spearheads that were used in battle with the Syrian Greek army. Rabbi Lau asked whether the Chashmonaim could really find nothing other than deadly weapons to use for their menorah, and he explained that this special menorah made the statement that even an instrument of death can create light, *Ki ner mitzvah, v'Torah ohr* (כִּי נֵר מִצְוָה, וְתוֹרָה אוֹר), "for a commandment is a lamp, and the teaching [Torah] is light" (Proverbs 6:23).

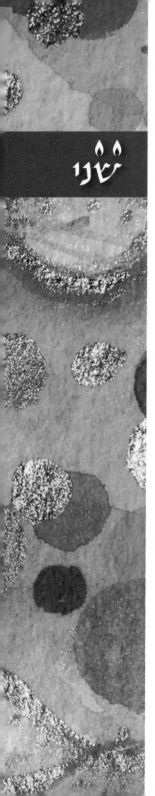

אשן

In an amazing expression of faith, the yeshiva commissioned a project to take the very Kassam rockets intended for destruction and death and fashion them into an object that would bring light — a menorah made from the very rockets aimed to destroy and to kill.

In doing so, they have brought the prophetic words of the prophet Isaiah to life. They have taken the spears of war and refashioned them into "ploughshares," a tool that brings hope and light to the world.

The Kassam Rocket Menorah is lit each year during the eight days of Chanukah. During these dark and cold nights, thousands of families in Sderot live under the threat of rocket fire. The menorah on the rooftop in Sderot illuminates the darkness with a message of hope. When lit up each night of the festival, the menorah is visible throughout the town of Sderot and even into Gaza. It offers a message of light and optimism to all who seek goodness and peace.

> "The heavens are the heavens of the Lord, but the earth He has given to the children of men" (Psalm 115:16).
>
> The Rebbe of Kotzk taught: "'The heavens' are in any case heavenly, 'but the earth He has given to the children of men,' to make earthly things heavenly."

FAMILY

"One person's candle is light for many."

TALMUD, SHABBAT 122A

SHALOM BAYIT
The Teaching of a Single Candle

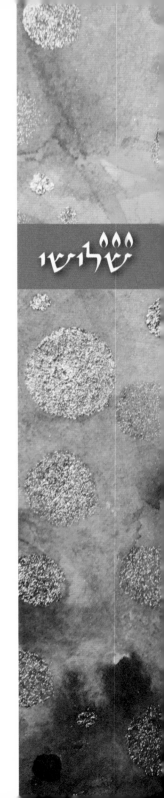

שלומו

IF A PERSON FINDS HIMSELF WITH ONLY ONE CANDLE ON FRIDAY AFTER-noon during Chanukah, should he light it as a Shabbat candle or a Chanukah candle?

It can't be both. One might suggest that he should light it as a Chanukah candle. After all, this light signifies the great miracle and spreads its light to tell of the great event in our history.

Yet Jewish law holds that, faced with such a choice, he should light it as a Shabbat candle.

Why?

The Rambam beautifully explains: "The Shabbat light takes priority because it symbolizes *shalom bayit*, 'domestic peace.' ...And great is peace, because the entire Torah was given in order to make peace in the world" (Laws of Chanukah 4:14).

Halachah, Jewish law, rules that if a person can light only one candle, the Shabbat light takes precedence. Peace in the home matters more than the great Maccabean military victory and even more than the miracle of the oil.

This teaching is beautifully exemplified by a wonderful story about one of the most beloved sages, the Chafetz Chaim (1839–1933). The

שלוחאו

world-renowned Rabbi Yisrael Meir Kagan had a rebbe, a mentor, who was not as well known as he was. His rebbe was a saintly man from the town of Horodna, Lithuania, named Rabbi Nachum Kaplan (1812–1879), known lovingly as Reb Nachum'ke.

The Chafetz Chaim made a point to observe carefully Reb Nachum'ke's every action and deed, for he knew that anything that Reb Nachum'ke ever did was done with forethought and good intent.

It happened one night during Chanukah that the Chafetz Chaim came to visit his rebbe.

The time for lighting Chanukah candles came, and the Chafetz Chaim waited for his rebbe to recite the blessings and to light the candles. Surprisingly though, Reb Nachum'ke let the time pass and made no move to light the menorah. The Chafetz Chaim was a bit baffled that his rebbe would let the time slip by and not light on time, but he didn't dare say anything.

More time elapsed, and still Reb Nachum'ke went about his regular routine without saying anything about the lighting of the Chanukah candles. An hour went by and then another hour; still the menorah was not lit. The Chafetz Chaim simply could not understand his rebbe's inaction and apparent inattentiveness to this mitzvah.

Finally deep into the night, there was a knock on the door. The rebbe opened the door. It was his wife. Almost immediately after she came in, Reb Nachum'ke began his introductory prayers, recited the appropriate blessings, and then lit the Chanukah menorah.

The Chafetz Chaim realized that there had to be a lesson here, so once the flames were flickering, he respectfully asked his rebbe to explain to him why he had let so much time elapse before finally lighting his menorah. Reb Nachum'ke explained patiently to his beloved student.

The Talmud (*Shabbat* 23b) poses a question: What is the law if a person has money to use for only one candle on the Friday night of Chanukah? Should he spend it on a Shabbos candle and fulfill the mitzvah of lighting

Shabbos candles, or rather spend the money on a candle for his Chanukah menorah, and thereby fulfill the mitzvah of Chanukah candle lighting?

Reb Nachum'ke answered, "The Talmud states unequivocally that one is obligated to spend the money for a Shabbos candle, the reason being that the Shabbos candle, aside from the mitzvah involved, adds to *shalom bayit*, peace and tranquility of the home. Thus, a candle that fosters *shalom bayit* takes precedence even over the mitzvah of lighting Chanukah candles.

"I have no doubt," continued Reb Nachum'ke, "that had my wife come home and realized that I did not wait for her with the Chanukah candles, she would unquestionably have been distraught. There would have been tension, and perhaps even anger on her part that I didn't show her the courtesy of waiting until she returned. Thus, I delayed until she came home.

"You see," added Reb Nachum'ke, "the Talmud itself used Chanukah candles as a focal point to emphasize the importance of marital harmony. Should I have taken these same Chanukah candles and through them diminished *shalom bayit*? Better to let the ideal time to light pass by and to fulfill the mitzvah of generating love and harmony in the home."

> Reb Aryeh Levin (1885–1969) was known for his sublime character traits of humility, kindness, and respect for all. Reb Aryeh was perpetually involved with deeds of charity and goodness. His concern for and devotion to his wife was also legendary. Reb Aryeh fulfilled the talmudic law that "one must love his wife like himself, and honor and respect her *more* than himself" (*Yevamot* 62b).
>
> Once Reb Aryeh brought his wife to the doctor because she was experiencing foot pain. When the doctor inquired as to the reason for their visit, Reb Aryeh told him, "My wife's foot is hurting us."

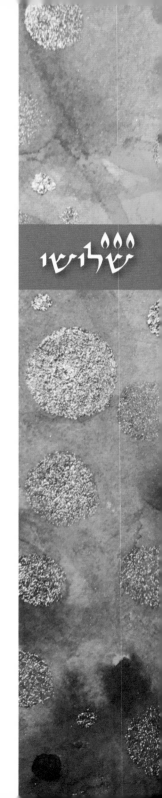

BUILDING A HOLY HOME

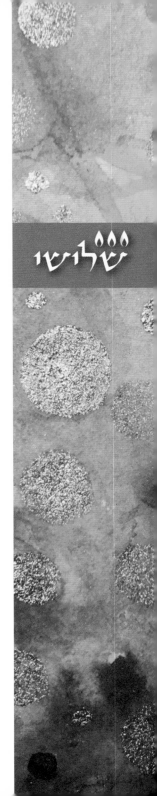

GOD COMMANDS US TO BUILD HIM A HOME. HIS HOME IS THE TEMPLE IN Jerusalem.

Three vessels of the Temple – the Ark, the Table, and the Menorah – parallel three essential furnishings that one would generally find in a home: a bed, a table, and a lamp.

The Ibn Ezra (1089–1167) suggests that like a bed, the Ark is a place of rest – God's place of rest; the Table is where we symbolically offer God sustenance; and the Menorah provides light. We would provide the same things for a guest visiting our own homes. Although God does not need us to provide for Him, we provide this setting for God, as it helps us more tangibly to feel His presence in our midst.

Two thousand years ago when the Maccabees entered the Temple and lit the Menorah, they celebrated a *chanukat habayit*, the rededication of the Second Temple in Jerusalem. The essence of the Beit Hamikdash or Temple was to make a house of God and to create a space for the presence of God to reside.

Rabbi Joseph Soloveitchik taught that this insight gives us an invaluable lesson about the purpose of our own homes: if the Temple could be transformed into a house, then the private home of a Jew can be transformed into a Temple.

שולחן

We welcome God into our homes by sanctifying the three corresponding objects: the bed, the table, and the lamp.

THE BED in our homes represents family purity and *shalom bayit*. God's presence resides in the home when there is a deep sensitivity and love shared between a husband and wife.

THE TABLE represents the mitzvot that surround the place of eating in our homes, such as eating kosher food, reciting blessings over food, and the mitzvah of welcoming guests. Our homes are sanctified when we transform our material blessings into spiritual sustenance for our family and those in need.

THE LAMP, which offers tangible light, is also a symbol of God's spiritual light, wisdom, and enlightenment. The light represents the study of Torah: "for a commandment is a lamp, and the teaching [Torah] is light" (Proverbs 6:23). When we learn and share the teachings of the Torah with our family and with all those who join us in our homes, we nourish the home with a spiritual dimension.

In Jewish life throughout the millennia, God has always been an honored presence in the Jewish home. Jews have always thought that God was a regular visitor in their homes and hearts, and therefore have taken the Divine Presence into account in their everyday behavior and speech. The Jewish people have always had the conviction that God was somehow present, calling out to His people in a challenging, comforting, encouraging, and inspiring way.

Concerning the Temple, the Torah says, "And there I will meet with you, and I will speak with you…" (Exodus 25:22). In the Sanctuary we were given the opportunity to experience God's presence. The same can be said of the Jewish home. When we sanctify our homes, by making them a sanctuary, then the Shechinah, God's presence, indeed finds a place to dwell.

It is interesting to note that the mitzvah of lighting the menorah is an obligation not on every *person*, but on every Jewish *home*. The formulation in the Talmud regarding this mitzvah is *ner ish u'veito* (נֵר אִישׁ וּבֵיתוֹ), "a candle to be lit *in each home*." The ancient custom was to place the menorah parallel to the mezuzah. This may suggest that it shares a characteristic of the mezuzah in that it is the home that generates the obligation. The home is crucial in executing the mitzvah.

Just as the miracle of the flame proclaims the presence of God in the Temple, the flames that burn in our windows each night proclaim that this house is a place of God's dwelling, a place imbued with a sense of God's presence.

Chanukah inspires the Jewish family to transform the stones and bricks of our homes into a familial temple, a home imbued with holiness.

On one of his travels, the townsfolk complained to the Baal Shem Tov that on Yom Kippur, the *chazzan* had chanted the *Al Chet*, the confessional prayer for sins, with a merry melody instead of a more appropriate somber refrain. When the Baal Shem Tov asked the *chazzan* why he did this, the latter replied, "If I were hired to clean the king's palace, wouldn't I be happy about making the palace more suitable for the king? When I confess my sins, I am sweeping away all the objectionable material within myself to make a place where God would wish to reside. Should I not rejoice over this?" The Baal Shem Tov was very moved by the explanation.

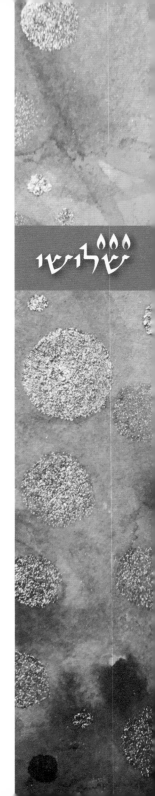

THE TREASURE OF CHANUKAH

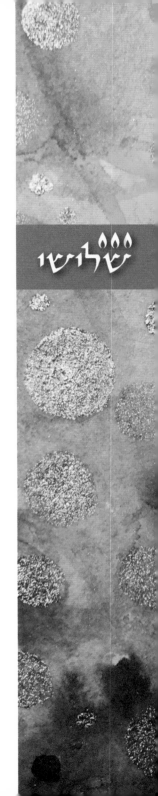

THERE WAS ONCE A POOR MAN BY THE NAME OF REB ISAAC BEN YAKIL of Krakow. He lived in poverty for many years, not knowing where his next crust of bread would come from. Still, Reb Isaac had complete faith that God would not let him starve, and that one day his suffering would end.

One night, he dreamed that there was a highly valuable treasure buried under a certain bridge in Prague. At first he paid the dream no attention, assuming it was mere wishful thinking. After all, who doesn't dream of riches?

But when the dream repeated itself night after night, he began to reconsider. Perhaps there was something to it? Could it possibly be true? So he set off on a long and tiring journey to Prague — only to discover that the bridge of his dreams was right near the royal palace and was heavily guarded at all hours. Soldiers marched up and down constantly, alert and ready, looking for any signs of danger or unusual activity. Digging under the bridge was clearly out of the question.

But Reb Isaac was not going to give up that easily. He returned to the bridge day after day until the guards began to recognize him. Soon they became curious. "Why do you come to the bridge every day?" one of the guards asked him. "Are you waiting for someone?"

Reb Isaac knew they wouldn't believe some half-baked excuse, so he told them about his dream. The guard listened, threw back his head,

– 89 –

and laughed heartily. "You came all this way because of a silly dream? You fool! I had a dream that some Jew, a Reb Isaac ben Yakil, has buried treasure under his stove, but do you see me going on a wild goose chase? Of course not!" and he laughed uproariously.

Hearing that, Reb Isaac hurried back to Krakow. Now he knew where to look. Sure enough, when he arrived, he immediately shoved the iron stove out of the way and began digging at the hard dirt floor. And to his great joy and astonishment, after some effort he uncovered a chest of gold coins! He used the money to build a magnificent synagogue for all to enjoy.

The essence of Chanukah is captured in this story. There is a treasure of light and of great blessing found right in our homes. It is a light that is meant for us to enjoy and to share with others.

A wealthy businessman who visited the Chafetz Chaim (1839–1933) was surprised to see that the sage lived in sparse quarters, and he offered to pay for a more spacious and comfortable dwelling.

The Chafetz Chaim asked him, "What is your home like?"

The visitor said, "I have a large salon, a spacious dining room, a study, several bedrooms, all beautifully furnished."

"And when you are away from your home on business, do you also have such accommodations?" the Chafetz Chaim asked.

"No," the man answered. "When I am on the road I have a room in a hotel."

"It is the same with me," the Chafetz Chaim said. "In the Eternal World I have a spacious home. But I am here on earth for a rather brief journey to earn my provisions for my permanent home. My stay on earth is like a business trip, and like you, when I am on the road, one room suffices."

Heroism

"There is no limit to the power of the soul.
It is a candle of the Divine in the world."

RABBI ABRAHAM ISAAC KOOK, *SHEMONAH KEVATZIM* 1:846

THE GREAT HEROINES

ARE WOMEN OBLIGATED TO PERFORM THE MITZVAH OF LIGHTING CHANUKAH candles?

The answer is yes. The Talmud (*Shabbat* 23a) explicitly obliges a woman, "since they, too, were part of the miracle."

Rashi says that not only were the women endangered like the men and experienced the redemption, but they played a critical part in the miracle.

Tosafot says that an extraordinary act by a woman named Judith or Yehudit played a major role in our miraculous salvation.

The high priest, Yochanan Kohen Gadol, had an extremely beautiful daughter by the name of Judith. The Greek king ordered that she come to his residence and be intimate with him. Judith was forced to go. Once she was alone with the king, she fed him cheese dishes so that he would become thirsty. She then had him drink wine and he became inebriated.

The king lay down and fell asleep. She then took a sword and cut off his head, which she brought to Jerusalem. When the Greek army saw that their leader was dead, they fled.

Judith's heroic act spearheaded the Maccabean revolt and their successful battles, victories, and the miraculous return to the Temple. To forever remember and honor her actions, there is a custom among Jews to eat dairy dishes and cheese on Chanukah, since the miracle came about through the milk that she fed the enemy (Rema, *Orach Chaim* 670:2).

The Talmud (*Shabbat* 23a) credits not just one woman but rather an

entire movement of hundreds if not thousands of Jewish women who were an essential part of the miracle.

One of the harsh decrees enacted by the Greeks against the Jewish people was that they were forbidden to circumcise their baby boys. A circumcision clearly marked the Jew as separate and distinct from his neighbors. In Greek culture, with its emphasis on the body, this was a dramatic distinction. It also provided a principal obstacle to marriage with non-Jewish women, something the Greeks desired in order to further assimilate the Jews away from their tradition and faith.

The Greeks were thus determined to put an end to the Jewish ritual of circumcision.

Women were at the forefront of this struggle. It was the Jewish mother, even more than the father, who was determined to ensure that their child would enter the covenant of Abraham in the fullest sense by receiving a *brit*, one of the most beloved and fundamental mitzvot. The book of Maccabees describes the self-sacrifice of mothers on behalf of their children: "And women who circumcised their sons were put to death by the king. The infants were hanged.... But they preferred death to violating their souls and violating God's covenant" (1 Maccabees 1:58–60).

Some have even suggested that Chanukah is an eight-day holiday specifically to commemorate the victory in the struggle over circumcision — which was led by heroic women.

> The Lubavitcher Rebbe called for a campaign encouraging Jewish women and girls to light Shabbat candles every Friday afternoon. He encouraged girls to begin lighting candles as soon as they were able to speak and to make the blessing. He taught that the prevalent spiritual darkness must be countered with as much light as possible. "And imagine how much light is added to the world every Friday," he said, "when women and girls worldwide light these millions of candles."

WHO WAS THE TRUE HERO OF CHANUKAH?

Some might say that it was Matityahu, the elderly pious man, who inspired and led the revolt against the Syrian Greeks. One day the henchmen of Antiochus arrived in the village of Modiin where Mattathias lived. The Syrian officer built an altar in the marketplace of the village and demanded that Mattathias offer sacrifices to Greek gods. Mattathias replied, "I, my sons, and my brothers are determined to remain loyal to the covenant that our God made with our ancestors."

He then gathered a following of loyal Jews and initiated a revolt against the enemy, invoking as his battle cry the same words that Moses cried in a time of danger: *Mi la'Shem elai* (מִי לַה׳ אֵלָי), "Those who are on the side of God, join me" (Exodus 32:26)!

Some might say that it was Judah the Maccabee, the son of Mattathias. Together with his courageous brothers, Judah assembled legions of Jewish warriors and defeated the enormous enemy army.

In the early days of the rebellion, Judah received the surname Maccabee, which means "hammer" or "sledgehammer," in recognition of his fierceness in battle. The name Maccabee (מַכַּבִּי) may also be an acronym for the Torah verse *mi ka'mocha ba'elim, Ado-nai* (מִי־כָמֹכָה בָּאֵלִם ה׳), "Who is like You, Lord, among the mighty?" (Exodus 15:11). This was his battle cry to motivate his troops.

רביעי

Still others might claim that it was the beautiful Judith, the daughter of Yochanan the high priest, who lured the Syrian Greek commander to sleep and decapitated him.

While these three historic personalities rightfully receive much attention, there is one other possibility to consider.

After their dazzling victory over the Syrian Greeks, the Maccabees found that the Temple was in total disarray. Even worse, the Temple had been desecrated and its holy vessels were badly damaged.

According to the Chatam Sofer (1762–1839), when the Jews first reentered the Temple, the Sanctuary was so defiled that on the first night the priests could not kindle the Menorah inside the Heichal or main Sanctuary. Instead they had to light it in the Azarah, the outer courtyard. This explains the curious phrase in the Al Hanisim prayer that states that they lit the Menorah *b'chatzrot kodshecha* (בְּחַצְרוֹת קָדְשֶׁיךָ), "in Your holy courtyard" (*Derashot Chatam Sofer L'Chanukah 5592*).

Those who first entered the Temple could easily have decided to wait until the Temple was purified and only then would they light the Menorah. And yet, one person searched the Temple, hoping to find a pure jug of oil, desperately wanting to light the Menorah that very night.

That person found the oil, and the Menorah was lit right away. God blessed that the lighting would last for eight days until new pure oil could be brought to the Temple.

Who was that person who was so determined to find oil and light the Menorah? Actually, we don't know. We have no record of that anonymous person.

But this anonymous *kohen*, presented with an easier path to do the ordinary, chose to do the extraordinary. As a result of his faithful initiative and his zeal for the mitzvah, the Menorah was miraculously lit for eight days. God responded to that leap of faith and blessed that lighting.

Five hundred years ago the Beit Yosef, Rabbi Yosef Caro (1488–1575), asked a now famous question: If there was enough oil to last one day, why do we celebrate the holiday for eight days? After all, the miracle only took place over seven days.

One answer suggests that we celebrate for seven days to symbolize the miraculous seven days that the oil lasted. And we celebrate an additional, eighth day in recognition of extraordinary initiative and faith — not the initiative taken by our three remarkable historical figures, but the faithful initiative of one anonymous *kohen* who was determined to make sure that the Menorah would be lit.

The ultimate hero of Chanukah might well be the unsung anonymous person who with faithful determination sought and found the oil that kindled the holy flames that have miraculously lasted until this very day.

> "The daughter of Pharaoh came down to bathe in the river…and she saw the ark among the reeds, and she sent her *amatah*, handmaid, to fetch it" (Exodus 2:5). Rashi offers a different explanation, that her *amatah* means her hand, which increased in length several *amot*, cubits.
>
> The Kotzker Rebbe asks: "From the outset, why did the daughter of Pharaoh extend her hand to take the ark when she saw it distant from her, and how did she know that a miracle would be performed for her, that her hand would become longer? Rather, this is proof regarding a commendable act, that a person must do to the extent of his capabilities without making calculations, and without acting in a purely logical manner. The main thing is the desire and the deed — the miracle will come about by itself."

NOAM'S ETERNAL FLAME

WE WOULD NEVER HAVE WITNESSED THE MIRACLE OF THE MENORAH were it not for the bravery and sacrifice of the courageous Jews, the Maccabees, who fought and defeated the powerful Greek army.

However, when thinking about Chanukah we generally don't think about the great many Jews who gave their lives in the many battles that were fought. In fact, of the five sons of Mattathias, only one child survived the war whose victory we celebrate.

In our own day, in the State of Israel we have been blessed with the heroism and bravery of the young Jewish men and women of the Israel Defense Forces. These modern-day Maccabees courageously protect our Jewish homeland and her people.

This is the story of one brave soldier who sacrificed his life, and whose story has a special Chanukah connection. On the night of December 27, 2002, the students at Yeshivat Otniel, in the Hebron hills, were ushering in Shabbat with food and song at the Friday night Shabbat meal. Four students had volunteered to be the evening's waiters and were busy in the kitchen preparing to serve the food.

A twenty-three-year-old soldier, a student in the yeshiva named Noam Apter, was among them. As Noam was loading food on a tray to bring into the dining hall, terrorists burst into the kitchen and sprayed the room with gunfire.

רביעי

Noam could have run from the room and saved his own life. Instead he sprinted to the door connecting the kitchen to the dining hall and locked it, leaving himself in the room with the terrorists. At the same time he had the presence of mind to hide the key where the terrorists could not find it.

One terrorist shot Noam in the back. Fatally wounded, Noam fell to the ground – but not before blocking the door with his body. On the other side of the door were close to a hundred students. After they had shot the four students in the kitchen – Yehuda Bamberger, Zvi Ziemen, Gabriel Hoter, and Noam – the terrorists tried to open the door of the dining room but failed. Next, they unsuccessfully attempted to shoot into the room through a small glass window.

Locking the door behind him, Noam had saved his friends' lives, while sacrificing his own. Noam was hailed as a hero by students and rabbis for his selfless bravery. Had he not locked the connecting door during his final moments, many more people would undoubtedly have been killed that night.

After Noam's death, his family discovered a collection of his own Hebrew poems in his desk.

Everyone has his own temple inside him.
In some, it's in ruins.
Some don't realize that it even exists.
But this temple is in every being.
It is our soul.
Someday, all the private temples within us will stand upright and then we will be prepared to bring the Shechinah into the world...

On that fateful night Noam revealed to us his inner temple, and just how pure a soul he himself was.

At the annual White House Chanukah celebration in 2004, US president George W. Bush requested that a menorah be lit to honor the heroic courage of a young man by the name of Noam Apter. The president had heard of his bravery and wished to honor his memory on Chanukah, a holiday of bravery and freedom.

A silver menorah was produced in Noam's memory. When the candles were lit, the president of the United States spoke of Noam and of the power of good defeating evil. Sitting at the side of the menorah was a picture of Staff Sergeant Noam Apter, of blessed memory.

For all its joy and beauty, the reality is that Chanukah is a bittersweet story, encompassing stories of self-sacrifice, heroic action, and the loss of many precious lives. So many of our brothers and sisters fought for our right to live with freedom and security, and gave their lives in this struggle.

When we gather to light our menorahs, we might choose to view the flames in part as memorial candles for the precious souls who have given their lives *al kiddush Hashem*, sanctifying God's name, so that the Jewish nation would survive.

We are inspired to emulate their courage.

We will never forget their sacrifice.

We will bring blessing to their memory.

Rabbi Aharon Lichtenstein (1933–2015), who was the leader of the Har Etzion Hesder Yeshiva in Israel, related a series of questions he had received from students serving in the Israel Defense Forces to his father-in-law, Rabbi Joseph Soloveitchik.

One student worked in the tank division and his job was cleaning out and maintaining the tanks. Often his uniform got covered in oil and grime. He wanted to know if he needed to change before the afternoon prayer, something that would be terribly inconvenient and difficult. Rabbi Soloveitchik looked at Rabbi Lichtenstein and wondered out loud, "Why would he need to change? He is wearing *bigdei kodesh*, holy garments."

רביעי

WHAT DOES THE WORD *CHANUKAH* MEAN?

AS EARLY AS THE FOURTEENTH CENTURY, IT WAS SUGGESTED THAT THE word *Chanukah* is actually a combination of two words: *Chanu*, which literally means "they rested" or "there was tranquility," and the two letters *chaf* and *heh*, which have the numerical value of twenty-five (Rabbeinu Nissim).

It was on the twenty-fifth day of the Hebrew month of Kislev that the victory was complete and we returned to the Temple to light the Menorah.

One word – *Chanukah* – captures both the great victory of the Maccabees over the Greek army and the date the celebration begins.

Known as the premier halachic authority during his lifetime, Rabbi Yosef Shalom Elyashiv (1910–2012), who lived to the age of 102, posed the following question regarding the meaning of the word *Chanukah*: If we wanted to emphasize the greatness of the Maccabean victory, why choose a name that reflects on the "tranquility," which only *followed* the battle?

The saintly rabbi of the holy city answered: a Jew never considers a victory in battle a cause for celebration, because war is never a goal unto itself. When we engage in battle, it is only as a means of restoring security and serenity. After all, we are commanded, "When your enemies fall, do not rejoice" (*Pirkei Avot* 4:24).

We dream only of peace.

The Sages intentionally named the holiday Chanukah so that they could share a moral message. They emphasized to the Jewish people in

רביעי

their time, and to the Jews for all time, that only the peace that follows the war is to be eternalized and celebrated for generations.

Chanukah celebrates the joyous return to Jerusalem and the reestablishment of Jewish sovereignty in the Holy Land. It was only then that we could once again fully embrace the precious mitzvot that were stripped away from us by the harsh decrees of the Syrian Greeks. We yearned to live peacefully so that we could engage in a life devoted to goodness, kindness, and service to our Creator.

Tranquility, brotherhood, and peace are our highest aspirations. Peace is so vital and precious that the word *shalom*, peace, is used to conclude the Amidah, the mourner's prayer of Kaddish, the Priestly Blessings, and the Birkat Hamazon or Grace after Meals.

The word *Chanukah*, the name given to this beloved holiday, reflects our deepest yearning for the blessing of *shalom* for us, and for all people.

One is required to take three steps back at the end of the Amidah before reciting the verse *oseh shalom*, the prayer for peace. Rabbi Chaim of Volozhin explained that this teaches us that making peace at times requires us to "take steps back" from our position, to be compromising and understanding.

MIRACLES

*"The difference between a miracle and a natural
event is only in frequency."*

RABBI SIMCHA ZISSEL BROIDE, THE ELDER OF KELM

THE GREAT CHANUKAH QUESTION

THE FOLLOWING PROVOCATIVE QUESTION WAS FIRST POSED FIVE HUNDRED years ago by the great Beit Yosef, Rabbi Yosef Caro: Why is Chanukah celebrated for eight days? Should it not be a seven-day holiday? After all, the cruse of oil found was sufficient to light the menorah for one day. Therefore, the miracle of the menorah was really only a seven-day miracle!

A memorable answer was given by Rabbi Simcha Zissel Broide, known as the Elder of Kelm: the difference between a miracle and a natural event is only in its frequency. For example, we consider the moon and stars appearing in the sky each night to be natural events and not supernatural, simply because we see them consistently.

In truth, "nature" is no less miraculous than "miracles." Actually, the very rules of nature are miraculous. The only difference between nature and the miraculous is that nature is what we are used to seeing and a miracle is what we rarely see. There is no intrinsic difference between the two.

The holiday of Chanukah was established by our Sages as an eight-day celebration with brilliant insight. Seven days of the holiday commemorate the revealed miracle, namely the oil lasting supernaturally for seven days. One additional day is added in order to commemorate that the oil burning the first day was also a miracle — a hidden miracle, which should be considered no less significant.

חנוכה

The great medieval sage the Ramban (on Exodus 13:16) put it this way: "Natural events should be viewed as hidden miracles, and miracles should really be called revealed miracles; both, however, should be viewed as miracles from God." He asserts that the purpose of open or revealed miracles is to alert us to the presence of the hidden miracles in the regular workings of nature.

When the priests in the Temple lit the Menorah in the time of Chanukah and saw the revealed miracle, they were reminded that in fact, the oil that naturally burned the first night was nothing less than a miracle as well.

The Elder of Kelm insists that we take inspiration from this teaching during the days of Chanukah and well beyond. Hidden miracles abound in our lives. God's guiding hand is present every moment. We determine whether an event is perceived as natural or miraculous.

> A maxim often attributed to the great physicist Albert Einstein posits "There are two ways to live your life. One, as if nothing is a miracle. The other, as if everything is a miracle."

QUALITY OVER QUANTITY

THE TORAH REQUIRES THAT *only* OLIVE OIL BE USED FOR THE LIGHTING of the Menorah in the Temple. Any other type of oil is forbidden to be used in the Temple's lighting.

When the Maccabees miraculously lit the Menorah in the Temple, some opinions say that all the olive oil burned the first night; there was no remaining oil. New oil replenished the Menorah each night.

If this was the case, then what was lit on the following nights therefore was *not* natural olive oil pressed from olives. The oil that filled the Menorah the remaining seven nights was, so to speak, miracle oil replenished miraculously by God.

The legendary Rabbi Chaim Soloveitchik (1853–1918) provocatively asks how this could have been used. Miracle oil, he points out, is not kosher for use in the Menorah; only natural olive oil can be used!

Reb Chaim explains that the oil from the first night was actually not fully consumed. On each of the eight days only an eighth of the oil burned. Indeed the miracle was that the very *essence* of the oil was altered, and the oil had changed its composition. Now, only a fraction of the oil was needed to fuel the flame for an entire day. The oil poured in the Menorah the first night became more potent so that the Menorah miraculously burned all eight nights.

This means that the miracle of the oil was not one of *quantity* but of *quality*.

Instead of the quantity of the oil increasing, it was the nature, the

essence, the quality of the oil that "increased" by changing. This meant that only one-eighth of the oil burned through the entirety of each night, for all eight nights.

Reb Chaim's teaching carries the beautiful message that as Jews we emphasize quality over quantity. Our teacher Moses himself highlights this point: "It is not because you are the most numerous of peoples that the Lord set His heart on you and chose you — indeed *you are the smallest of peoples*" (Deuteronomy 7:7).

Chanukah emphasizes the power of the few to overcome the many, as articulated in the Al Hanisim prayer: "the many into the hands of the few." A small group of Maccabee soldiers were victorious in overcoming a massive army. A small cruse of oil fueled the Menorah for eight consecutive days.

In other words, our greatness is not to be found in our quantity, but in our *quality*. Our determination to do good, our dedication to kindness and devotion to morality has empowered us with unique strength. Being small in numbers lends itself to creating a sense of importance and uniqueness in the group. The realization that there is a sense of urgency and responsibility in one's actions is enhanced by the comprehension that one is part of a very small group, and therefore every individual counts enormously in the fate and success of the whole people.

In the mystical teachings of the Kabbalah, oil symbolizes Torah wisdom. Much like the oil that fuels the flame, the Torah fuels our people. The Greeks tried to defile the oil and to destroy our loving devotion to the Torah. They attempted to erode our very essence and darken the pristine light found at our core.

But the pure light of the Jewish soul can never be snuffed out. Its flame will endure with a potency that continues to shine bright for the world.

Rabbi Yisrael Salanter (1809–1883), the great leader of the *mussar* movement of self-improvement and mastering one's personal moral conduct, was once asked to speak between Minchah and Ma'ariv in a congregation. He sensed that his audience was not in the most receptive mood.

Reb Yisrael simply said to them: "If only one Jew is moved by even one word of my speech to pray the evening service tonight with more *kavanah*, with intensity of concentration; and even if it's only one word of prayer; and even if that one Jew is just this speaker, then my speech will have been worthwhile."

חמישו

MAKING A MIRACLE GREAT

NES GADOL HAYAH SHAM (נֵס גָּדוֹל הָיָה שָׁם), "A GREAT MIRACLE HAPPENED there." These beloved words are symbolized by the four initials *nun* (נ), *gimmel* (ג), *heh* (ה), *shin* (ש), which appear on the dreidel, referring of course to the miracle of Chanukah.

Moses stands at the burning bush and observes a miracle. The bush is on fire and astonishingly the leaves and branches are not consumed. Moses witnesses his first miracle. In response he says, "I see a great sight" (Exodus 3:3).

Rabbi Joseph Soloveitchik asks: "Why did Moses not call it a *nes*, a miracle? Why did he simply say, 'I see something great'?"

Although Moses was aware that he was witnessing a miracle, that is not what intrigued him. Rather, what riveted Moses was the message that he heard. It was a great sight for one reason: because Moses responded to the call of God.

Simply seeing something supernatural did not impress Moses. The burning bush was "great" in his mind and heart because in that extraordinary interaction, Moses took on a new challenge and charted a new course in his life. The moment was transformative. Moses accepted a new mission.

Rabbi Soloveitchik taught, "It is not always necessary for an event to

be miraculous in order to be great, and not every miraculous event is a great event." An event is great only if the following things occur: it fosters change, it impacts the person, it ushers in a new era, and it produces great things. Whether or not the event was miraculous or natural is not critical.

No matter how miraculous an event is, it is very "small" if it is wasted.

This teaching speaks directly to the great miracle of Chanukah. These events were great because they produced a transformation of the Jewish people. The Jews proved that not only could they defeat a fierce enemy on the battlefield, but they could also purify the spiritual defilement of a whole population, a nation that overwhelmingly had sunk deeply into the impurity of the soul and contamination of the spirit.

The events witnessed during the days of Chanukah inspired change. Life did not remain the same as before. During the days of Chanukah, the Jews took advantage of the new opportunity that was offered to them: a spiritual revival and a rededication to religious values and to a committed life — truly a great thing.

The Jewish people engaged in a national rededication to the Torah and tradition. "Rededication" is the very meaning of the word *Chanukah*.

The Sages waited a full year before they declared Chanukah a holiday. Why did they not establish the holiday immediately after the great miracles of the disproportionate battle and the eight-day burning of the one flask of pure oil in the Menorah?

The Sages waited to see whether the change was lasting. Had the Jewish people truly transformed their lives? Only then, when the Sages saw the life-changing impact, did they consider this story to be great, worthy of celebration for all time.

The Jewish people, in the days of Chanukah, acted heroically, not only on the battlefield, but also in renewing and strengthening their allegiance to God and to the Torah.

As we celebrate these events each year, we should also aspire to emulate this remarkable kind of heroism in our own lives.

The Hebrew word for miracle, *nes* (נס), can also be translated as "banner." A *nes*, a banner raised high, calls out with a message. A banner is in public view and is meant to have impact and impart an important directive.

Rabbi Joseph Soloveitchik taught that when we speak of the *nes gadol* that occurred in the days of Chanukah, we mean that there was "a great banner," a great message that was heeded by the Jewish people. There was a spiritual awakening, and the Jewish nation was elevated to new heights.

חנוכה

YEDIDYA'S LIGHT

THIS IS THE TRUE STORY OF A LITTLE BOY BY THE NAME OF YEDIDYA, who made aliyah with his family to the city of Hebron, south of Jerusalem. Hebron is a small, tight-knit community. Only ninety Jewish families live in the city.

It is not an easy or hospitable place for Jews to live. Nevertheless, these heroic families live in this sacred setting because they passionately believe in the holiness of this biblical city.

Hebron is the city where Abraham and Sarah lived for much of their lives. It is the place where Sarah died, and where Abraham purchased a cave and field so that he could bury his wife and establish burial plots for his family.

The cave is known as Me'arat Hamachpelah, which means "the cave of the couples." It is where the fathers and mothers of the Jewish nation are buried. Abraham and Sarah, Isaac and Rebecca, Jacob and Leah were laid to rest in this place over three thousand years ago. According to Jewish mysticism, it is also the burial place of Adam and Eve.

Well, beautiful little Yedidya was a special young boy, loved by all the families of Hebron.

At the age of three and a half, Yedidya was diagnosed with autism. He could not communicate with words; sadly, he did not speak. By the age

חמישי

of three, he had still not uttered a full word. His parents prayed each day for his health and well-being. If only he would begin to speak.

Yedidya's father prays each day in the Me'arat Hamachpelah. He serves as the director of tourism for the Jewish community in the city. One afternoon Yedidya joined his father on a tour of the Me'arat Hamachpelah. Even at this young age, Yedidya knew his way around the cave.

While his father was praying the afternoon service, Yedidya went off on his own, as he often did. That day he ran in the direction of the burial place of Abraham.

The area where Abraham is buried does not have an accessible entrance. People generally stand outside it and look through steel-gated windows. It is common for people to stand by these openings and peer through these spaces and offer prayers.

Suddenly, policemen who keep watch on the goings-on inside the cave gathered around the area of Abraham's burial place. There was commotion.

The guards called out, "Get your son out. Please get him out! He must get out!"

There *was* a little boy sitting on the ground, inside the gated area. How he got in is unclear, but he had found his way inside. Incredibly, Yedidya had somehow climbed through the bars.

And he was in no mind to leave. Little Yedidya sat on the floor, totally unaware of what was happening around him. He did not hear the shouts of the police, nor did he sense the commotion.

Yedidya was sitting on the floor, smiling and completely at ease.

And then, for the first time in his life, Yedidya spoke.

He loudly said two words: *Ohr poh*, "Light here." He excitedly repeated these words: "Light here, light here," and he was pointing to Abraham's burial place.

Amazingly, little Yedidya sensed light emanating from this holy spot.

When we are spiritually sensitive, we can perceive a light from beyond the physical world.

There is light where there is joy.

There is light where there is kindness.

There is light when there is love shared between people.

Yedidya uttered just four more words before he was removed from the burial place: *Abba poh, Ima poh*, "Father is here, Mother is here." He was pointing to the burial place of Abraham and Sarah.

Yedidya sensed the aura found in this holy place — earth that contains within it the very roots of the Jewish people.

There is light when we are deeply connected to our wondrous past and to our noble roots.

If we let them, the candles of Chanukah will remind us of this magnificent spiritual light.

> Rabbi Menachem Mendel Schneerson, the Lubavitcher Rebbe, said, "The innocent faith of a child touches upon the utterly simple essence of God."

SEEING WITH CHANUKAH EYES

THE REMARKABLE REBBE NACHMAN OF BRESLOV TAUGHT THAT THE HOLIDAY of Chanukah is a time of the "fixing of the eyes."

The mitzvah of Chanukah requires lighting and seeing the candles lit. The holiday reminds us to have an *ayin tov*, literally "a good eye," to use our eyes to see only the good in others, which is considered an extremely important character trait (*Pirkei Avot* 2:12).

Reb Shlomo Carlebach, following Reb Nachman's insight, taught that Chanukah is a chance to correct the ways we fail to see the good that is really in front of us, and to correct the way we often see with distorted vision. Chanukah is indeed the holiday for the "fixing of the eyes."

The following story told by Rabbi Shlomo Carlebach beautifully captures this idea:

One of the greatest of the Chassidic masters was the Kozhnitzer Maggid, Rabbi Yisrael Hofstein. He was the holiest of the holy. One morning there was a knock on the Maggid's door. He opened the door to find standing there the rabbi of the nearby town of Czenslochov. He was crying from the depths of his heart.

"My dear rabbi," said the Maggid, "please sit down. What hurts you? What can I do to help?"

The rabbi sobbed, "I feel like I am at the end. My wife and I have been married for so long, almost twenty years. But we never have been able to have children. And the pain of being without a child...I just

can't stand it anymore... Please, Holy Master, help us. Can you pray for us to have a child?"

The Maggid thought for a moment. This is what he then said: "There is one person...all the gates of heaven are open for him. But I warn you, it's not easy to see him. Tell me, my dear friend, have you ever heard of a man who lives near your city named Schwartzer Wolf?"

"Schwartzer Wolf! You can't mean that disgusting woodcutter who lives in the forest! Why, he is so vulgar, so brutal...nobody wants anything to do with him. He almost never comes to town or prays in the shul. And when he does, everyone tries to avoid him."

"Yes, that's him," the Maggid said quietly. "I want you to know that he is a very holy man. He is one of the *lamed vavnikim*, the thirty-six holy people who keep the world alive, resting upon their goodness. If you can get an invitation into his home for even one meal of the Shabbat and he gives you a blessing...he is the only person I know of who can open the gates of heaven for you."

So the next Friday afternoon, the rabbi asked some townspeople directions to Schwartzer Wolf's house, and then plunged into the forest.

He found the path he'd been told about, and after following it for what seemed like hours, he finally saw in the distance a dirty, broken-down shack. This must be it. The sun was going down. The rabbi looked up to heaven and whispered a silent prayer. The rabbi knocked on the door of Schwartzer Wolf.

For a few minutes nothing happened. Nobody came to the door. He knocked again. Still nothing. The rabbi could not believe it...all this way and nobody was home.

The rabbi had just turned away from the house, trying to figure out what he could possibly do next. Suddenly, a loud crashing sound made him jump in fear.

Trembling, he turned around. The door of the house was thrown open. The wife of Schwartzer Wolf was standing there. And — *oy gevalt —*

was she ugly! She was the most disgusting woman he had ever seen in his life! She had a baby on her hip, and three more children hanging on to her filthy, torn skirt. Usually the rabbi delighted in children. But these children looked as obnoxious and repulsive as their mother did!

Now, you need to know this about the *lamed vav tzaddikim*, the thirty-six hidden righteous people: they are so holy that they perfectly mirror whoever is looking at them. If when you look at them you think they're disgusting looking, it's because you are disgusting. If they seem ugly, that means that you are ugly — not just on the outside, but in the deepest depths. Only if you are pure and holy can you see their beauty and their light.

The rabbi turned to the woman and asked, "Please could I stay with you for Shabbos? It's too late for me to make it back home now."

She looked at him coldly and spoke. "My friend, there is no way you're spending Shabbos in this house. If you have to…you can stay in our stable. But let me warn you, don't even think of coming near this house."

The rabbi made his way to the stables. He had set aside in his bag two candles, a little wine and challah. "What a way to spend the holy Sabbath," he thought as he looked around. "In a smelly stable with a horse and two dogs, sleeping on dirty old hay. But at least I am close to the house…and after all, there are three meals on Shabbos. Maybe I can still find a way to get in…"

Suddenly, the door of the stable burst open, and Schwartzer Wolf stalked in. The rabbi was frozen in fear. The man's hair and beard were wild and dirty. He was very tall and looked incredibly strong. The rabbi trembled before the sheer power of his physical presence.

Schwartzer Wolf went up to the rabbi and stood towering over him: "I want you to know that if it had been up to me, you'd still be wandering around the forest. Since my wife let you in, you can stay. But if you so much as open this door — or even look out the

window — I will strangle you with my own hands. As soon as Shabbos is over, I want you out of my stable." With this he spun around and walked out, slamming the door so hard that the whole building shook.

All that night the rabbi from Czenslochov poured out his heart to God: "Master of the World, please have mercy. Please help me become worthy enough for Schwartzer Wolf to give me his blessing…" The rabbi prayed harder than he ever had in his life. And by the first light of day, he was beginning to feel that he had repented for everything he had ever done wrong.

Early in the morning the rabbi heard Schwartzer Wolf going off to pray in the forest. All day long he stayed in the stable, crying and waiting; finally, in the late afternoon he heard Schwartzer Wolf come back into his house.

By now the rabbi was desperate. It was getting later and later; he knew that time was running out. The sun was getting low in the sky. Shabbos would soon be over. He hadn't gotten the blessing. He hadn't even made it into the house. It looked like he had lost his one chance to have children.

The rabbi of Czenslochov sank to the ground, burying his head in his hands and sobbing from the depth of his broken heart. He cried out to God and said, "Ribbono shel Olam, there is no one who can help me but You. I know that I'm not worthy. But I am begging You and begging You — please have mercy. Please don't let me die without having children…"

Just at that moment, he felt the gentle touch of a hand on his head. He looked up through his tears. It was Schwartzer Wolf. And yet, he seemed like a different man. If yesterday he had seemed so gruesome, so frightening, right now he was shining with holiness and radiant with light. And he said, so kindly and sweetly, "My dearest friend, would you do me and my family the honor of joining us for the third meal of the Shabbos?"

The rabbi went with Schwartzer Wolf back to his house. And he couldn't believe his eyes. If the day before the wife and children had seemed totally disgusting, now they were absolutely beautiful. The rabbi joined the family in the ritual hand washing, and they all ate some challah and fish. The rabbi was so lost in the exalted holiness of the moment that he could hardly swallow the food, much less open his mouth to ask for a blessing. But it really didn't matter because Schwartzer Wolf turned to him and said, "My sweetest rabbi, I know why you came to my house. I know what's in your heart. I'm sorry I had to be so cruel to you at first, but I had to bring you to the point of desperation so that you would pray as you have never prayed before. I bless you and your wife to have a son. But there is one condition — that when you have a child, you name your son after me..."

For a moment the rabbi was confused. Surely the *tzaddik* knew that we don't name children for anyone who is still living. He wanted to say something, but with the awe of the whole experience, he simply found he could not speak. So he just nodded. After the Havdalah prayers marking the end of the Sabbath were said, he went home full of joy to his wife. He walked through the door and told her, "God is truly merciful. Schwartzer Wolf has blessed us with a son."

The next morning the rabbi went as usual to the synagogue for the morning prayers. As soon as he walked in, he saw that something strange was going on. The *shammes* was going around from person to person, asking everyone to do something. But they were all shaking their heads no. The rabbi went over to the *shammes*: "What's the problem here?"

"Nothing to worry about, Rabbi. It's just that somebody died last night, and I am having trouble getting a minyan together for his funeral."

The rabbi felt a shiver of dread. "Tell me, who died?"

"That disgusting woodchopper, the one who lives in the forest.

People call him the Schwartzer Wolf." The rabbi began to cry. He whispered, "The holy, the exalted Schwartzer Wolf!"

He ran to the front of the shul and shouted, "My friends, do you know who the Schwartzer Wolf really was? He was the most holy. He was the head of the *lamed vav tzaddikim,* one of the thirty-six people who hold up the world." He told everyone about what had happened over Shabbat in the forest. And then he said, "We were guilty. We ignored him. We insulted him. We laughed at him. We were afraid of him. Oy, we treated him so badly. The least we can do now is go with him to his final resting place." So everyone in the city went to the funeral of the holy Schwartzer Wolf.

And exactly nine months later the rabbi's wife had a son. The joyous father kept his word to the hidden *tzaddik,* and named his little baby boy Schwartzer Wolf.

When Rabbi Shlomo Carlebach concluded telling the story, he would beg everyone to keep telling the story and always remember the lesson of Schwartzer Wolf.

Reb Shlomo would then say, "We need to have the *eyes* to see the holy in others. There are Schwartzer Wolfs everywhere we go. Sometimes they are revealed to us. Often they are hidden and their goodness remains concealed from us. It is so important…we need to have the right eyes to see."

> "They could not drink the water of Marah, for it was bitter" (Exodus 15:23).
>
> The Kotzker Rebbe taught: Since they themselves were bitter, the bitterness sprang from within, and therefore they sensed the taste of bitterness.

HOPE

"The salvation of God comes in the blink of an eye."

PESIKTA ZUTRATA, ESTHER 4:17

IN PRAISE OF THE ROOSTER

ONE OF OUR MORNING PRAYERS MIGHT SEEM TO BE A STRANGE THOUGHT with which to start the day: "Blessed are You, Lord our God...Who gives the rooster understanding."

Why do we single out the rooster for praise?

Some say it reflects the way we once experienced the new day — being woken by the crow of the rooster. This blessing would then be recited giving thanks to God for a new day and expressing some gratitude to the rooster for helping us to partake of it.

The great German rabbi and scholar Samson Raphael Hirsch (1808–1888), in his commentary on the prayer book, offers a beautiful insight. He sees within this blessing a metaphor for the Jewish people: When the world is enveloped in darkness, the Jewish people act as a "rooster" that awakens others to the light of the Divine. This small people, whose size is miniscule compared to the world's population, serves to spread its light to the four corners of the world.

Amazingly, the rooster does not actually wait until daybreak to commence its crowing. It somehow senses that the day is about to begin just before the first rays of the sun break over the horizon. The rooster begins its mission while it is still dark, intuiting the imminent light from within the darkness.

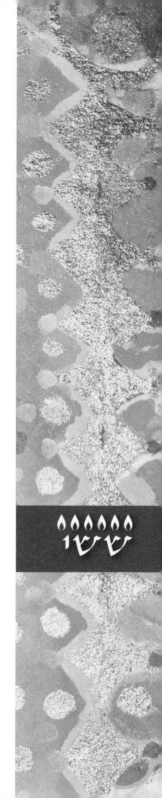

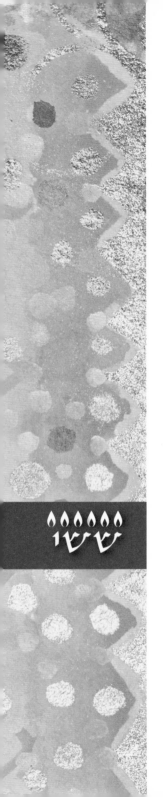

So too with the Jew. Within our collective soul, we intuit the coming of the first glimmer of light, even while it is still dark, and we never give up our eternal hope for a better future.

It takes a special strength and vision to look beyond the darkness to see the light that ultimately awaits us.

This is the strength and vision found in Chanukah. The Maccabees — and the Jewish people who supported them — heroically went into a physical and spiritual battle against a dark and foreboding enemy. Though there was little hope left for a people dominated by an intimidating and ruthless regime, amazingly, they were victorious. In thankful celebration, they lit the Menorah on the first night with a faith that it would illuminate the night.

Ultimately, the rooster's crow means more to us than just nature's alarm clock. For Jews it symbolizes an attitude that we try to incorporate into our own lives: an attitude of optimism, hope, and yearning for a new day, an attitude that finds the silver lining in every cloud and fends off the darkness with the power of light.

It is with that first morning blessing, the blessing of the rooster, that we articulate our belief in renewal and a better tomorrow. We wake up each morning to a new day filled with a profoundly positive attitude and eternal hope.

> In 1992 a writer preparing a story about the Lubavitcher Rebbe's upcoming ninetieth birthday asked the Rebbe what message he would like to convey in connection with his birthday. "Ninety is the numerical equivalent of the Hebrew letter *tzaddik* (צ), meaning 'righteous,'" the Rebbe explained. "We must all constantly strive to be more righteous. Today we must be better than yesterday, and today we must prepare for a better tomorrow."

CHANUKAH: A NEW BEGINNING

HOW DO WE UNDERSTAND THE REASON THE GREEKS FORBADE THE JEWS from celebrating Rosh Chodesh, declaring and honoring the new month?

Why did the tyrant Antiochus focus on this particular practice?

The Rebbe of Sochatchov, Rabbi Shmuel Bornstein (1856–1926), offered this explanation about the deeper meaning behind this decree against the Jews.

The Syrian Greeks attacked this observance because they wanted to quash two of the defining qualities of the Jewish soul, namely, its powers of resilience and renewal.

These qualities are the essence of celebrating the new Jewish month. Each month the moon is revitalized, increasing its light each day. This process is representative of the light in the Jewish soul that has the perpetual power to reemerge and revitalize. The soul of man is created with a unique ability to be reenergized, endowing man with remarkable inner strength.

Rabbi Shlomo Carlebach tells the following poignant story, which captures this unique idea.

> I was sitting on a plane going from New York to Boston. Next to me was sitting a non-Jewish brother. We started talking to each other. He saw that I was sitting with a book open in front of me. He noticed that it was in Hebrew. He said to me, "What are you reading?"

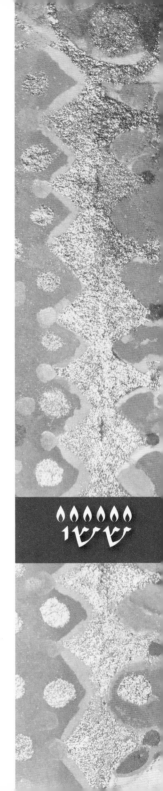

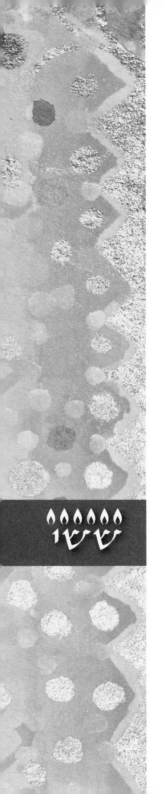

I was studying the portion from the Torah of B'reishit. It was the portion for the upcoming Shabbat.

I asked him, "Dear brother, did you ever study the Bible?" He told me that he lives in Maine and there is a whole group who broke away from his church because the priest does not teach "Torah" on a deep enough level. I said to him, "I am also a dropout! I am also looking for deep Torah teachings. The *chevra*, the friends, that I am with are also searching for Torah on the deepest level. Hey, maybe you should join my synagogue!"

So we had two more minutes until landing. I said to him, "Let me share a Torah thought that I am now studying. The Torah begins with the word *b'reishit*. Most translate the word to mean 'in the beginning.' We know that the first verse says, 'In the beginning God created the heaven and the earth.' But let me ask you a question: We already know that God created the world in the beginning of time, so what are we being taught?

"Do you know what *b'reishit* means? Says the ancient mystic Rabbi Shimon bar Yochai (c. 70 CE): Not *at* the beginning; rather, *with* beginnings. God instilled in the heavens and the earth *beginnings*.

"Even if you fall, and fall again, you can always get up, you can always begin again. The first word in the Torah does not only mean 'in the beginning'; it means that when God created the world, He filled it with beginnings. Nature itself gives you strength to begin again. You are sad — you wash your face with water and you are less sad. Within nature itself God planted newness. You stand in the wind and when you feel the wind is blowing in your face, it gives you so much hope. God instilled in the heavens and earth beginnings."

Listen to what then happened.

Ten years later I was finishing giving a concert near Boston. Suddenly a man walks in with his wife and his little daughter. I thought that I recognized him — he looked familiar. He was crying. He came over to me and hugged me. His wife was also crying and his daughter had tears in her eyes. The woman began telling me the following. "Do you remember this non-Jewish brother? He sat next to you on the plane to Boston about ten years ago." I looked at him, "Yes, my man! You are the fellow who broke away from his church. Of course I remember you."

His wife then turned to me and said: "When I first met my husband he was a multimillionaire. We got married. We had a child. We were living a dream life. A few years later we went bankrupt. I didn't know it but my husband had hit rock bottom. He didn't have the strength to endure the shame. He bought himself a pistol and decided to take his own life. He had nothing left. He decided that at five o'clock, at the end of his day at work, he would end it all.

"He finished work that day. It was a quarter to five. He had fifteen minutes. What would he do for the last fifteen minutes?

"He decided to open the drawer where he had his Bible. He opened the book to the first page and began to read. He read the first word. He then looked at it again. He whispered to himself: 'In the beginning...' Suddenly he remembered the Torah of Reb Shimon bar Yochai. 'No, it does not mean "in the beginning." It means "with beginnings." God created the world with beginnings... There is always another beginning...there is always a second chance. God gives you the strength to start again.'"

A minute later he called his wife and daughter and with tears in his eyes he said, "I didn't tell you this, but I was planning to end my life, I was going to shoot myself...but, thankfully, now I am not. At the last moment I opened the Bible and remembered a teaching from a holy rabbi from two thousand years ago. One can always begin again. And if you fall – and fall again – you can always get up...you can always start over."

The woman turned to me and said: "My husband and I owe you

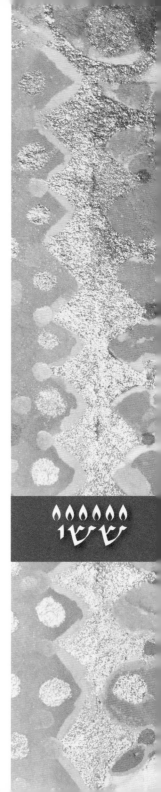

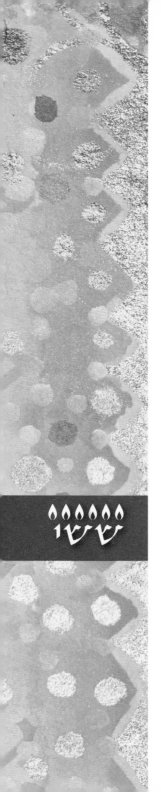

his life because you were the messenger who taught him that God gives us the strength to never give up."

When Reb Shlomo Carlebach shared this story, he would ask everyone to be little messengers of Reb Shimon bar Yochai and bring to others the first message of the Torah: that the world was created *with* beginnings.

The waxing and waning of the moon that we celebrate each month is a symbol of the revitalizing force found in the soul. Even when the moon reaches its weakest point and seemingly disappears, suddenly a thin crescent reappears and grows stronger, becoming more and more luminous.

Chanukah is a unique time to experience a spiritual recharge and inner renewal.

During the long, dark nights of winter we light candles that remind us of our inner resolve and resilience. Embedded in the *neshamah*, soul, of every person is an inextinguishable light that propels us to overcome adversity, conquer challenges, and emerge stronger.

> The Midrash says that God created and destroyed many worlds until He created ours (*Genesis Rabbah* 3:7). This Midrash presents a puzzling teaching. The question is obvious: Why was all this necessary? Why did the Holy One, blessed be He, need to create many worlds until He formed the one He wanted?
>
> Rabbi Soloveitchik explained: Naturally, God did not need practice. He could have made it right the first time. But He deliberately "failed and failed again" to teach us human beings a lesson that would apply to our own lives. Do we not also attempt to build worlds in our own personal lives that sometimes get destroyed? We put time into our relationships and our careers. Sometimes they get unraveled and sometimes they are shattered. Then it can be so hard to pick up the pieces and muster the energy to go on and

create again. Each and every one of us, in our lives, experiences loss and tragedy. How do we move forward? How do we start over?

It is as if the Holy One is telling us: "Don't despair. Don't give up. Follow in my footsteps. I did it. I know what it is like. You can also do it. I started again after many worlds were destroyed. You too can be successful in creating a new world for yourself that will be strong and lasting."

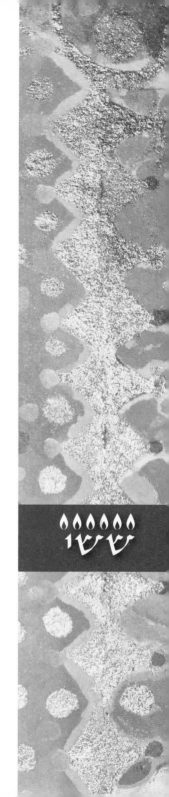

WHY WE LIGHT AT NIGHT

WE ARE ACCUSTOMED TO THE SECULAR NOTION THAT A NEW DAY BEGINS with sunrise.

However, in Jewish law and practice, the new day begins at night.

Why? Why does Shabbat begin at nightfall? Why do we begin the Passover Seder at night? Why do we begin to celebrate each new day of Chanukah with the candle lighting as the sun sets?

Our source for this practice appears in the beginning of the Torah: "And there was evening and there was morning, one day" (Genesis 1:5). This verse in the Torah says that nightfall precedes the morning, hence the new day begins at night. The twenty-four-hour period that commences with the sun setting is the Jewish definition of one full day.

What is the deeper reason that the Jewish day consists first of night, followed by day?

This unique Jewish definition of a day reflects our hopeful and optimistic approach. The night is only temporary. Darkness precedes light. Darkness is only a stage that leads us to sunrise and the brightness of day. This stands in contrast to the way the rest of the world defines a day.

Rabbi Jonathan Sacks teaches that the Greeks, who believed in many gods rather than one loving God, gave the world the concept of *tragedy*. They posited: we strive, we struggle…at times we might achieve greatness, but life has no ultimate purpose. The universe neither knows nor cares

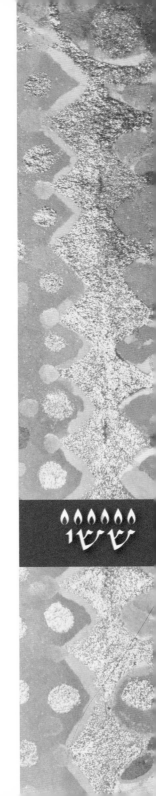

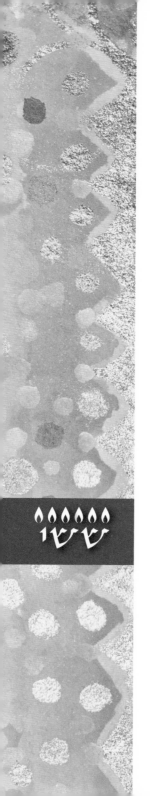

that we are here. In Greek dramas, man is typically brought to ruin, and his life ends in sorrow.

Ancient Israel, on the other hand, gave the world the idea of *hope*. We are here because God created us in love, and through love we discover the meaning and purpose of life.

Tragic cultures eventually disintegrate and die. Lacking any sense of ultimate meaning, they lose the moral beliefs and the resulting norms and rituals on which continuity depends. They sacrifice true happiness for fleeting enjoyment, refusing to defer pleasure for the sake of critical tasks in the here and now. They thereby forfeit the future for the present.

Inevitably, they lose the passion and energy that brought them greatness in the first place. This was the story of ancient Greece.

By way of contrast, the Jewish sentiment of hope and renewal is captured in a beautiful vignette in the Talmud (*Berachot* 1:1). Two sages – Rabbi Chiya and Rabbi Shimon – were walking side by side. They were walking in the valley of Arbel, in northern Israel. Together they saw the dawn, whose light began to slowly burst forth. Rabbi Chiya turned to his dear friend and observed: "So will be the redemption of Israel. First it comes little by little and then becomes greater and greater…until it bursts forth with great brightness."

The moments before the dawn are typically the darkest time of the night. As the dawn begins to break, there are moments when the darkness and the light seem to mingle with one another. Soon the light breaks through.

It often requires a long process for the light to shine brightly – a process that can feel unending. But the Jewish people remain ever hopeful. We know that the sun must inevitably rise. A new day, carrying the promise of renewal and the potential for joy and goodness, will come.

At nightfall when darkness surrounds us, Jews gather around the menorah. The candles bringing light to the darkness are symbols of a deep and abiding faith in the potential for a better day to come and the hope for the final redemption.

A parable: There was once a king who was growing older in years. He wished to choose one of his three sons to take over his kingdom. He came up with the following idea.

There was a small shack in the middle of a field. "Whoever can fill the shack to capacity," the king exclaimed, "will take over my throne."

The oldest child went first. He filled it with rocks and stones of all shapes and sizes. When there was no room left, he filled the cracks and crevices with small pebbles.

It was then the second son's turn. He carried bags of feathers, dumping the feathers into the shack. Before long the shack was filled with feathers from top to bottom.

Finally, the youngest son had his opportunity. In the evening the third son walked into the shack. Surprisingly, he was empty-handed. He reached into his pocket and took out a match and a candle. He lit the candle and the room was filled to capacity with light. The king smiled. "You, my child, will take over my throne."

The truly wise son understood how to fill a vacuum; where there is emptiness, we are to fill that space with light.

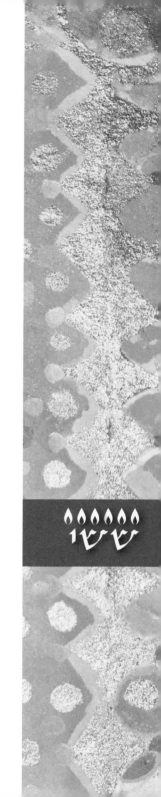

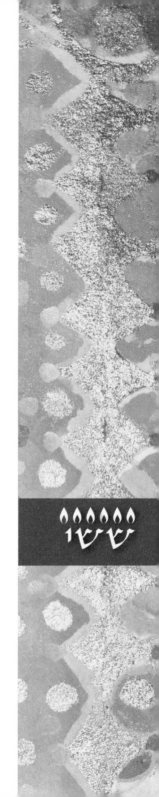

THE ARCH OF TITUS
From Splendor to Degradation and Back Again

It is hard for a Jew to look up at the Menorah on the Arch of Titus in Rome without feeling deep emotions. This is especially true on Chanukah.

The Arch of Titus in Rome was erected around 81 CE to commemorate the Roman triumph over the Jews. It was built to commemorate the defeat of Judea, culminating in the destruction of the Temple in Jerusalem in 70 CE.

On the arch are carved bas-reliefs depicting the Temple's vessels being carried through the streets of Rome by Roman soldiers wearing celebratory wreaths on their heads. The Menorah, in the center of the carvings, is certainly the most prominent of the treasures. They were also once colored brightly. The Menorah was painted with gold.

These carvings mark the end of a long historical saga that actually began with the revolt of the Maccabees two hundred years earlier. In the days of Chanukah, in 166 BCE, Antiochus Epiphanes, the Greek ruler of Judea, hoped to transform the Temple into a pagan cult center. In 70 CE, just over two hundred years later, Titus completely destroyed the Temple.

According to the Talmud, not only did Titus commit the most vile acts of sexual impurity in the holy of holies, but he also personally set fire to the Beit Hamikdash, thus starting its destruction.

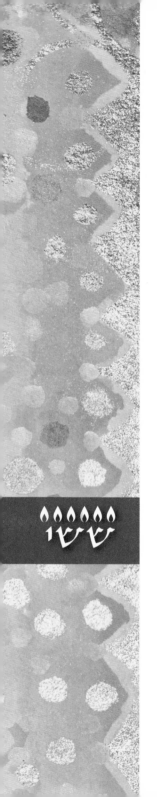

The Arch of Titus depicts reveling heathen soldiers in a triumphal parade, reminiscent of the foul acts of their leader.

In a heroic show of faith, Holocaust survivors in Rome, in 1947, walked through the arch from west to east, symbolically carrying the Menorah back to Zion, as they celebrated the United Nations vote to establish the Jewish state. In doing so, they redeemed the Arch of Titus from being a symbol of Jewish degradation into an icon representing a brighter Jewish future.

This transformation was completed in 1949, when the newly born State of Israel, searching for a symbol that would serve as the emblem for its recently created modern state, chose the image of the menorah, the symbol of hope and light. With unmistakable symbolic intent, the founders fashioned the emblem after the menorah that appears on the Arch of Titus. The Arch of Titus, which was meant to tell the story of the demise of the Jewish people, would now be used to represent the Jewish people's determination and miraculous survival.

The menorah on the Arch of Titus tells yet another amazing story that powerfully depicts the story of Israel. This message may be summed up best by the lessons of Chanukah: the few over the many, the holy over the profane, the ascent in holiness over the descent to nothingness, and increasing light over darkness.

Rabbi Abraham Isaac Kook, the first chief rabbi of Israel, once noted that the modern Hebrew word for "history," הִיסְטוֹרְיָה, spelled with a *tet* (ט), would have been more appropriate if spelled with a *tav* (ת), הִיסְתוֹרְיָה. When written with a *tav*, the word could be read as a combination of two separate words, namely, הֶסְתֵּר-יָ-ה (*hester Yah*), meaning "hidden God." This would indicate that it is our obligation to see God through the unfolding of history and the redemptive process.

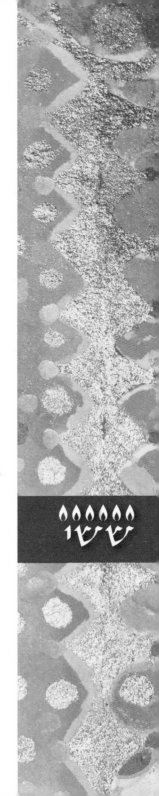

BEAUTIFYING OUR *TZEDAKAH*

ON CHANUKAH MANY HAVE THE CUSTOM TO INCREASE THEIR *TZEDAKAH*, giving additional charity to the poor (*Kitzur Shulchan Aruch* 139:1). When we celebrate the unity of the Jewish people, the mitzvah of *tzedakah* is an especially suitable one, as it brings Jews closer to one another.

Tzedakah shares a unique component with the mitzvah of Chanukah: *hiddur*, the concept of *beautifying* the mitzvah. While one can perform a mitzvah according to its most basic requirements, there is also the opportunity to enhance the mitzvah and make its performance that much more beautiful.

When it comes to the lighting of the menorah, although the Talmud says one may fulfill the basic mitzvah with one candle per family, we choose to fulfill the mitzvah in the most ideal form, adding one candle each night.

Other ways of beautifying the mitzvah include kindling the menorah using pure olive oil rather than candles, or using a beautiful menorah. Indeed, the Sages highlight two observances to explain the halachic concept of *hiddur* (beautifying the mitzvah): the observance of Chanukah and the giving of *tzedakah*, both which we are to do in as beautiful a way as possible.

The following story is told about a modern-day Chassidic Rebbe known for his exceptional kindness to the poor.

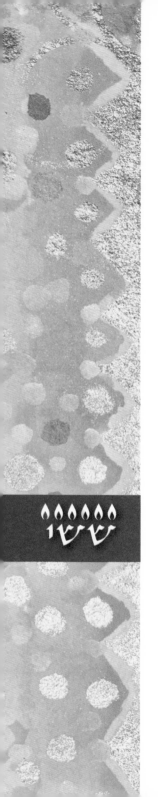

עשׂו

During the first days after Rabbi Shlomo Carlebach's death, clusters of homeless people from Broadway and Riverside Park on Manhattan's Upper West Side congregated in front of his synagogue, weeping. Members of the shul, crying inside, were astonished at the depth of feeling the street people had for Rabbi Shlomo, and wanted to assure them that they would not be forgotten.

A man was dispatched from the members to deliver a message to the throng outside. "Don't worry," he said to the group of homeless people, "you don't have to cry…we will continue to give you money."

"Is that what you think?" replied one woman in tatters, pulling herself up indignantly. "That we're crying because of the money?"

"We're not crying because of the money we're no longer going to get from the Rabbi," yelled a ragged man. "We're crying because now that Shlomo Carlebach's gone…who is going to come to us at 2:00 in the morning and sing to us and tell us stories, and hold our hands?"

There is no greater mitzvah than *tzedakah*. But there are some types of *tzedakah* that are very special, particularly when one truly empathizes with the recipient.

The Rambam (Laws of Charity 10:7) famously lists eight levels of charitable giving, one higher than the next. The highest level involves restoring someone's sense of self-worth.

Tzedakah can be given begrudgingly or it can be given with a warm and open heart. This teaching is hinted to with the word the Torah uses (Exodus 30:12) for giving *tzedakah*: *v'natnu* (וְנָתְנוּ).

In Hebrew the word ונתנו is a palindrome; that is, it reads the same from both directions (Baal Haturim, Exodus 30:12). The Torah teaches us that when fulfilling the mitzvah of *tzedakah*, we should be concerned with the thoughts and feelings of both parties: the giver should be sure to offer gifts with care and kindness, and we should ensure that the receiver feels cared for and loved.

The *tzaddik* Reb Chaim Halberstam, "the righteous one of Sanz," was lavish in his giving of *tzedakah*. When he gave to a person who was known to be a scoundrel, some of his followers protested that the scoundrel did not deserve the *tzaddik's* bounty.

The saintly Rebbe said, "If I give even to people who are undeserving, then I may hope that God will give to me even though I am undeserving. But if I restrict my *tzedakah* only to people who are worthy of it, how can I ask God to give anything to me?"

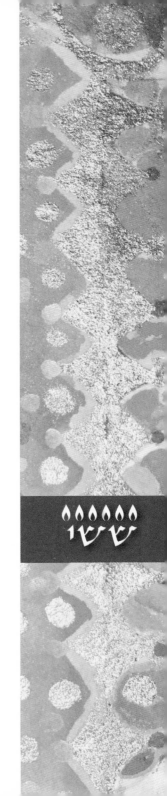

THE CANDLE THAT WOULD
NOT BE EXTINGUISHED

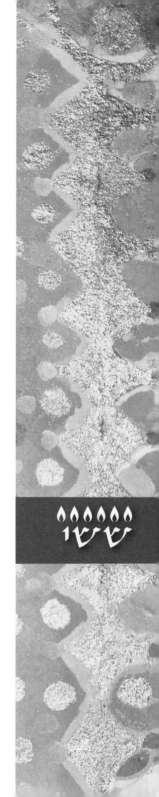

RABBI SHLOMO CARLEBACH HEARD THE FOLLOWING REMARKABLE STORY from someone who witnessed it firsthand:

> The year was 1942 and I was in Auschwitz. We were so many poor souls clinging together, hungry and afraid. We could barely find enough support for ourselves, much less anyone else. But there was one man in our barracks who was different from all the rest. He was a *tzaddik*, a righteous person.
>
> His name was Reb Naftali. For the entire time I knew him, I never once heard him complain. It was the deepest Hell, yet he never uttered a bad word.
>
> In fact, he managed to give help to others. There was a small group of us who clung to him, followed him around. What could we do? He was the only warmth and light that we had.
>
> Winter came, and it was bitterly cold. There was such hopelessness in the air. Then came the dreaded announcement. Several days before Chanukah, the Germans declared that anyone found lighting candles would be shot.
>
> We could not dream of facing that threat with defiance. But what about Reb Naftali? We whispered amongst ourselves: Could it be that Chanukah would pass and Reb Naftali would fail to bless the lights? No, that would be impossible. But where would he get the candles?

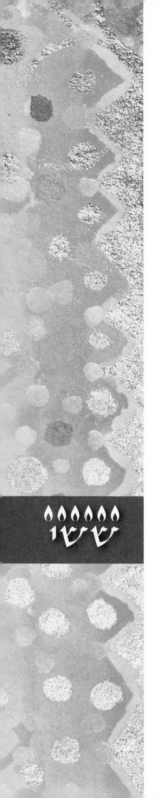

The first night of Chanukah arrived. Our little group kept our eyes on him.

We weren't going to let him out of our sight. All night we had to stay in the barracks. If they caught someone outside, they would shoot him.

Nine o'clock came.

Ten o'clock came.

Then eleven o'clock.

I started to doze off. When I caught myself, I realized that Reb Naftali had slipped out. I roused the others and we stole out after him.

We followed his tracks in the snow, but somehow they looked strange.

We found him in a little building, protected from the wind. He wasn't wearing shoes. Auschwitz in the winter without shoes!

"Reb Naftali, where are your shoes?"

"I traded them in for a candle."

"Please, Naftali," we begged, "don't do it. They'll kill you."

"Listen," he said sternly, "tonight is Chanukah. On Chanukah Jews light candles. That's what we do. The Maccabees weren't afraid — why should we be?"

He took out a little pencil-thin candle, made the blessings, and lit it. We all stood there, frightened and excited. Who would have ever dreamed that one small flame could give so much light?

There was a tension in the air. We felt as though we should run. Then suddenly, a German soldier came walking out of the night. In one hand he held a whip, in the other, a pistol.

"Who lit that candle?" he barked at us. Reb Naftali stepped forward. "I lit it," he said. The German whipped him across the face. "Blow it out!" he yelled. "Blow it out!"

Reb Naftali just stood there. He didn't move. He didn't even lower his eyes.

Then the German took out his gun and shot him. Just like that!

He killed him right on the spot. We stood in fear, not believing our eyes. "You," he shouted at one of my friends, "drag him this way." He dragged poor Naftali through the snow into the darkness. The German walked away.

But you know what...the candle was still burning. The Chanukah menorah of Reb Naftali remained lit.

And for all of us who experienced this, Reb Naftali's candle is still burning. It was never extinguished.

When Reb Shlomo Carlebach finished telling this story, he said: "The Maccabees passed on to the generations a great light. So great that the candle is still burning...it is still burning. Let's also become a great army; let's kindle the light! The blessing of the *haftarah* says, *she'lo yichbeh nero l'olam va'ed* (שֶׁלֹּא יִכְבֶּה נֵרוֹ לְעוֹלָם וָעֶד), 'the light will burn forever.' God swore to us that the light would burn forever...

All the holidays extend from the night to the day. We eat the matzah on Pesach both at night and during the day. On Sukkot we sit in the *sukkah* both at night and during the day. However, Chanukah is the one holiday where the unique ceremony of that holiday takes place only at night. Chanukah gives us the strength to bear the sometimes long, sometimes blackest of nights. Because God swore to us that in the morning the light will come; the light will continue to burn."

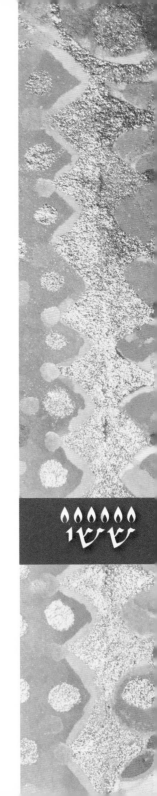

The Chassidic master the Sfat Emet, Reb Yehuda Leib Alter of Ger, teaches that each letter of the Hebrew word for soul — *nefesh* (נֶפֶשׁ), spelled *nun* (נ), *feh* (פ), *shin* (שׁ) — represents the components of the candle: *ner* (נר), "flame"; *petilah* (פתילה), "wick"; and *shemen* (שמן), "oil."

On Chanukah, perhaps more than any time of the year, the Jewish soul is stirred. One can access one's inner strength and spirit. There is a light that is embedded in each and every person — a light that is good, and that can lead us to good deeds and thoughts.

UNITY

"Your mission is to light up souls."

RABBI MENACHEM MENDEL SCHNEERSON,
LUBAVITCHER REBBE

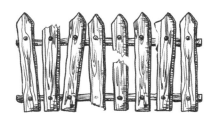

MENDING FENCES ON CHANUKAH

THE MENORAHS THAT WE LIGHT IN OUR HOMES TODAY ARE REMINISCENT of the very first Menorah, which was lit each day by Aaron the High Priest during the Israelites' travels in the wilderness.

Amazingly, but not surprisingly, it was Aaron's direct descendants, the *Chashmonaim*, who led the way in the battle against the Greeks. They were the ones who once again lit the Menorah when reentering the Temple on Chanukah.

The Sfat Emet suggests that the personality of Aaron has a special place in our hearts during the days of Chanukah. This is true not only because Aaron was the great Menorah lighter, but also because Aaron, the brother of Moses, was the greatest peacemaker in the world (*Pirkei Avot* 1:12).

He sought out people who were quarreling and made peace between them. When Aaron met one of the quarrelers, he would say, "I just met your acquaintance and he is very sorry for what he did; you should know, he wants to make up with you."

Aaron would sit with husbands and wives who had marital problems, and also with those who had separated due to marital strife. He would not rest until he did everything he could to make peace between them and to help bring them back together.

Not infrequently it happened that after the couple would reunite, another child would be born to them. They would often give honor to

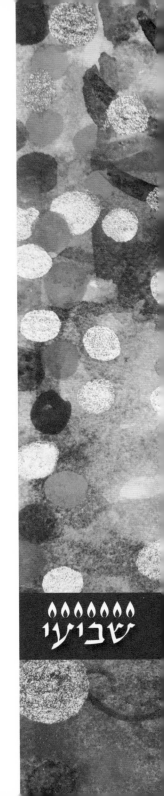

אֶשְׁבּוּ

– 153 –

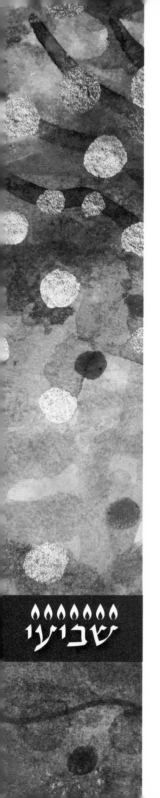

אביעזר

their peacemaker by naming their child after him. In fact, our Sages teach that more than three thousand children were named after Aaron during his lifetime (*Avot d'Rabbi Natan*)!

The Sfat Emet explained that Aaron believed deeply that within the heart of every person there is a place that sincerely yearns for reconciliation and peace. There is nothing that can defile this pure place. Love is locked in the heart securely and eternally.

The small jar of oil that was sealed by the high priest gave abundant light to the Menorah. This can be likened to the pure place in the heart of a Jew. This yearning for peace cannot be spoiled or defiled.

During the ancient days of Chanukah there was ultimately a renewed sense of brotherhood and bonding among the Jewish people. The Greek onslaught and determination to actively assimilate the Jews had created terrible divisiveness among our people. Jewish Hellenists and traditionalists took opposing sides. Thankfully, the miraculous military victory and the miracle of the lights brought a renewed brotherhood and love throughout the nation of Israel.

The Rambam strikingly concludes his laws of Chanukah with a teaching about the beauty of peace and brotherhood: Peace is great; the entire Torah was given to bring about peace within the world, as it states, "Its ways are pleasant ways and all its paths are peace" (Proverbs 3:19).

In Jerusalem there is a long-standing custom of gathering for special meals on the nights of Chanukah. At these gatherings feuding families often join together. Friends who quarreled during the year are reconciled at these meals.

Chanukah is an auspicious time to come closer to one another and for reconciliation. Chanukah is the great holiday of peace.

When the saintly sage of Jerusalem Rabbi Shlomo Zalman Auerbach (1910–1995) passed away in 1995, three hundred thousand people attended his funeral. Before his death Reb Shlomo Zalman had asked his family that nothing be said about him at the funeral, except for one thing. His son Rabbi Aryeh Leib stood before the massive crowd and said the following: "My father asked me to request one thing from all of you. He wanted me to say the following in his name: 'If I, God forbid, offended you or did not treat you with proper respect, please forgive me today. I can't bear to stand before God burdened with the sin of having been insensitive to my fellow person.'"

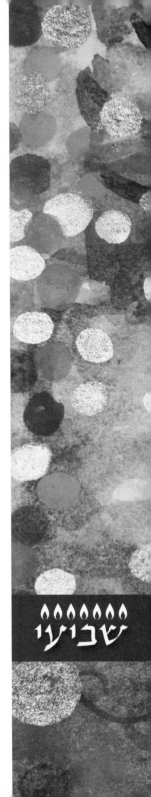

שבועו

JOSEPH AND CHANUKAH

THERE IS MEANING AND SYMBOLISM IN EVERY DETAIL OF THE JEWISH calendar. Chanukah always falls on the Shabbat when the Torah reading tells the story of Joseph and his brothers.

Rabbi Joseph Soloveitchik believed that this bears witness to the fact that there is a link between the events surrounding Joseph's experience and our Chanukah celebration...even today.

The story of Joseph tells of the devastating breakup of the sons of Jacob. Joseph is hated by his brothers and ostracized from the rest of his family.

However, ultimately there is a reconciliation. The brothers regret their unfortunate actions. Joseph heroically forgives his siblings. Joseph does not simply forgive them and suppress his resentment for their abuse of him. Rather, he loves them and cares for them as if nothing had happened, telling them that he feels toward them as he does toward Benjamin, who was not involved in the kidnapping (Rashi, Genesis 45:12). The family – the children of Israel – are reunited; they are one.

Like the biblical story of Joseph and his brothers, the Chanukah story echoes a similar drama. There was a rift within the Jewish people. There was a severe clash of ideas and ideals between two factions. There were

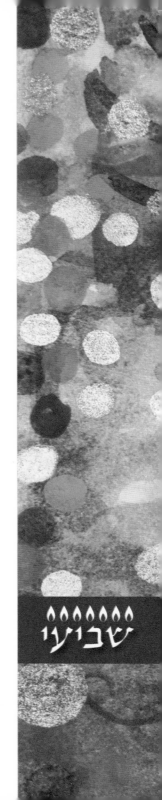

עבורו

the Chashmonaim — those who held fast to Torah law — on one side and the assimilating Hellenists on the other. Significant numbers of Jews preferred to live their lives as Hellenists. They followed Greek fashions, adopted their language, changed their Hebrew names, and frequented Greek arenas and gymnasia. This was a dangerous schism that split the Jewish people and threatened our very survival as a nation.

Chanukah not only celebrates a military victory and the return to the Temple in Jerusalem. Maybe more importantly, Chanukah celebrates a fractured people coming together again — a reconciliation and a return to brotherhood.

The Talmud (*Shabbat* 22b) says that the Sages waited a year until they established Chanukah as a new holiday. Why? asked Rabbi Soloveitchik. They waited to see if there was a true reconciliation between the Jewish people. It was insufficient just to remove the physical *tumah*, impurity, from the Temple; the spiritual *tumah*, the impurity of divisiveness and strife, had to be removed as well. The nation of Israel had to make peace with one another, which thankfully they did.

Chanukah teaches us that making peace is an essential ingredient toward redemption. Joseph made peace with his brothers; the Chashmonaim and the Hellenists came together once again and unified our people. This is the great celebration of Chanukah!

Rabbi Abraham Isaac Kook, when he was the chief rabbi of Palestine, had many detractors. His critics slandered him and hung posters criticizing his positions on matters of policy and religious observance. When he walked through the narrow streets of the holy city, his enemies would even go so far as to empty their chamber pots on him.

It once came to pass that one of Rabbi Kook's most rancorous opponents needed a letter that had to be signed by none other than the chief rabbi himself. Too embarrassed to face Rabbi Kook directly, the man sent a messenger in his stead. The messenger went to the rabbi's office and asked him to write the letter. Rabbi Kook sat down right away to fulfill the request. When he finished, he put down his pen and gave the messenger the letter, but almost immediately asked for it back.

Rabbi Kook opened the letter and reread it word for word. He then gave it back to the messenger, who left before Rabbi Kook could change his mind again. Rabbi Kook's assistant, puzzled by this, asked, "Why did the Rabbi want to see the letter he had just written?"

Rabbi Kook answered. "I reread the letter because I wanted to be certain that it did not appear to be written with any lack of enthusiasm, and I wanted to make sure that even subconsciously I did not hold back in any way from supporting this person."

The lesson of this story may be best captured in the beloved words of Rabbi Kook himself. He said, "The Temple was destroyed due to senseless hatred; it will therefore be rebuilt with senseless love."

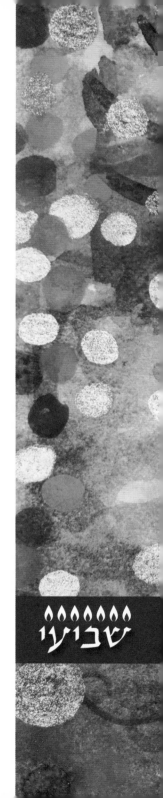

שבועי

WHERE TO PLACE THE MENORAH

THE TALMUD (*SHABBAT 22A*) STATES THAT THE IDEAL LOCATION FOR THE menorah is on the left-hand side of the front door. Jewish law establishes that the menorah sits on the left and the mezuzah is on the doorpost on the right (Rambam, Laws of Chanukah 3:4). In this way, say our Sages, when he enters the door a Jew is completely surrounded by mitzvot.

For generations this custom has been challenging to observe. Placing the menorah outside one's home was at times ill-advised, and often even dangerous. We therefore placed the menorah in the window, or somewhere else in the home, and performed the mitzvah in this way.

One of the great modern decisors of Jewish law, Rabbi Yechiel Michel Epstein (1829–1908), in his classic work *Aruch Hashulchan* (*Orach Chaim* 671, par. 5), notes that the custom of his day was to light indoors, simply because winter weather in Europe made outdoor lighting impractical.

However, the chief rabbi of Jerusalem, Rabbi Zvi Pesach Frank (1873–1960), held that Jerusalemites should reestablish this beautiful custom. Today throughout the holy city of Jerusalem, the ancient custom cited in the Talmud has returned, as many homes are adorned with the menorah on the outside, next to the doorway.

The great Chassidic master and first Rebbe of Ger the *Chidushei HaRim*, Rabbi Yitzchak Meir Rotenberg (1799–1866), asks: "Does it not seem

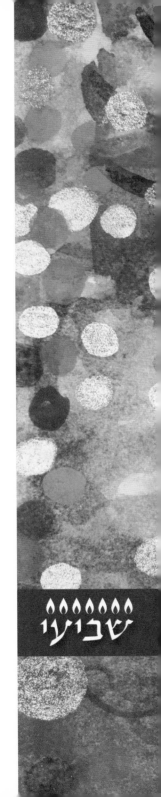

שבועון

odd to place the menorah on the *left* side? After all, in Jewish law, the *right* side is always given prominence, as it is seen symbolically as the place of strength and power. Why therefore would we not place the menorah on the right side, in order to more aptly express the power and strength of the lights?"

The Rebbe answers his own question: "You are making a mistake. It may be true that when one enters the home, the menorah is on the left; but when one *exits* the door, the menorah is in the right side! The purpose of the menorah is to spread its light *beyond* the home. We are to share its light with those on the outside. The menorah is in the most appropriate place — it is on the right side after all. The light of the menorah is meant to pour out of our homes into the streets."

The Lubavitcher Rebbe, Rabbi Menachem Mendel Schneerson, would greet thousands of people, one by one, each Sunday morning in his Crown Heights shul in New York. He would offer them blessings as well as a dollar for *tzedakah*. During the days of Chanukah, a woman who came to visit stepped up and wished the Rebbe a happy Chanukah. The Rebbe responded with the following blessing: "Your home should become a light that illuminates the entire street and community. Make sure you are sharing your lights with others. They are not meant for yourself. Give your light to others."

THE WINDOW SHUTTERS
OF CHELM

MANY PEOPLE HAVE THE CUSTOM OF LIGHTING THE MENORAH IN THE window. By placing the menorah in public view, we share the miracle with all those who pass by and see the light emanating from our homes.

Speaking of windows, the following "wisdom of Chelm" story comes to mind.

In the small village of Chelm there was a beloved man who served as the *shammes*, the sexton of the town. His job was to take care of all the needs of the synagogue, including the task of waking the townspeople early each morning for the Shacharit prayer service.

Even before the sun began to rise, he would walk through the town and knock on the shutters of each house. He would give a rap or two on a shutter until someone from inside would open it, or at least he heard some response. He would then move on to the next house.

This daily duty was not the most pleasant thing for the *shammes*, trudging through town early each day, often in inclement weather, be it heat, snow, or rain. Conversely, the men in the town never liked the banging on their windows.

Time passed, and as the *shammes* of the town was aging, it was becoming increasingly difficult for him to circulate through the entire town of

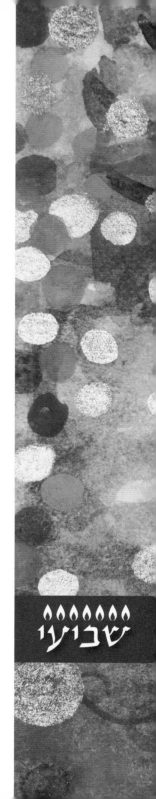

שביעי

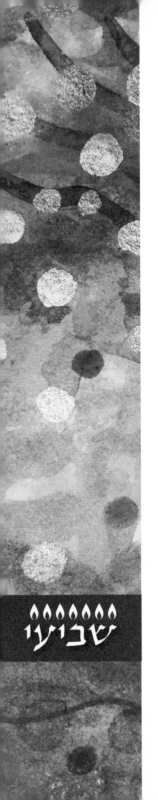

Chelm each morning. The wise men of the town convened an important meeting to make plans as to how the *shammes* would be able to carry out this function without unduly exerting himself.

After much discussion, one of the elders proposed the following idea: "There are two things we need to keep in mind. One is how difficult it has become for the *shammes* to make his rounds now that he is elderly and weak. Secondly, we the townspeople really do not like being disturbed each morning with the banging on our window shutters, especially so early in the morning.

"I have an idea that will solve both problems: We will ask everyone in the town to remove their shutters from their windows, and then we'll gather all the shutters and bring them to the home of the *shammes*.

"When the *shammes* wakes up in the morning, he will not have to leave his home and go out in the cold or rain. In the comfort of his own home he will be able to simply walk over to all the shutters and knock on each of them. This will solve everything. He will be happy not having the grueling walk each morning, and we will all be happy not being bothered by his disturbing knocking."

The wise men of Chelm were so impressed with this idea that they voted unanimously to put it into practice right away!

This classically humorous and absurd story offers us a joyful way to reflect on the message of Chanukah. When each of us places the menorah by the window and opens the shutters, we share the unique light of our own menorahs with the world. Every person and every home has a unique light.

The great poet and mystic Rabbi Abraham Isaac Kook expressed this idea with these words:

> *Everyone must know*
> *That within burns a candle.*
> *No one's candle is like someone else's;*
> *No one lacks a personal candle.*

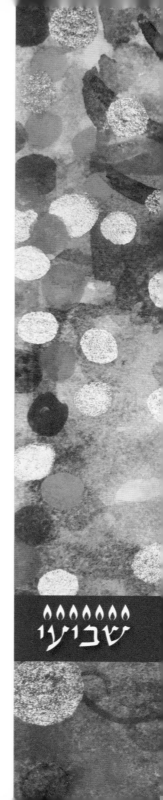

We all must know
That it is our task to reveal our light to the world,
To ignite it until it is a great flame
And to illuminate the universe.

The light from our windowsills unites with the light that shines from every other Jewish home, spreading great illumination and warmth to all people.

The Chassidic master Rebbe Shlomo Karlin (1740–1792) had a personal custom to light with wax candles. He felt that when the wax drips and the liquid hardens, an imprint is made that lasts well beyond the eight days of Chanukah, whereas oil simply burns and nothing of it remains. Wax candles symbolize the lesson that Chanukah must make a lasting impression on the soul.

One year he was unable to procure wax candles and that year he kindled his menorah with oil. It so happened that the menorah toppled over and a small fire broke out. It left dark burn marks on the wall. Reb Shlomo was not bothered by it. On the contrary, he was pleased because the mitzvah had left its mark on the house.

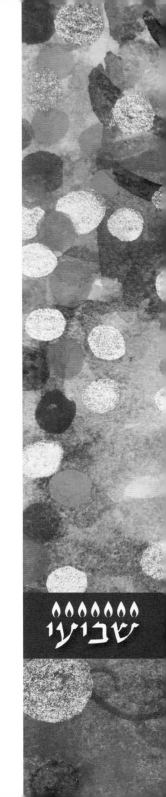

GIVING THE GIFT OF LIGHT

WHAT IS THE CONNECTION BETWEEN CANDLES AND SPIRITUALITY? WHAT is the deeper significance of lighting candles?

Of course, we light candles to usher in Shabbat and the Jewish holidays. And on Chanukah the lighting of the menorah is the essential mitzvah of the eight-day celebration.

But there is more to the lighting than just greeting the holiday or performing a mitzvah. The Chassidic masters taught the following: When you give away something physical, it is no longer yours. The more money you spend, the less money you have. The more gas you use driving your car, the less gas in your tank. As you eat the food in your refrigerator, you will soon need to go to the market to restock.

But in the spiritual world it works the opposite way. Spiritual resources become even greater the more they are used and the more they are shared with others. When I share wisdom when teaching a student, the student learns and I too become wiser. When I share love with another, that person receives the love and my love expands.

When I share a spiritual gift with another — an act of kindness, a smile, an uplifting word — the one who receives the gift gains, and the giver loses nothing.

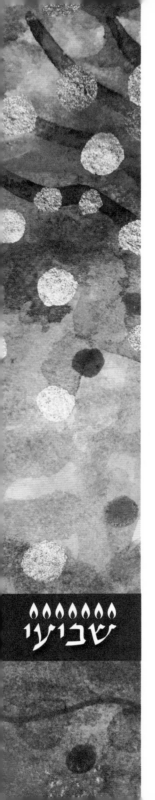

Rabbi Jonathan Sacks taught this lesson from a well-known dispute in the Talmud (*Shabbat* 22b) on the following question: *Madlikin mi'ner l'ner o lo?* (מדליקין מנר לנר או לא), "Is it permissible to take one Chanukah candle and use it to light another?"

On this there is a debate between Rav and Shmuel. Rav says no, Shmuel says yes. Rav says no because "you diminish the mitzvah." If I take a light to light another light, then I'm going to spill a little of the oil or a little of the wax, and the result is that I will diminish the first light.

But Shmuel doesn't worry about this. Now, we know in general, in any dispute between Rav and Shmuel, *Halachah k'Rav*, "The law is always like Rav against Shmuel" — with only three exceptions. And this is one of them!

What is at stake? What were they arguing about? And why in this case is the law not like Rav but like Shmuel?

The answer you will find in today's Jewish world. Imagine two Jews, both keeping the mitzvot. But there's a big difference between them; one of them says, I have to look after my light, and if I get involved with Jews who are not religious, who are not committed, my *yiddishkeit*, my religiosity, will be diminished. That is the opinion of Rav, a spiritual giant.

But Shmuel dared to say otherwise. He said, when I take my light to set another Jewish soul on fire, I don't have less light, I have more! Because while there was once one light, now there are two, and maybe from those two will come more! And on this the *halachah* is like Shmuel.

This is what it is to be a Jew, to walk in the path of Shmuel, to know that when we reach out to Jews who are less committed than we are, our light is not diminished; the result is that we create more light in the world.

This is the spiritual element found in a flame. When one takes a candle and shares its fire with another person's candle, the first candle remains as strong and as potent as before; the flame in no way is diminished by sharing it with another candle. The result is that there are two flames that together exude double the light. The two flames bring greater light and remove darkness.

The lights we kindle on Shabbat, for the festivals, and perhaps most poignantly during Chanukah symbolize the pure light, the soul, found within each of us. The more we give of ourselves, the more we share blessing with others, the more potent is the blessing that we bring to others and ultimately to ourselves.

In Yiddish there is an idiom, *a tzaddik in peltz*, "a righteous person in a fur coat." There are two ways one can have warmth in frigid weather. One can wear a warm coat, or one can build a fire that radiates heat. The first way provides warmth only for oneself, while the second method provides warmth for others as well. The *tzaddik in peltz* is one who seeks his own salvation, while allowing others to go to their doom. Lighting a fire is a means of sharing one's blessing with others.

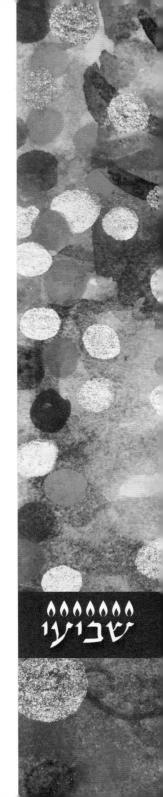

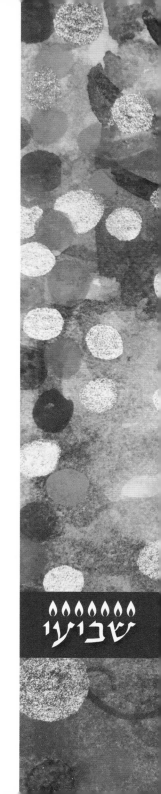

BLACK FIRE ON WHITE FIRE

REB MENDELE VORKER (1819–1868) AND RAV AVREM'L, THE TRISKER Maggid (1806–1889), were the best of friends. Even after they became the rabbinic leaders of different towns, they still kept in touch. They had made a pact to write to each other every week.

There was one special Jew, a Chassid of Reb Mendele Vorker, whose job it was to deliver letters between the Trisker and Reb Mendele every Friday. He would visit his Rebbe's home Friday morning to pick up his letter for the Trisker Maggid. He would then walk for several hours through the forest to the Trisker.

In Trisk, he would deliver the letter to Reb Avrem'l, who would go into his room, read the letter, and then write a reply. The man would wait for him to finish and then bring this letter back to Rav Mendele Vorker.

This Chassid felt privileged to do his job, and carried it out faithfully every week for many years. During that whole time, he never dared to open one of the letters and violate the intimate bond between the two *tzaddikim*.

However, one Friday morning, after the man had left with his Rebbe's letter, he was struck with a bizarre *yetzer hara*, evil inclination. He felt compelled to open the letter and read what the *tzaddik* had written to his lifelong friend.

He carefully opened the letter so that he would be able to close it

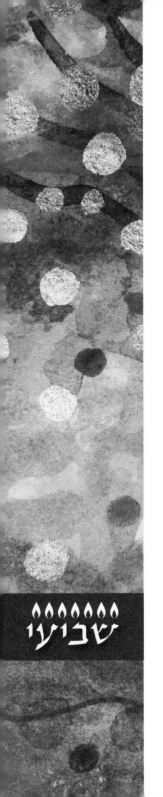

again without the Trisker being able to tell that it had been tampered with. When he did, he was shocked to see what was on the paper: nothing! It was completely blank.

At first he felt confused, and then he was hurt and angry. Was this some sort of trick that his Rebbe had been playing on him all of these years? He wondered if he had been sacrificing for his Rebbe, walking dozens of miles every Friday in hot summers and cold winters, all as part of some practical joke at his expense.

With a heavy heart, he closed the letter and continued his delivery to Trisk, wondering what would happen next. When he got there, he delivered the "letter" to the Maggid as he always did; the Rebbe took it and went into his room. A little while later, the Trisker emerged from his room with a flushed face. He handed the Chassid a letter. The Chassid headed out of town back to Vorka to deliver the Trisker's letter to his Rebbe, and to spend Shabbat in Vorka.

He had barely left the border of Trisk when he tore open Reb Avrem'l's letter to see what was inside. And sure enough, this letter was also blank! The Chassid was bewildered, hurt, and upset. He was now convinced that the two *tzaddikim* were playing some sort of terrible joke on him. With a broken heart, he walked back to Vorka and went straight to his Rebbe's house. He couldn't even bear to look his Rebbe in the face as he delivered the Trisker's "letter."

The Chassid returned home and resolved that the Vorker Rebbe would no longer be his Rebbe. He was just too hurt. Delivering these letters was "his" mitzvah. It had been what he took pride in and what he felt privileged to do for two great *tzaddikim*. If it was all for nothing, the pain was just too great. He didn't go to Reb Mendele Vorker's *tisch*, table, that night, and he didn't go to the Rebbe's Seudah Shlishit, the third meal of Shabbat, either.

By the time Shabbat was over, the Chassid just couldn't bear the pain anymore; he could not go on living without his Rebbe. He had to speak to him about what had happened.

He came to the Rebbe's house after Shabbat and waited for the Rebbe to see him. When he finally came in, he stood silently for a minute and then burst out crying. The Rebbe saw that he was clearly very upset about something and asked the Chassid to tell him what was bothering him.

The Chassid told his Rebbe that he was ashamed to admit what he had done, but that he had to confess. He had opened the Rebbe's letter on the way to Trisk the previous morning. "And what," the Rebbe asked him, "did you see?"

The man answered that of course, he had found a blank letter. "And what did you do then?" the Vorker Rebbe asked him.

"I delivered the 'letter' to the Trisker Maggid and waited for his return letter."

"And what happened when the Trisker gave his letter to you?" his Rebbe asked.

"I opened that letter too as soon as I left Trisk."

"And what did it say?"

He told the Rebbe what he already knew: the Trisker's letter was also blank.

"And what did you think when you saw the two blank letters?"

"I didn't know what to think! I felt that I was delivering the Rebbe's letter for nothing. Like it was all a waste."

"Let me explain something," the Vorker Rebbe said. "Every one of the black letters written in a Torah scroll is an expression of Hashem's love for the Jewish people. But these letters only express the part of Hashem's love that can be put into words. Now, the blank spaces between the letters... this is how Hashem expresses his love for us which is so great, and which bursts forth to such an extent that it cannot possibly be expressed in words.

"Most of the time, I am able to express the feelings of love I have for my friend, the holy Trisker, with words. At those times, I am able to express that love with the words I write to him in the letters. There are other times when the love I feel for the precious Reb Avrem'l is so

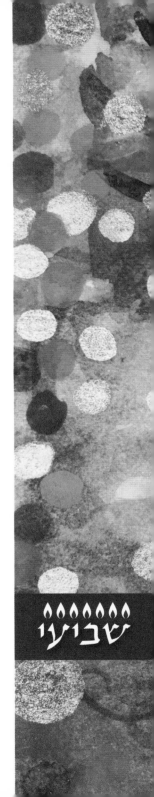

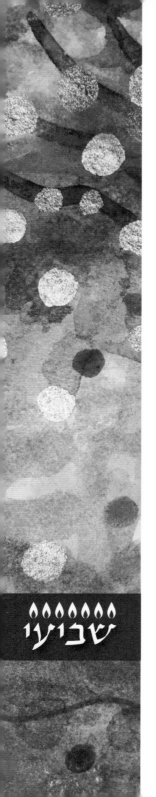

great, so powerful, that it cannot be expressed in words. At those times, the only way I can tell him how much I love him is with blank spaces…"

This powerful connection between the black fire and the white fire, the letters and the spaces, goes all the way back to the giving of the Torah at Mount Sinai.

The Jerusalem Talmud (*Shekalim* 6:1) says that the Torah given to Moses was written with black fire on white fire. And of course, our Torah scrolls reflect this relationship, with the letters written in black ink, surrounded by the white spaces around each letter.

In Judaism, fire often symbolizes the Divine Presence on earth, such as when Moses saw a burning fire inside the bush from where the voice of God emanated. Similarly, fire encompassed Mount Sinai when God revealed Himself to the Jewish people.

So it is for us at Chanukah. When gazing at the fire of the menorah, we are reminded of God's presence. We are reminded of the Shechinah, God's providence and closeness to us.

The Jewish people have been granted the precious gift of *black fire*, the Torah and mitzvot, laws that guide us and direct us through life. We have also received the precious gift of *white fire*, the gift of God's loving embrace and presence, which fill our lives.

The *white fire* symbolizes our Father in heaven Whom we turn to in prayer and Who turns to us; it is the shoulder of the Almighty to rest on when we feel weary and weak; ultimately, the Holy One is our dearest friend, with whom we share our most joyous and fulfilling moments in life.

Rebbe Yisrael of Ruzhin (1796–1850) said that there were two people who were devoted friends. One was falsely accused of treason and was sentenced to death. The friend intervened, saying, "He is innocent! Free him! It was I, not he, who committed the treason, and it is I who should be executed, not he."

The other friend said, "Don't believe him! He is just trying to protect me. I was the traitor."

When the king heard of this, he said that someone who is willing to give up his life for another could not be guilty of treason, and he freed the man. He then called both friends and said, "I have never seen such a devoted friendship. I will free both of you on one condition, that you take me into your circle. I wish to be a part of such a selfless relationship."

This is the meaning of the verse *V'ahavta l'reacha kamocha: Ani Hashem* (וְאָהַבְתָּ לְרֵעֲךָ כָּמוֹךָ: אֲנִי יְהֹוָה), "You shall love your fellow as yourself, I am God" (Leviticus 19:18). Said the Rebbe, "If you love your fellow as yourself, then I, God, wish to be in the relationship with you."

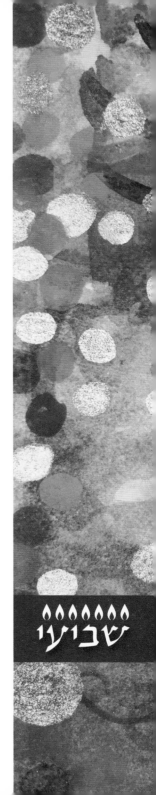

שביעי

BELLS AND POMEGRANATES

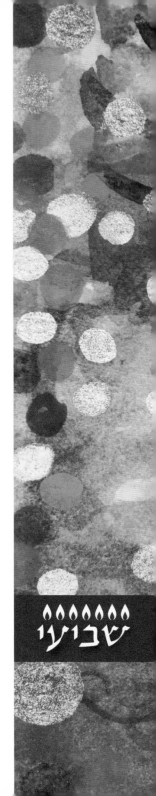

THE MIRACLE OF CHANUKAH TOOK PLACE IN THE TEMPLE IN JERUSALEM, where the flask of oil was found and the menorah was lit. The *kohanim*, the priests of the Temple, inspired the revolt against the enemy and led the Jewish people to victory.

Strikingly, the *kohen gadol*, high priest, wore eight unique garments, yet another example of the transcendental significance of the number eight. Furthermore, the Torah uses over eighty verses to describe the clothing of the priests. The sheer volume of the information clearly indicates an important message embodied by the garments — but what is that message?

The Talmud (*Zevachim* 88b) teaches that each garment atones for a particular sin of the Jewish people. The sin of *lashon hara* or speaking slander, literally "evil tongue," is forgiven through the wearing of the outer garment, the *me'il* worn by the high priest.

On the hem of the *me'il* is a row comprised alternately of bells made of gold and pomegranates spun from thread. When the *kohen gadol* walked, the ringing of the bells at the hem of the *me'il* was audible. Says the Talmud: "Let an item that makes a sound atone for the sin that involves sound, namely, the sounds of *lashon hara*."

The Talmud indicates that the Jewish people are forgiven for the sin of *lashon hara* simply by virtue of the high priest wearing this piece of clothing.

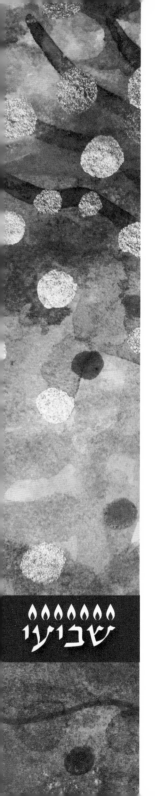

One of the great early sages, Rabbi Isaac Arama (c. 1420–1494), known for his classic Torah commentary *Akeidat Yitzchak*, explains that the matter is not that simple. He teaches that the atonement gained for the Jewish people's sin by the high priest's garment is only effective when the Jewish people learn their lesson and heed the message of that garment.

What then is the message to be learned from the bells and the pomegranates?

Next to each bell is a pomegranate. The Talmud (*Berachot* 57a) tells us that the pomegranate is an expression of everything that is good about each Jew: "Even the empty ones are full of mitzvot, like the pomegranate is full of seeds." How can a person be "empty" and "full of good deeds" at the same time?

The answer is simple. We choose what we want to see. Do we look to find fault or do we look to see the positive?

If you ignore the good points in each person, you will see the person as empty. If you look for the best in others, you will find an abundance of good qualities and good deeds.

Thus the Torah says to place a pomegranate next to the bell. If you want to make a "sound" about your fellow, when you "ring your bell," make sure that you are speaking of your fellow as a "pomegranate," seeing the good in him or her.

Highlight the positive in others. Uplift and build up others with your words. We rectify the sin of *lashon hara* only when we learn to choose words that are good — not words of hurt, but words that heal.

Rabbi Samson Raphael Hirsch's philological genius is evident in his commentary on the Torah.

The Hebrew word for "unfaithful behavior" is *me'ilah* (מְעִילָה). Rabbi Hirsch suggests that the close similarity to the word *me'il* (מְעִיל), the cloak worn by the high priest, is not incidental. He supports his thesis with the fact that the word *beged* (בֶּגֶד), a garment, is spelled exactly the same as the word *boged* (בֹּגֵד), which, like *me'ilah*, refers to deception and violation of trust.

That both these words have similar double meanings, Rabbi Hirsch contends, cannot be coincidental. A garment, Rabbi Hirsch says, is something in which a person presents himself to the world. One cannot know the true essence of a person merely by his external appearance. The *me'il* may be a cloak that is masking the true essence, which is called *me'ilah*. The Torah is cautioning us not to deceive others with a false facade and, most importantly, not to deceive ourselves.

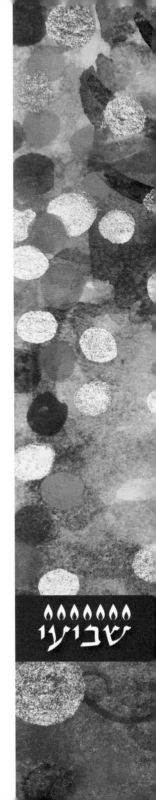

שביעי

HOLINESS

"A little bit of light pushes away much darkness."

Rebbe Shneur Zalman of Liadi, first Lubavitcher Rebbe

WHY EIGHT?

THE MYSTICAL MASTERS OF THE KABBALAH TEACH THAT THERE IS HIDDEN meaning in numbers.

When it comes to Chanukah, the number eight is significant: the menorah has eight lamps; we celebrate the festival for eight days.

What is special about the number eight?

The sixteenth-century sage and kabbalist the Maharal of Prague (1525–1609) offers a brilliant exposition of Chanukah. The Maharal notes that the number seven represents the realm of nature; seven parallels the seven-day cycle of the week, which is based on the seven days of creation.

In contrast, the number eight represents that which is beyond the natural order. The number eight represents elevation to a realm beyond this physical world. The number eight symbolizes that which transcends nature.

Three examples, among many, from the Torah:

1) Circumcision occurs on the eighth day of a baby boy's life, when a boy becomes a member of the Jewish nation and joins its miraculous destiny.

2) The Jewish people traveled for seven weeks in the wilderness after leaving Egypt. In the eighth week they received the Torah

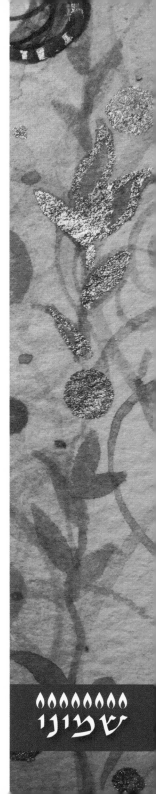

אֱמוּנָה

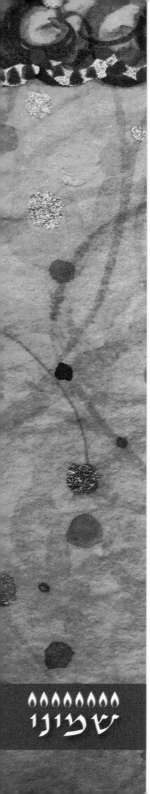

from God as the heavenly wisdom was received by Moses and the children of Israel at Sinai.

3) Precisely eight garments were worn by the high priest in the Temple. It was his unique role to represent the entire nation of Israel and come closest to God.

One other remarkable example of the significance of the number eight: Rabbi Israel Meir of Radin, the Chafetz Chaim, wrote a volume called *Ahavat Chesed*, Loving Kindness. The opening page cites eight verses in the Torah that require a Jew to live a life emulating the ways of God. Eight times the Torah instructs the Jew to "walk in His ways" (Deuteronomy 8:6, 10:12, 11:22, 13:5, 19:9, 26:17, 28:9, 30:16). We emulate God with acts of kindness, mercy, and sensitivity toward others. As the Talmud (*Shabbat* 133b) says, "Just as God is full of mercy, so too, you should be in your conduct."

When we live a life filled with kindness, we transcend this physical world. We enter the sphere of the Divine, the realm of "eight." When we practice compassion and mercy, we come closest to our most Godly selves.

On Chanukah we celebrate two remarkable miracles: the Maccabean battle in which we overcame impossible odds, and the small jug of oil fueling the Menorah for eight nights. The number eight, which is central to Chanukah, poignantly captures the theme of this holiday of miracles.

Every Jew is obligated to light the eight candles. Chanukah teaches that every Jew is to aspire to reach the eighth rung; we have the ability to transcend a purely earthly existence. When lighting the eight-branched menorah for eight days, we become more aware of the inherent holiness that emanates from the Divine *neshamah*, soul, that every person possesses.

Rabbi Chaim of Volozhin, the leading disciple of the great Vilna Gaon, quotes the verse "And let them make Me a sanctuary, that I may dwell *within them*" (Exodus 25:8). He taught that the verse does not say that the Divine Presence will dwell *in the Sanctuary*, but rather it says *within the people* — "within each and every one of them."

With this statement God is saying: "Do not think that My ultimate intention is the construction of the Sanctuary edifice; rather my entire purpose in desiring a sanctuary and its vessels is merely so that you should infer from it how to mold *yourselves*."

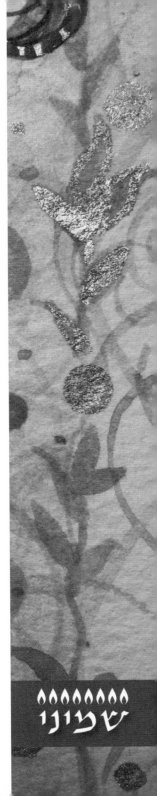

A TREE OF LIGHT

ROOTS, BRANCHES, BUDS, FLOWERS, AND FRUIT ARE ALL COMPONENTS OF a fruit tree.

These same components describe one of the most beloved of all Jewish objects: the Menorah.

Rabbi Samson Raphael Hirsch describes the Temple Menorah as "a light-bearing tree."

The Menorah in the Temple consisted of the following: a base, similar to the root of a tree, a central shaft similar to the central trunk of a tree, and branches extending outward from the center. The Torah text (Exodus 37:18) uses the word *branches*: *K'nei Menorah* (קְנֵי מְנֹרָה). On each branch of the Menorah there were flower cups called *gevi'im meshukadim* (גְבִעִים מְשֻׁקָּדִים), "almond-shaped cups" (Exodus 37:19), each with a *kaftor* (כַּפְתֹּר), knob, shaped like an apple, and a *perach* (פֶּרַח), flower.

What is the symbolism of a tree-shaped Menorah?

The Menorah, fashioned in the likeness of a beautiful blossoming tree with flowers and fruit, represents growth and vitality. The lights that emerge from the top of each branch represent the joy and exuberance that a life committed to the Torah provides for each of us.

Rabbi Hirsch teaches that light, when it is mentioned in the Torah, is a metaphor for the pulsating joy of living. Joy is essentially "the feeling of awareness of a blossoming life."

– 187 –

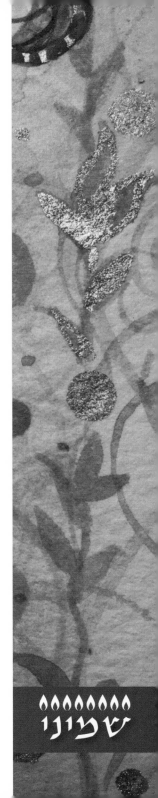

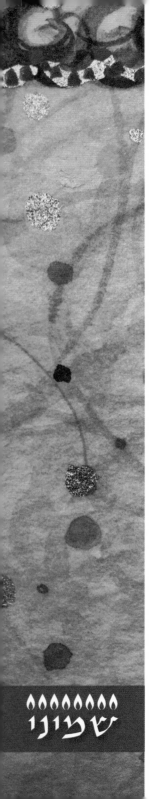

Light is a symbol of growth, energy, an unfolding and a flowering of progress, dynamism, happiness, and joy. As an example, in the book of Esther (8:16), when the Jews were saved, we are taught, "For the Jews there was *light* and joy, gladness and honor." The light described here refers to joy.

Viewing the Temple's Menorah as a whole, its roots, branches, flowers, and fruit symbolize exuberance and vitality.

Rabbi Hirsch brilliantly notes that the Hebrew words for joy and growth are closely related: the word for "happy," *sameach* (שָׂמֵחַ), is almost identical to the word *tzomeach* (צֹמֵחַ), "growing." In addition, *sees* (שִׂישׂ), which means "joy," is almost identical to the word *tzitz* (צִיץ), which means "blossom."

One of the most beloved verses, which we sing as the Torah is returned to the Ark, compares the Torah itself to a tree: *etz chaim hi* (עֵץ־חַיִּים הִיא), "it is a tree of life" (Proverbs 3:18).

This metaphor suggests that the Torah is not only a source of ancient wisdom, but also that it is dynamic and ever relevant. Its laws are lights that continue to nurture and enrich us. The eternal teachings of our tradition are a source of strength that encourage spiritual blossoming and personal growth.

Chanukah celebrates this vitality and vibrancy of the Torah and also contains the recognition that we as people cannot grow and prosper without remaining committed to the Torah's ideals and teachings. Indeed, Chanukah celebrates the indispensability of God in our lives.

As we gaze at our menorah, our "light-bearing tree," may we become more attuned to the precious gift of Judaism that enriches and ignites our lives.

Rabbi Joseph B. Soloveitchik suggested that Judaism rests on three attributes of the individual, signified by the *head*, the *hand*, and the *heart*.

The head involves the intellectual discipline inherent in

Judaism. One who has the will but has no knowledge at all of Judaism cannot be a good Jew. The ideal of Torah study involves the highest level of logic – the ability to think abstractly, analytically, and conceptually. The learning of Torah is therefore nothing less than the sanctification of the mind through intellectual struggle.

The hand involves performance of mitzvot. Diligence in the observance of mitzvot with precision requires great commitment. Through such performance, a person's hands are sanctified.

Although one can find the first two attributes in abundance today, it is the third aspect that Rabbi Soloveitchik found most challenging in our day and age. The heart involves experiencing God emotionally. As our Sages say, "God desires the heart" (Talmud, *Sanhedrin* 106b).

One must feel the emotional pull of the Master of the universe.

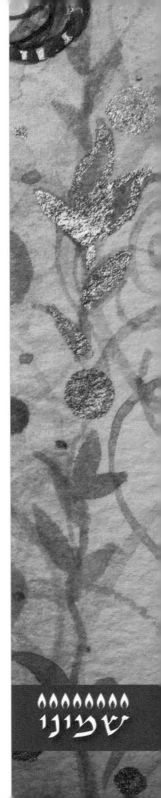

אשׁוּוּן

THE PURITY OF CHANUKAH

PURITY IS A MAJOR MOTIF OF CHANUKAH.

Three examples:

1) The Maccabees found one jug of *pure* oil to light the Menorah.

2) The Syrian Greeks required Jewish brides to be taken to the general before consummating their marriages with their husbands on their wedding nights. In this way they attempted to destroy the *purity* of the Jewish home.

3) Finally, the Chanukah prayer Al Hanisim refers to Syrian Greeks as defiled and the Jewish people as the *pure* people.

What does it mean to be pure? How do we recognize purity? How do we attain it?

The following story, told by Rabbi Shlomo Carlebach, gives us a glimpse into how to make purity a practical part of our lives.

"There are Jews who find it very important to go to the mikveh, the ritual bath. Mikveh water is water that is untouched, pure rain water. Not only does the body need washing, but also the soul needs washing. The idea of mikveh is that it is to be used for a "spiritual washing."

For Chassidim this is a very strong custom. Some go every day, and some go at least on Friday before sunset. You wash your soul off as you enter Shabbat. So when I travel across the world I often call up the local synagogue in the city before arriving for Shabbat and ask them if there is a mikveh in their city.

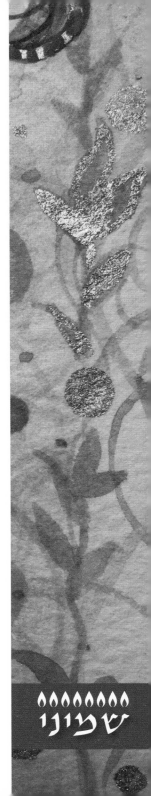

אזוינו

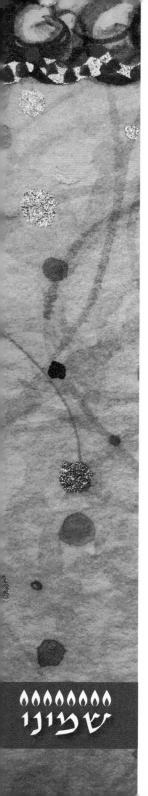

I once came to a city in the "wild West," somewhere in Texas. Usually when I go to a mikveh in such a place, I am the only one there on a Friday afternoon. So I am in this "way out" city and it's Friday afternoon. I'm just about to leave the mikveh when in walks a man wearing a big black cowboy hat. He does not look like someone who would use the mikveh. I say to myself, could it be that this fellow is going to the mikveh? He must be in the wrong place.

He turns to me and he greets me...in Yiddish!

And after he used the mikveh, he told me his story.

He said, "You're probably wondering what I'm doing here. Most people who use the mikveh on Friday afternoon are preparing for Shabbos. But I'm not the most observant Jew, and I don't always keep Shabbos.

"I grew up in a small town in Eastern Europe.

"When I was about eight years old, my father took me for a Shabbos to a town called Vizhnitz. He wanted me to see the Rebbe, Reb Yisrael of Vizhnitz. The Rebbe was known to be a very great man, and he was known also for his humility.

"In Vizhnitz there were thousands of people who came for Shabbos. Friday night everyone gathered to hear the Rebbe speak at his table. My father wanted to protect me from the huge crowd, so he tucked me under the table at his feet, near the Rebbe.

"There were lots of children under the table. The Rebbe knew we were there and he gave us challah and soup and chicken. I happened to be the closest to him so I was being fed all night. I began to feel as if the Rebbe knew that I was there.

"The Rebbe began to teach profound Torah that was beyond my understanding. But at one point he raised his voice and said the following: 'I need to teach you something critical that you must always hold on to. Sometimes we have the impulse to immerse ourselves in holiness, but the "other side," the *yetzer hara*, our evil inclination, says to us: "Who do you think you are? You're no *tzaddik*. You weren't acting so holy yesterday, and you won't be acting so holy tomorrow, so don't even try to be holy now.'"

"I saw from under the table that the Rebbe jumped up, and he was yelling with fire in his voice and he said, 'Tell your "other side" to have compassion. Tell it, "Just give me five minutes to be close to God."' And then the Rebbe sat down. He reached under the table and he put his hand on my head and he told me to never forget.

"Not long after this encounter with the Rebbe, we moved to America. As a child I didn't get a Jewish education. I never had a chance to learn Torah or very much about being Jewish. Today I don't keep many of the laws of Judaism. But sometimes I just feel like I want to do something holy. And I think about how the Vizhnitzer Rebbe said to tell my 'other side' to let me be close to God...even if it is just for five minutes.

"So, my friend, this morning I woke up and wanted to feel some holiness in my life. I may keep Shabbat tonight, I may not. But right now I had a longing to feel a little purity."

Reb Shlomo Carlebach, when telling this story, added: "Sometimes we look to add holiness in our lives — please don't let the 'other side' say, 'Well, does it really fit into your life? Is it for real? Do you really need it? It's not going to last anyway.'

"Do you know how special it is to have five minutes of holiness? Those few minutes of purity connect you with endless light, with the eternal. There is no way of qualifying the joy one has and the reward one receives for even a minute of holiness."

A man once said to the great Chassidic master Rabbi Levi Yitzchak of Berditchev, "It says in the prayer of the Shema that we will be punished for our sins. But just look at me! I am a

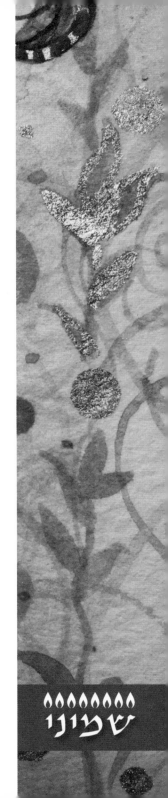

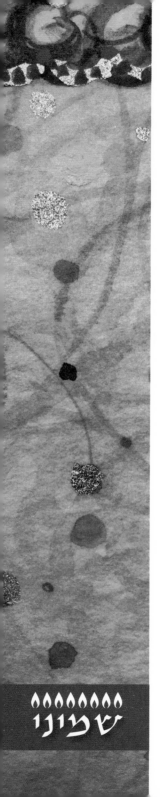

sinner, but I have great wealth and a very enjoyable life. So you see it is not true."

Rabbi Levi Yitzchak responded, "My dear friend, the only way you could make this statement is because you have recited the Shema. There is not enough wealth in the entire world to adequately compensate anyone for reciting the Shema even a single time."

BEING A CHILD ON CHANUKAH

CHANUKAH IS A MAGICAL TIME FOR CHILDREN. CHILDREN LIGHT THE menorah, play dreidel, and receive *gelt* (money) and gifts, making this an especially beloved time of year.

But is being a child on Chanukah only for the young?

When our matriarch Sarah passed away, she was 127 years old.

Actually, the Torah reports it this way: "She was one hundred years, twenty years and seven years" (Genesis 23:1).

Rashi teaches that when she was one hundred, she was like a twenty-year-old woman. When she was twenty, she was like a seven-year-old child. Although Sarah aged, she remained young at heart. At every stage in her life she retained the best qualities of being young — both the qualities of a child and the qualities of a young woman.

She approached each day with vitality and vigor. The maturity of Sarah never diminished the special childlike qualities within her. As an adult she may have reached the greatest intellectual heights, but this did not impinge on her purity of faith. For her, the experiences of different ages did not merely occur in sequence. Rather, they existed simultaneously within her.

Rabbi Soloveitchik taught that childlike qualities are necessary in order to fulfill the essentials of a Jewish life: namely, prayer, faith, and love of God.

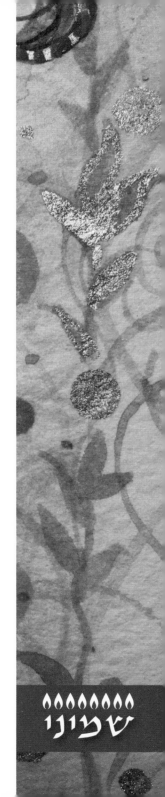

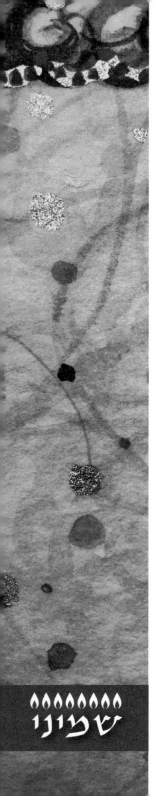

PRAYER. Prayer requires a sense of total reliance, even helplessness, like a child who is incapable of functioning on his own without a caring parent. Prayer is surrendering. The only one who knows how to pray is a little child, the child who realizes that his or her existence is dependent on someone else.

FAITH. Only a child is capable of pure and simple faith. Faith is the complete reliance on and trust in someone. A little infant, for example, has absolute faith in his mother. Without the mother's presence the child feels alone and afraid. This is what it means to have faith in God, to have total reliance on Him. Faith means the suspension of judgment and even of logic, especially when confronted with life challenges that are beyond our comprehension.

LOVE OF GOD. The Rambam (Laws of Teshuvah 10:3) describes the love that a Jew has for God: "And what is the love that is befitting? It is to love the Eternal with a great, an exceeding love, so strong that one's soul shall be bound up with the love of God, and one should be continually enraptured by it, like a lovesick individual whose mind is at no time free from his passion for a particular woman, the thought filling his heart all the time."

Love of God, in this passage, is compared to the intense passion of lovers, the romantic love shared by the young. Fulfilling the mitzvah "You shall love your God with all your heart" can only be actualized when one is engaged in a "romantic relationship" with the One Above. Sarah was like a woman of twenty regarding her devotion to God and her passionate relationship with Him.

Perhaps more than any other holiday of the Jewish year, Chanukah is a children's holiday. In this rare instance children participate in the mitzvah of the festival. Jewish law recommends that even the youngest should light the menorah.

For children everything in life is still new and unexpected, worthy of curiosity and examination. For a child there is still a magical world, even a spiritual world, viewed from a different place of perception and thought. The Chassidic masters suggest that the word *Chanukah*, which means rededication or renewal, refers to a personal sense of renewal and newness that we engage in during these eight days.

There are times in life when we need to see the world through the pure eyes of a child; Chanukah is such a time.

When Rabbi Aaron Soloveitchik (1917–2001) of Yeshiva University was six years old, he was standing and davening on a fast day next to his illustrious grandfather, Reb Elya Pruzhener (1842–1928).

The ark opened and the congregation was reciting the prayer responsively. As Reb Elya cried out each verse with emotion, little six-year-old Aaron recited the prayers with as much fervor as a six-year-old can muster.

When they came to the verse "Do not cast us away in old age," Reb Elya exclaimed it with the same passion as the other verses. The little boy, however, lowered his voice and recited the verse almost in an undertone.

After the prayers Reb Elya said to his grandson, "I noticed that there was one verse that you did not say with the same enthusiasm you gave to the others."

Little Aaron was surprised at his grandfather's attentiveness. "Zeide," he replied, "those words are not for me. I'm only six years old!"

Reb Elya smiled at his grandson's perception and said, "Let me tell you what intent lies in these words besides their literal meaning. At times when an elderly person is confronted with a challenge, he says, 'I am too old and tired to deal with this problem.

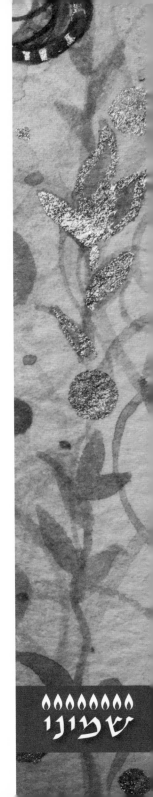

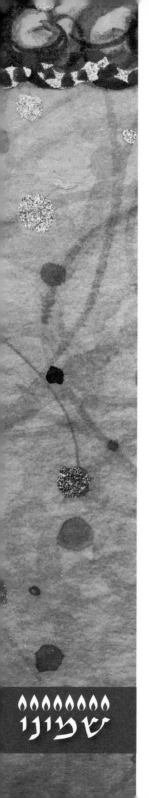

Let others take charge. I don't have the strength or the willingness to get involved.'

"With older people," said Reb Elya, "it is understandable. But sometimes even young people give up when they have a problem. They say, 'I can't deal with it. I'm too tired and it's too hard. Let others do it.' They have been smitten with the mindset of the elderly. We therefore ask God, 'Do not let us develop the attitude of those elderly people who have lost their enthusiasm to accomplish.'"

HOW LONG MUST THE LIGHT LAST?

RABBI AVRAHAM DOV OF THE CITY OF AVRITCH (1765–1840) IN THE Ukraine was known for his extraordinary humility. At the age of sixty-five he fulfilled his lifelong dream of making aliyah and living in the Holy Land. He wrote his Torah insights in a volume entitled *Bat Ayin* (The Eye Within). He refused to publish this work until he arrived in Israel and made the final edits. The Rebbe was determined to expose the pages of his teachings to the sacred air of the Land before printing the book.

This beloved work, *Bat Ayin*, contains the following Chanukah message.

The Talmud (*Shabbat* 21b) asks, "How long must the candles stay lit?" It answers, *ad she'tichleh regel min hashuk* (עַד שֶׁתִּכְלֶה רֶגֶל מִן הַשּׁוּק), "until such time as people stop walking in the marketplace." The purpose of the candles is to broadcast the message of the miracle to others. Once there are no longer pedestrians on the street, there is no one to see the lights of the menorah, and there is no need for the candles to be lit.

The saintly Rebbe of Avritch suggested a deeper explanation.

He creatively suggested that the word *regel* has the same root as the word *ragil*, regular or habituated. Based on this, he reinterpreted the phrase as follows: one must light the menorah, *ad* – until – *she'tichleh regel*, to the point where one's habituation ceases.

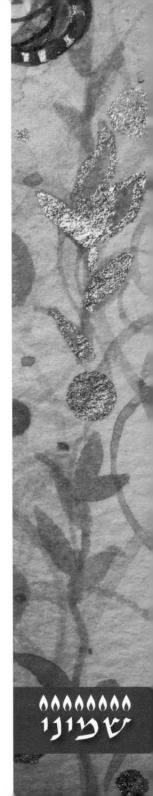

שמעון

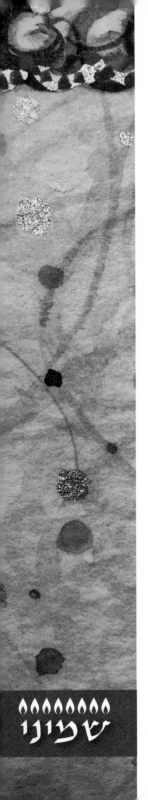

In other words, the Chanukah candles must remain lit, in our own minds and hearts, until we have obliterated the idea that the world functions only with *regel*, regularity, without *hashgachah pratit*, God's providence and miraculous oversight. The lights of Chanukah need to remain burning until they help us to remove the all-too-human habit of applying only rationality and reason when relating to our circumstances and to the world.

Our spiritual vision should allow us to perceive the presence of God in our lives. The lighting of the menorah must awaken us to see the miracles that surround us and to invigorate our belief and faith in the Holy One.

The Avritcher Rebbe's explanation was embodied in the following episode that is told by Rabbi Shlomo Carlebach about the Rebbe's aliyah to Israel.

Rebbe Avraham Dov of Avritch was unique among the Chassidic masters. He left his home and his followers to fulfill the dream of making aliyah and to begin a new life in Israel. The Rebbe moved to the city of Tzfat, where he embarked on leading a new community to whom he served as rabbi and teacher.

One day, a stranger entered the courtyard near his home, and Rebbe Avraham Dov ran to greet him. The Chassidim watched this encounter. They couldn't hear what they spoke of, but as soon as the stranger left, the Rebbe returned to his study and strangely did not emerge from his home for many days.

The Chassidim were puzzled: Who was that person? What did he and the Rebbe discuss? Why did the Rebbe lock himself in his study for many days? Their puzzlement grew when the Rebbe finally emerged and commanded his Chassidim to prepare the most amazing *tisch*, a festive meal at the Rebbe's table.

The Chassidim did as they were told. They ate and drank, sang and danced. But the whole time, all they really wanted to know was who was the stranger? What did he and the Rebbe discuss? Why did the Rebbe lock himself in his room for so long?

Finally, one of the Chassidim mustered up the courage to ask the Rebbe, "Why?"

The Rebbe silenced them and began: "Many years ago, while still in the town of Avritch, I would always sit for hours with anyone who came from Eretz Yisrael. I would question them about the Holy Land and what it was like to live there.

"One day a charity collector came to town and we talked endlessly. When he stood to leave, I begged him, 'Please, tell me more!'

"He said to me, 'I've told you everything.'

"But I insisted, 'Tell me more!'

"He said to me, 'What more can I tell you? When you stand at Me'arat Hamachpelah along with the Patriarchs and Matriarchs in Hevron, you will know.' And he turned to leave.

"I begged of him, 'Please, tell me more!'

"He said, 'What more can I tell you? When you stand at *Kever Rachel*, at Rachel's tomb, and cry with her, you will know.' And again he turned to leave.

"I continued to beg, 'Please, tell me more!'

"He said, 'I've told you all I can. When you get there you will see for yourself — even the stones are precious stones. Even the stones are made of emeralds and rubies and diamonds!' And with this he left.

"So you see," the Rebbe turned to his Chassidim, "when I arrived, everything was exactly as he said it would be. Everything but the stones — they were regular stones, they weren't precious stones at all. I could never understand why he lied to me. The last thing he told me was not true!

"So a number of days ago, he walked into the courtyard, and despite the passage of twenty years, I recognized him immediately. I ran to him and said, 'Everything you told me was true, except the part about the stones! Why did you tell me that they were precious stones when they are not?'

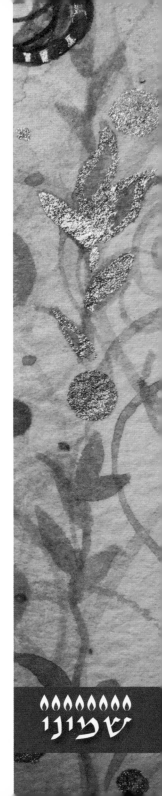

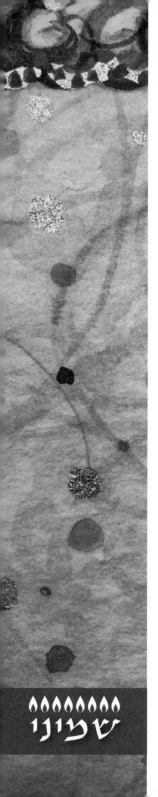

"He looked at me and said with dismay and surprise, 'What? They're not? You don't also see the jewels?'

"So I locked myself in my study and I began to cry. Every day I would cry and look out at the stones, hoping to see the jewels. Today, finally, while looking out the window I realized that every stone was precious. Every stone was an emerald or a ruby or a diamond!"

On Sunday afternoons, the Lubavitcher Rebbe, Rabbi Menachem Mendel Schneerson, would stand outside the door of his office to greet and bestow a blessing upon anyone who came to see him. He often would stand for hours, as thousands of people filed by, many of them seeking a blessing or advice about a personal matter or a spiritual dilemma.

The Rebbe was once asked how he had the strength to stand all day, sometimes for seven or eight hours, to accommodate everyone. "When I see all these people, it is like counting diamonds," he replied with a smile. "One doesn't grow weary or weak when counting something as beautiful as diamonds."

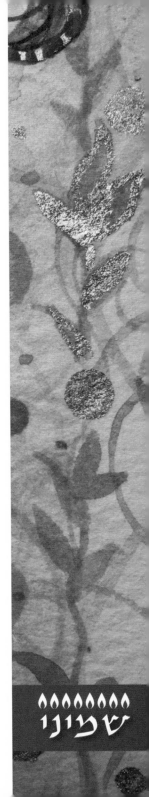

A KISS FROM ABOVE

THE SPECIAL LOVE WE HAVE FOR CHANUKAH WAS ARTICULATED A THOUSAND years ago by the Rambam: "The commandment to kindle the Chanukah lights is an exceedingly precious mitzvah" (Laws of Chanukah 4:12).

Many have asked why the Rambam, in his code, never refers to the observance of other mitzvot – such as Shabbat or *kashrut, sukkah* or shofar – using the phrase "an exceedingly beloved mitzvah," and yet he does so regarding Chanukah.

Having miraculously won the war against the Syrian Greek army, the Jews returned to the Temple. Whether or not the Menorah was lit was not critical. If they had to wait a few more days to attain pure oil, that would have been fine.

So why then was it necessary for there to be a miracle in the first place? Wasn't the miracle, in effect, the military victory against all odds?

The Rebbe of Slonim, Reb Shalom Noach Berezovsky (1911–2000), answered that it was not necessary from our perspective. However, from God's perspective it was! God wanted to express His thanks, love, and admiration for His people. God wished to display His gratitude for the Jewish people's self-sacrifice, courage, and commitment. The Temple miracle was a heavenly response to the heroic self-sacrificing and idealism of the Maccabees.

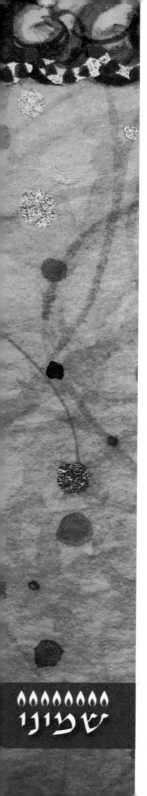

Rabbi Shlomo Carlebach would often say: "I know that Jews believe in God, but do Jews know how much God believes in them!"

The light of the Menorah which miraculously shone for eight days revealed God's feelings of *chavivut*, fondness or love. In a word, the miracle of the Menorah demonstrated God's eternal love for His people, Israel. As the Sages explained, "The fire of the Menorah is testimony that the *Shechinah*, God's presence, was with the Jewish people" (Talmud, *Shabbat* 22a).

The Slonimer Rebbe taught that this is what the Rambam had in mind when he referred to the mitzvah of the Menorah as *chaviv* – a most beloved mitzvah. Beloved because the miracle of the Menorah was an expression of God's deep affection for His people. The purpose of the oil lasting eight days was none other than to show God's love for Israel.

It is also remarkable to find that the *halachah* is very strict regarding the obligation to light the menorah. It requires that a poor person must extend himself to the point of borrowing money and even selling the shirt off his back in order to purchase candles for the mitzvah of lighting.

Why such stringency? Jewish law wanted to ensure that everyone, regardless of financial situation, be included in this mitzvah which uniquely expresses God's love for the Jewish people.

Each night of Chanukah we are reminded of God's love. This is what makes the mitzvah of kindling the menorah so special in our eyes and in the eyes of the Holy One.

Rabbi Chaim Shmuelevitz (1902–1979) said that the miracle of the oil lasting eight days in the menorah was the way God "placed a kiss on the head" of His precious child. Like a mother who wishes to express her boundless love for her child with a kiss, especially at a moment when the mother is so proud, God wished to express His endearing love to His children. God shone His light and love through the light of the Menorah for all of us to see.

CELEBRATING THE UNIQUENESS
OF EACH OF US

ALTHOUGH THE CHANUKAH MENORAH IS CUSTOMARILY KINDLED IN THE synagogue, the essential observance of Chanukah is celebrated when each person lights his or her menorah, preferably at home, when each family gathers to kindle the menorah in its window or front doorway.

The Ishbitzer Rebbe, Rabbi Mordechai Leiner (1801–1854), taught that the holiday of Chanukah uniquely emphasizes the greatness that lies within every individual.

The Sages did not choose to commemorate Chanukah with public gatherings. Strikingly, the menorah lighting is designated to be done at home, *ner ish u'veito* (נֵר אִישׁ וּבֵיתוֹ), "a candle for each member of the household." The language of the Talmud is telling. Regarding the lighting of the menorah it says, *ner l'chol echad v'echad* (נֵר לְכָל אֶחָד וְאֶחָד), "a candle for each and every individual," meaning that each member of the household is responsible to light the menorah.

The emphasis of the ritual of Chanukah is on the contribution of each person.

Chanukah exemplifies an important pillar of Judaism: every person counts. Every person has something unique to contribute to perfect the world.

In a small village called Modiin in the Judean Hills, not far from Jeru-

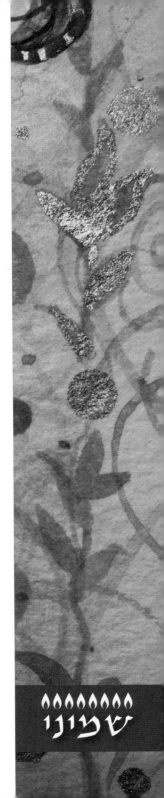

שִׁיעוּר

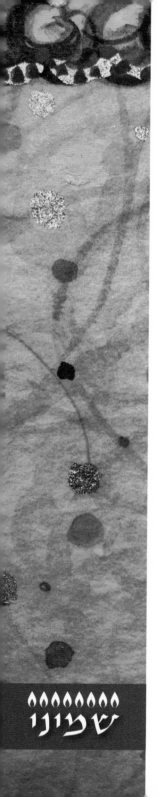

salem, a small family resolved to challenge one of the greatest armies on earth. In the Chanukah prayer of Al Hanisim we highlight the name of one individual, Mattathias the son of Yochanan. Together with his sons and their followers, they became known as the Maccabees. With his five sons – Yehudah, Shimon, Elazar, Yochanan, and Yonatan – Mattathias sparked a revolt that continued for three years.

Weighing their odds, victory was virtually impossible; however, one passionate man and his dedicated family were determined to do all they could, regardless of the outcome.

And of course we know what that outcome was: the Maccabees liberated Jerusalem, reclaimed the Temple, and heroically lit the glorious flames of the Menorah.

But it all started with one person, with one family.

In a most memorable Chassidic teaching, it was said of the great Rebbe Rabbi Simcha Bunim of Peshischa (1765–1827) that he carried two slips of paper, one in each pocket. On one he wrote: *Bishvili nivra ha'olam* (בִּשְׁבִילִי נִבְרָא הָעוֹלָם), "For my sake the world was created." On the other he wrote, *V'anochi afar va'efer* (וְאָנֹכִי עָפָר וָאֵפֶר), "I am but dust and ashes." He would take out each slip of paper as necessary, as a reminder to himself.

On Chanukah we focus on the trait of *gevurah* – courage and heroism. These are days that reenergize every individual with Jewish pride and confidence as ambassadors of the Divine who can accomplish great things.

Mattathias and his sons could not have guessed what great awe and respect their struggle would garner over the millennia. They could not have known how their spirit would illuminate centuries of darkness and how they would encourage their descendants to follow their example by liberating Jerusalem and creating a homeland for the Jewish people.

Chanukah's candles are our own individual and unique lights. The potential for greatness knocks at our door and summons each of us to be confident and courageous in our own Jewish living.

Rabbi Jonathan Sacks told the following anecdote at the gala banquet of the Conference of Chabad-Lubavitch Emissaries.

Friends, I once heard a beautiful story from a *shaliach* (an emissary of the Rebbe) who had gone to a little town in Alaska, where he asked at the local town hall, are there any Jews there?

They said to him there are no Jews there. So he asked — in order not to go back having not done anything — could he go and visit the local school and give a talk to children? The head of the school said fine.

And he went into a classroom — this little town in the middle of Alaska — and he said, "Children, have any of you ever met a Jew?"

And one little girl put up her hand and she said, "Yes."

And he said, "Who?"

And she said, "My mother."

And he was thinking to himself, "What do I say to this girl? She's the only Jewish child in this school; the only Jew in the entire city. I will be leaving town. What can I say to this girl now that will lead her to stay Jewish?"

And this is what he did: he asked her to light Shabbos candles every Friday before Shabbos. And he said this to her: "I don't know if you know this, but Alaska is the most westerly place in the world where there are Jews. It is the last place in the world where Shabbos comes. And when every Jew lights Shabbos candles, they bring light and peace to the world. So every Shabbos the whole world is waiting for your Shabbos candle — the last of all to be lit."

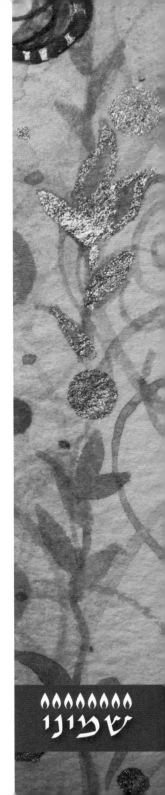

WINGS TO FLY

THE CLASSIC FAIRY-TALE WRITER HANS CHRISTIAN ANDERSEN TELLS THE following story about a baby bird that had just hatched.

The bird looked around him and saw all the other birds flying, and decided to try it himself. He jumped up as high as he could but came straight down again. After trying this a few times, he realized what his problem was: he had two appendages at his sides that were weighing him down. He figured that if only he could find some way to get rid of them, surely he would be able to fly with no trouble at all.

However, when he shared this idea with an older bird, he was shocked to discover that those very things that he had thought were weighing him down were actually what gave him the ability to fly.

Interestingly, the Talmud (*Shabbat* 49b) compares the Jewish people to a bird, and states that the mitzvot are the wings that give the Jewish people the ability to soar. This teaching is reflected in a custom observed by many when wrapping *tefillin*. We wind the straps to each side, creating the image of the wings of a bird.

Mitzvot are the wings for the Jewish people. When we view the Torah commandments as chores or burdens that weigh us down, we are failing to see their richness and preciousness.

Our Sages teach that there were three mitzvot in particular that the Greeks forbade the Jews from observing: Shabbat (observing the Sabbath),

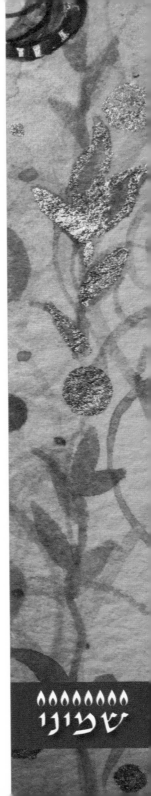

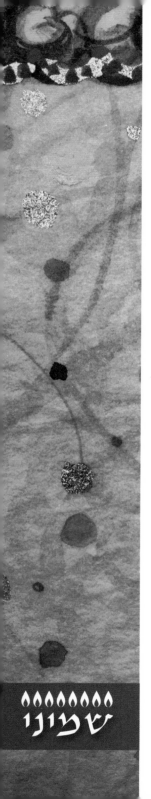

Rosh Chodesh (calculating and celebrating the new Jewish month), and *brit milah* (circumcision).

All three relate to endowing the physical world with spirituality and divine holiness. These three mitzvot each highlight the special relationship that God has with His chosen people — and this idea was anathema to the ancient Greeks.

The Syrian Greeks saw these observances as distinguishing the Jewish culture from their own. The Jews functioned on a different schedule with their observance of Shabbat. The Jewish festivals are based on establishing the new months of the lunar calendar. And circumcision is a permanently branded sign of Jewishness.

Under the rule of the tyrant Antiochus, those who were caught observing these commandments were severely punished. The Greeks sought to impose their culture and ideology, at times by means of debate and at times through violent force.

The Greeks, like many of our enemies before and after, sensed that it was the mitzvot that gave the Jews their uniqueness and their strength. With mitzvot we thrive; without them, we quickly lose our uniqueness and vitality.

We learn, "The tablets were the work of God and the writing was the work of God, *charut* (חָרוּת), engraved, upon the tablets" (Exodus 32:16). Our Sages explain, "Do not read *charut*, but rather *cherut* (חֵרוּת), freedom, for there is no one who is truly free who does not engage in Torah" (*Pirkei Avot* 6:2).

The Sages who taught this wanted us to see a paradox. The Torah and its commandments bind us to laws that have been imposed upon us, yet our greatest freedom comes from the acceptance of Torah and these very laws. True freedom comes from choosing to engage in a disciplined way of life. Observance of mitzvot assists us in finding mastery over ourselves and fulfilling our highest aspirations. Judaism teaches us to become the champions of our own lives.

The sacred commandments are meant to be our wings, providing us with the means to reach great heights.

The Syrian Greeks forbade the observance of the Sabbath, Rosh Chodesh, celebrating each new month, and circumcision. Amazingly, the observance of Chanukah recalls all three of these mitzvot. The new Jewish month of Tevet always occurs during Chanukah; every Chanukah has at least one Sabbath; and Chanukah is eight days long, which alludes to the mitzvah of circumcision, performed on the eighth day.

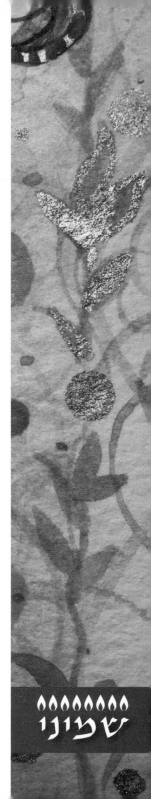

שמיני

Customs &
ברכת המזון
Birkat Hamazon, Grace after Meals

CUSTOMS OF CHANUKAH – DEEPER INSIGHTS

Placement of the Menorah

Jewish law records the custom to light the menorah at the doorway in a low place, within a few feet from the ground.

The following anecdote reveals an insight into this custom:

All his Chassidim strove to be present when Rabbi David of Tolna kindled his Chanukah lights. It was a powerful event.

One year, on the first night of Chanukah, just before the time to light the flame, the Rebbe was standing before the menorah, involved in his last-moment inner preparations. The crowd of Chassidim pressed around him. Unexpectedly, the Rebbe turned to a certain Chassid and said, "I know that your wife is quite short. When you need to speak with her, what do you do? Do you bend over towards her or does she raise herself up to your height?"

Immediately upon uttering this remarkable question, the Rebbe began his recital of the Chanukah blessings and lit his golden menorah.

The Chassidim were bewildered. What did the Rebbe wish to convey?

The young Rabbi Mordechai Dov of Hornosteipel spoke up, offering to explain what the Rebbe, who was his great-uncle, had said:

"It is taught in *Kabbala* that 'The Divine Presence never descends lower than ten (*tefachim*, or handbreadths from the ground).' The one exception is the Chanukah light. According to its law, ideally it should be lit at a height of less than ten *tefachim* [about two feet] above the ground. Then the Divine Presence will descend to 'lower than ten.'"

The Holy One bends down to His beloved, the Jewish people. While at times God may feel distant and removed, during the holy days of Chanukah His presence descends from above, bends down low, and yearns to be close to us.

Sufganiyot, Donuts, on Chanukah
A Thousand-Year-Old Custom

There is an amazing thousand-year-old teaching from the father of the Rambam, Rabbi Maimon ben Yosef (c. 1110–1170), which stresses the importance of the Jewish people maintaining and not compromising their special customs.

Many attribute the custom of eating *sufganiyot* (i.e., dough fried in oil), to a passage authored a thousand years ago by the father of Maimonides, Rabbi Maimon (*Sarid Ve-Palit*, 1945). He writes:

אין להקל בשום מנהג ואפילו מנהג קל ויתחייב כל נכון לו עשית משתה ושמחה ומאכל לפרסם
הנס (של חנוכה) שעשה השם יתברך עמנו באותם הימים ופשט המנהג לעשות סופגנין בערבי
אלספלנג והם הצפחיות לדבש ובתרגום האיסקריטין והיא מנהג הקדמונים משום שהם קלויים
בשמן זכר לברכתו

One should not be lenient regarding any custom, even the lightest of customs. And one is obligated to make every effort to prepare festivities (*mishteh ve-simcha*) and actions to publicize the miracle that God did for us on those days. It has become customary to make "*sufganin,*" known in Arabic as "*alsfingh*" … This is an ancient custom (*minhag ha-kadmonim*), because they are fried in oil, in remembrance of His blessing.

Apparently, Rabbi Maimon felt that the custom of eating fried dough is rooted in the miracle of the *pach ha-shemen*, the flask of oil which burned for eight days. Seemingly, this custom could be fulfilled by eating other fried foods, such as *latkes*, as well.

Putting a New Spin on Chanukah: Why We Play Dreidel

The *sevivon* or dreidel is perhaps the most famous and popular custom associated with Chanukah. A well-known explanation maintains that young Jews played with dreidels in order to fool the Greeks if they were caught studying Torah, which had been outlawed. If the enemy soldiers approached, the young Jews would quickly take out their tops and trick the Greeks into thinking they were playing an innocent game.

SYMBOL OF AN OVERT MIRACLE

The nineteenth-century Galician Rebbe Zvi Elimelech Shapira, known as the Bnei Yissaschar, compares the dreidel and the Purim *grogger*:

He notes an interesting distinction between the two. The grogger is spun from the bottom, while the dreidel is spun from the top.

The Bnei Yissaschar claims that this is indicative of a fundamental difference in the identities of these two holidays. In the Purim story, the role of God is a hidden one. God's name is not in the Megillah [the book of Esther] at all; the narrative takes place through human actions alone. God's actions in the story take place organically, from the ground up, through the agency of mankind. This is represented by the swinging the grogger "from below."

On Chanukah however, we celebrate more explicit miracles: God acts openly in the story of the oil, and even in the victory of the small band of ragtag Maccabees over the Greeks. This is God acting from above, which we symbolize in spinning the dreidel from above.

Spinning the dreidel is thus a symbol of the "hand of God," Who openly initiated miracles for all to see the salvation from on High.

A LESSON FROM THE DREIDEL

The Vizhnitzer Rebbe, the Damesek Eliezer (1890–1945), once reflected on the custom of playing dreidel on Chanukah.

"The dreidel is small. On the four sides of the dreidel are found the initials that symbolize the phrase *Nes gadol hayah sham* (נֵס גָּדוֹל הָיָה שָׁם), 'A great miracle happened there.'

"Is it not a bit strange," asked the Rebbe, "if we wanted to publicize the miracle should we not plaster the words expressing the miracle on large signs or on poster board and hang them in the street for all to see?"

The Rebbe answered, "We can learn a valuable lesson from the dreidel. Although it is very small and humbly only contains a few Hebrew letters, because it spins and perpetually moves, the dreidel is far superior to a static sign, lacking vitality, that simply hangs on a wall. Where there is energy, where there is motion and momentum, great things can happen, and with God's help, even the miraculous."

Why We Give Chanukah *Gelt*

There is a custom of giving Chanukah *gelt*, coins, to our children. One explanation suggests that when the Maccabees returned to Jerusalem they relit the Menorah and struck coins to show that they were a free people. Our version of symbolizing these coins is with the giving of Chanukah *gelt*.

CHANUKAH *GELT*: A DEEPER IDEA FROM THE BELZER REBBE

The mitzvah of Chanukah requires that every person light a menorah. The mitzvah of *pirsumei nisah* (פרסומי ניסה), publicizing the miracle, is so important that no one should be left out. The Chanukah celebration is incomplete without every person participating.

The Rambam therefore writes that a poor person needs to sell the shirt off his back in order to fulfill the mitzvah (Laws of Chanukah 4:12).

The Belzer Rebbe taught that we want to ensure that no person, especially a poor person, feels embarrassed about receiving *tzedakah*, charity. That is the reason we give out *gelt* each night — so that if someone unfortunately needs to receive *tzedakah* in order to purchase materials for the lighting, it will be camouflaged through the giving of *gelt* to everyone.

WHAT GIFT TO GIVE

Many wonderful stories are told about the Jerusalem *tzaddik*, the saintly Rabbi Aryeh Levin.

His renowned son-in-law, Rabbi Yosef Shalom Elyashiv, told the following family story.

The bride and groom following the ceremony under the *chuppah* enter the privacy of the *yichud* room. There is a widely held custom that the groom gives a gift to the bride when they are alone for the first time on their wedding night.

Rabbi Aryeh Levin was so poor that he could not afford to buy a present. When he sat together with his new wife he said to her, "I am so sorry that I did not have the means to buy you a gift that you are so deserving of. But there is another gift I wish to give you tonight: I promise you that whenever we have a difference of opinion, I will defer to you. My gift to you is that we will never argue with one another."

Her response was, "I would like to reciprocate with a gift to you. I will always concede to you. Please accept this gift from me so that we will never argue with one another."

Gift giving can come in many different forms. We can give the kind of gift Reb Aryeh gave his wife. Gifts of kindness. Gifts that can't be bought with money, but rather the kind that enrich and uplift those around us.

BIRKAT HAMAZON –
GRACE AFTER MEALS

IT IS PRAISEWORTHY TO HAVE A FESTIVE MEAL ON CHANUKAH, ESPECIALLY WHEN it is filled with words of gratitude and teachings related to the festival. It is also proper to engage in Torah-related conversations during the Chanukah banquet. Participating in such a festive meal adds to the fulfillment of joyfully celebrating these special days.

Jewish law teaches that we recite a blessing after anything we eat. Following a meal with bread we recite Birkat Hamazon, the blessing after a meal, or as it is commonly called, "Grace after Meals."

There is something seemingly paradoxical, or at least counterintuitive, about the nature of our blessings over the foods we have eaten. We make a shorter blessing for non-bread items. The shortest blessings of all are those we make after we eat items that God creates and provides for us – for example, the blessing *Borei nefashot* after a banana or an apple.

The longer and more elaborate blessing that we recite after eating, the full Grace after Meals, is only recited for a meal that includes bread. Bread requires man to put a considerable effort into creating. Why is there a longer blessing after eating bread? Should we not be more thankful for that which has been given to us without much effort?

Rabbi Joseph Soloveitchik explains that when it comes to fruits and vegetables, human beings merely do the harvesting, but it is God Who has done most of the work. Fruits and vegetables grow by the laws of nature, subject to the will of God. During the period of growth, people are basically passive, and when the fruit has grown, we merely have to gather it in.

Bread, however, is very different. While the wheat also grows by itself, it is up to human beings to do the work of plowing and planting, harvesting and grinding, sifting and kneading, and of course, baking.

The fuller and more elaborate Birkat Hamazon, Grace after Meals, is most appropriate because it signifies the noblest act of man, namely, *partnering* with God. The world can be viewed as an uncompleted creation that God made deliberately imperfect in order to leave room for human creativity. Man's charge is to complete creation, thereby acting as a cocreator with God.

A Story

The Baal Shem Tov asked that it be revealed to him who would be his companion in Paradise, and he was given the name of someone who lived in a remote village. His curiosity having been aroused, he traveled to the village to meet this special person, expecting to find a pious scholar, well versed in the Talmud and Kabbalah.

Imagine then how astonished he was to discover his designated heavenly partner to be a boor, who indulged in nothing but working and eating. "Certainly this man must be one of the hidden *tzaddikim*," the Baal Shem Tov thought, and decided to study his behavior carefully in order to unmask the disguise of boorishness that he exhibited.

Alas, there was nothing extraordinary about this very simple person, except that he ate voraciously. The Baal Shem Tov then decided to confront the man directly. "Tell me the truth about yourself," he demanded. "Who are you, and who were your teachers?"

The man responded, "I don't know what you are talking about. I have no teachers, and I have never learned anything beyond reading the Siddur. I am a lumberjack. I cut trees for my living, and that's all I know."

"Then tell me why you eat so voraciously," the Baal Shem Tov said. "You have the appetite of a dozen men."

"I will explain that," the man said. "When I was a young boy, my father was a vassal to a feudal lord. One day the lord insisted that all his vassals must convert to his faith. When my father refused, he was severely beaten. Being a very thin, weak man, he could not put up much resistance. My father died from his beating.

"Right then and there I decided that this would never happen to me. I would eat a great deal to make my body strong so that if anyone tried to make me deny God, they would have a formidable opponent to reckon with."

The Baal Shem Tov now understood why this man merited so lofty a position in Paradise. Where else in the world could you find a person for whom every morsel of food was a preparation for a *kiddush Hashem*, bringing sanctity to God in heaven?

Eating thus becomes a great mitzvah when our intentions are that it enable us to follow God's will and to bring honor to His name in this world.

BIRKAT HAMAZON

בִּרְכַּת הַמָּזוֹן

Shir Hama'alot

שִׁיר הַמַּעֲלוֹת

שִׁיר הַמַּעֲלוֹת בְּשׁוּב יְיָ אֶת שִׁיבַת צִיּוֹן הָיִינוּ כְּחֹלְמִים. אָז יִמָּלֵא שְׂחוֹק פִּינוּ וּלְשׁוֹנֵנוּ רִנָּה אָז יֹאמְרוּ בַגּוֹיִם הִגְדִּיל יְיָ לַעֲשׂוֹת עִם אֵלֶּה. הִגְדִּיל יְיָ לַעֲשׂוֹת עִמָּנוּ הָיִינוּ שְׂמֵחִים. שׁוּבָה יְיָ אֶת שְׁבִיתֵנוּ כַּאֲפִיקִים בַּנֶּגֶב. הַזֹּרְעִים בְּדִמְעָה בְּרִנָּה יִקְצֹרוּ. הָלוֹךְ יֵלֵךְ וּבָכֹה נֹשֵׂא מֶשֶׁךְ הַזָּרַע בֹּא יָבֹא בְרִנָּה נֹשֵׂא אֲלֻמֹּתָיו.

A Song of Ascents. When the Lord brought Zion out of captivity, we were like dreamers. At the time, our mouths were filled with laughter and our tongues with cries of joy; at the time it was said among the nations, "The Lord has done great things for them." The Lord had done great things for us; we were happy. Let our captivity, Lord, be a thing of the past, like dried-up streams in the Negev. Those who sow in tears shall reap in joy. The man who weeps as he trails the seed along will return with cries of joy, carrying his sheaves.

הָיִינוּ כְּחֹלְמִים – *Hayinu k'cholemim,* **"We were like dreamers"** Rabbi Joseph Solo-veitchik suggested this interpretation: In our own lives, each of us has dreams and aspirations. As young people we dream about what we will be when we grow up. As we mature, we dream about the kind of life that we will live and the great things that we will accomplish. However, as we all know, so many of these dreams go unfulfilled; so many of our aspirations are never realized.

Nevertheless, when it comes to the promise of our return to Zion, we are taught that our dreams will be actualized: *hayinu k'cholemim,* "we were like dreamers." King David, the author of Psalms, is saying that although the many dreams in our lives are not fulfilled, *this* dream will be. Our aspirations for the great future and messianic times will be fulfilled.

As we offer this prayer today, almost two thousand years since we were driven into exile from the Land of Israel, we have never lost faith that this awesome day will soon come.

הַזֹּרְעִים בְּדִמְעָה בְּרִנָּה יִקְצֹרוּ – *Hazorim b'dimah b'rinah yiktzoru,* **"Those who sow in tears shall reap with joy"** Rabbi Samson Raphael Hirsch emphasized that it is Israel's mission to sow God's seeds – implanting spirituality, morality, and integrity in a hostile world. The process of nurturing the seeds until they are ready for harvest can be agonizing and frustrating, but the achievement of the ultimate success brings incomparable joy. So too is it with Israel: the seeds of its mission may become drenched in tears of unbearable suffering, but the crop – the eventual harvest of homage to truth and righteousness – will be reaped with joy.

Zimun: Inviting Others to Give Gratitude at the Meal

המזמן אומר: רַבּוֹתַי נְבָרֵךְ.

המסובים עונים: יְהִי שֵׁם יְיָ מְבֹרָךְ מֵעַתָּה וְעַד עוֹלָם.

המזמן חוזר: יְהִי שֵׁם יְיָ מְבֹרָךְ מֵעַתָּה וְעַד עוֹלָם.
בִּרְשׁוּת (אָבִי מוֹרִי) / (בַּעַל הַבַּיִת הַזֶּה), (מָרָנָן וְרַבָּנָן וְרַבּוֹתַי),
נְבָרֵךְ (במניין: אֱלֹהֵינוּ) שֶׁאָכַלְנוּ מִשֶּׁלוֹ.

המסובים עונים: בָּרוּךְ (במניין: אֱלֹהֵינוּ) שֶׁאָכַלְנוּ מִשֶּׁלוֹ וּבְטוּבוֹ חָיִינוּ.

המזמן חוזר: בָּרוּךְ (במניין: אֱלֹהֵינוּ) שֶׁאָכַלְנוּ מִשֶּׁלוֹ וּבְטוּבוֹ חָיִינוּ.

Leader: My friends, let us bless.

Others: May the name of the Lord be blessed from now and forever more.

Leader: May the name of the Lord be blessed from now and forever more. With permission of the distinguished people present, let

us bless Him (if there are 10 men present add: our God) whose
food we have eaten.

Others: Blessed is He (our God) Whose food we have eaten and
through whose goodness we live.

רַבּוֹתַי, נְבָרֵךְ – *Rabotai, nevarech*, **"My friends, let us bless"** Our Midrashic tradition speaks of Abraham having entrances to his home on all four sides, welcoming to all wayfarers. He served travelers food and drink. When they had finished, he told them to give thanks for what they had eaten. When the guests began to thank Abraham, he corrected them: "The food was not mine. It was given to us by God, and you must thank Him for it." In this way he was able to motivate people to believe in the true God (Talmud, *Sotah* 10b).

We are called upon to follow in the footsteps of Abraham. When we call to guests at the table to offer thanks, with the words of the *zimun*, we invite others to attribute the meal to the goodness of the Creator. In this way we positively influence and teach about God's goodness to all who have joined us around the table.

רַבּוֹתַי, נְבָרֵךְ – *Rabotai, nevarech*, **"My friends, let us bless"** Hunger, more than any other craving, can turn people into self-centered creatures battling all others for survival. The very word *lechem*, bread, is related to *milchamah*, war.

For this very reason it is likely that the Sages instituted this element of a communal blessing of God for having provided us with food. Rabbi Samson Raphael Hirsch points out that by proclaiming that the entire group thanks God for its sustenance, we remember that our neighbor is not a competitor to be feared, fought, and defeated. Rather we are all guests at God's table, and His beneficence is sufficient for us all.

The first blessing of Birkat Hamazon was composed by Moses in gratitude for the manna with which God sustained Israel daily in the desert (Talmud, *Berachot* 48b).

בָּרוּךְ אַתָּה יְיָ אֱלֹהֵינוּ מֶלֶךְ הָעוֹלָם, הַזָּן אֶת הָעוֹלָם כֻּלּוֹ בְּטוּבוֹ
בְּחֵן בְּחֶסֶד וּבְרַחֲמִים, הוּא נוֹתֵן לֶחֶם לְכָל בָּשָׂר כִּי לְעוֹלָם
חַסְדּוֹ. וּבְטוּבוֹ הַגָּדוֹל, תָּמִיד לֹא חָסַר לָנוּ, וְאַל יֶחְסַר לָנוּ מָזוֹן

לְעוֹלָם וָעֶד. בַּעֲבוּר שְׁמוֹ הַגָּדוֹל, כִּי הוּא אֵל זָן וּמְפַרְנֵס לַכֹּל וּמֵטִיב לַכֹּל, וּמֵכִין מָזוֹן לְכָל בְּרִיּוֹתָיו אֲשֶׁר בָּרָא. בָּרוּךְ אַתָּה יְיָ, הַזָּן אֶת הַכֹּל.

Blessed are You, Lord our God, King of the universe, Who provides food for the entire world in His goodness, with grace, kindness, and mercy. He supplies bread for all living beings, for His kindness is everlasting. Because of His great goodness, we have never lacked food, nor will we ever lack it on account of His great name since He is God who feeds and provides for all and is good to all and who supplies food for all His creatures which He brought into being. Blessed are You, Lord, Who provides food for all.

The second blessing, beginning *nodeh Lecha*, "we thank You," is known as the blessing for the Land and was composed by Joshua (Talmud, *Berachot* 48a). When he was privileged to enter the Land of Israel, Joshua composed this blessing in its honor.

נוֹדֶה לְךָ יְיָ אֱלֹהֵינוּ עַל שֶׁהִנְחַלְתָּ לַאֲבוֹתֵינוּ אֶרֶץ חֶמְדָּה טוֹבָה וּרְחָבָה, וְעַל שֶׁהוֹצֵאתָנוּ יְיָ אֱלֹהֵינוּ מֵאֶרֶץ מִצְרַיִם, וּפְדִיתָנוּ מִבֵּית עֲבָדִים, וְעַל בְּרִיתְךָ שֶׁחָתַמְתָּ בִּבְשָׂרֵנוּ, וְעַל תּוֹרָתְךָ שֶׁלִּמַּדְתָּנוּ, וְעַל חֻקֶּיךָ שֶׁהוֹדַעְתָּנוּ, וְעַל חַיִּים חֵן וָחֶסֶד שֶׁחוֹנַנְתָּנוּ, וְעַל אֲכִילַת מָזוֹן שָׁאַתָּה זָן וּמְפַרְנֵס אוֹתָנוּ תָּמִיד, בְּכָל יוֹם וּבְכָל עֵת וּבְכָל שָׁעָה.

We thank You, Lord our God, for having given the heritage to our fore-fathers of a desirable, good, and spacious land, and for having brought us out, Lord our God, from Egypt, and for rescuing us from slavery, and also for Your covenant which You sealed in our flesh, as well as for Your Torah which You taught us, and Your laws of which You told us,

> and for the life, grace, and kindness You have granted us, and for the food which You supply and provide for us constantly, every day, all the time, and at every hour.

נוֹדֶה לְּךָ – *Nodeh Lecha*, "We thank You"   The Hebrew language often uses one word to express two different concepts. Rabbi Yitzchak Hutner (1906–1980) teaches that the word *hoda'ah* is used to thank someone. It is also used to acknowledge that someone else is right. This linguistic partnership is rooted in the fact that hidden in every person's psyche is a yearning for independence, for not being dependent or reliant on someone else. When a person thanks a friend for a favor, inherent in these thanks is an acknowledgement that he wasn't able to solve or satisfy his need by himself. Every thank-you is in its depth an acknowledgement of a need for the generosity of someone else. This pertains in far greater measure when we think of the appreciation and acknowledgement an individual owes his Creator.

עַל שֶׁהִנְחַלְתָּ לַאֲבוֹתֵינוּ – *Al she'hinchalta la'avoteinu*, "for having given the heritage to our forefathers"   The Land of Israel is referred to as *nachalah*, a heritage, implying that it remains eternally the inheritance of the Jewish people. Therefore, centuries of exile dispersed in other lands means only that we were not living in the Land, not that it ceased to be ours.

Rabbi Joseph Soloveitchik taught that this is one of the great miracles of our return to Israel after close to two thousand years. "The Land of Israel did not betray the Jewish people. It was loyal to them, awaiting redemption throughout the years. There is a sense of loyalty on the part of the Land; she will never betray her people."

אֶרֶץ חֶמְדָּה טוֹבָה וּרְחָבָה – *Eretz chemdah tovah u'rchavah*, "A desirable, good, and spacious land"   We offer these three adjectives in praise of the Land of Israel in this paragraph of the Grace after Meals. The Land of Israel is described as a "desirable, good, and spacious" land: *chemdah, tovah, u'rchavah*.

Rabbi Joseph Soloveitchik points out that two of the three terms are mentioned directly in the Torah when describing the beautiful qualities of Israel: *tovah*, "good," and *rechavah*, "spacious," both of which are found in a verse in the Torah (Exodus 3:8). However, the first term, *chemdah*, is found only later, appearing in the book of Jeremiah (3:19).

Why did the Sages choose the term *chemdah* as the opening adjective praising the Land?

The meaning of the word *chemdah* is "yearning," which describes the inseparable attachment of Jews to the Land of Israel. It is a yearning that is not rational, a longing that cannot be explained in logical terms.

Rabbi Soloveitchik shared this insight on Israel's twentieth Independence Day, in 1968, and spoke of the inspiring example of the *chalutzim*, the first Jews to settle modern-day Israel. These early pioneers took bold risks to establish the land; the *chalutzim* led the way for all of our people. Although they faced great hardships and dangers, they were drawn back to the Land and were determined to return, settle, and rebuild our Jewish homeland. They personified *chemdah*, yearning for and desiring the Land of Israel.

A Jew's deep connection to Israel cannot be explained rationally; it is a reflection of a profound inner longing for the Promised Land.

עַל הַנִּסִּים וְעַל הַפֻּרְקָן וְעַל הַגְּבוּרוֹת וְעַל הַתְּשׁוּעוֹת וְעַל הַמִּלְחָמוֹת שֶׁעָשִׂיתָ לַאֲבוֹתֵינוּ בַּיָּמִים הָהֵם בַּזְּמַן הַזֶּה.

בִּימֵי מַתִּתְיָהוּ בֶּן יוֹחָנָן כֹּהֵן גָּדוֹל חַשְׁמוֹנָאִי וּבָנָיו, כְּשֶׁעָמְדָה מַלְכוּת יָוָן הָרְשָׁעָה עַל עַמְּךָ יִשְׂרָאֵל לְהַשְׁכִּיחָם תּוֹרָתֶךָ וּלְהַעֲבִירָם מֵחֻקֵּי רְצוֹנֶךָ, וְאַתָּה בְּרַחֲמֶיךָ הָרַבִּים עָמַדְתָּ לָהֶם בְּעֵת צָרָתָם, רַבְתָּ אֶת רִיבָם, דַּנְתָּ אֶת דִּינָם, נָקַמְתָּ אֶת נִקְמָתָם. מָסַרְתָּ גִבּוֹרִים בְּיַד חַלָּשִׁים, וְרַבִּים בְּיַד מְעַטִּים, וּטְמֵאִים בְּיַד טְהוֹרִים, וּרְשָׁעִים בְּיַד צַדִּיקִים, וְזֵדִים בְּיַד עוֹסְקֵי תוֹרָתֶךָ, וּלְךָ עָשִׂיתָ שֵׁם גָּדוֹל וְקָדוֹשׁ בְּעוֹלָמֶךָ, וּלְעַמְּךָ יִשְׂרָאֵל עָשִׂיתָ תְּשׁוּעָה גְדוֹלָה וּפֻרְקָן כְּהַיּוֹם הַזֶּה. וְאַחַר כֵּן בָּאוּ בָנֶיךָ לִדְבִיר בֵּיתֶךָ, וּפִנּוּ אֶת הֵיכָלֶךָ, וְטִהֲרוּ אֶת מִקְדָּשֶׁךָ, וְהִדְלִיקוּ נֵרוֹת בְּחַצְרוֹת קָדְשֶׁךָ, וְקָבְעוּ שְׁמוֹנַת יְמֵי חֲנֻכָּה אֵלּוּ, לְהוֹדוֹת וּלְהַלֵּל לְשִׁמְךָ הַגָּדוֹל.

We thank You for the miracles, for the liberation, for the mighty acts, for the victories, and for the wars which You waged for our ancestors in those days at this time.

It was in the days of Mattathias, son of Yochanan the high priest, a Hasmonean, and his sons, that the wicked Hellenistic regime rose up against Your people Israel to make them forget Your Torah and to drive them away from the laws of Your will. Then You, in Your great mercy, stood up for them in their time of trouble. You pleaded their cause, argued their case, and avenged their wrong; You delivered the strong into the hands of the weak, the many into the hands of the few, the impure into the hands of the pure, the wicked into the hands of the righteous, and the wanton into the hands of those immersed in Your Torah. Thus You made Yourself a great and holy name in Your world, and for Your people Israel You brought about a great victory and liberation on this day. And afterwards, Your children came to the sanctuary of Your house, cleared Your holy place, purified Your Temple, and kindled lights in Your holy courts, and they established these eight days of Chanukah to thank and to praise Your great name.

עַל הַנִּסִּים – *al hanisim,* "for the miracles" This prayer is a declaration of gratitude for God's miracles on the holidays of Chanukah and Purim. Therefore it is inserted here, in the section of Birkat Hamazon that is likewise devoted to expressions of gratitude.

וְעַל הַמִּלְחָמוֹת - *v'al hamilchamot,* "[thank You] for the wars" The basic meaning for this phrase is our thanks to God for helping us be victorious in the battles. This text follows the custom of Ashkenaz. However, in the text adopted by the Sephardic tradition in the Al Hanisim prayer we find "for the wars" replaced by *al hanechamot* (עַל הַנֶּחָמוֹת), "for the consolations."

It is suggested that it is not fitting to ever give praise for war. No wars are good. Even wars that must be fought inevitably bring great pain and suffering. And no victory, however great, comes without a heavy price.

The Talmud (*Ta'anit* 22b) explains the verse "And a sword will not cross your land"

(Leviticus 26:6), describing the ideal blessing in the Land of Israel, to mean "not even a sword of peace." In other words, we hope never to have to engage in battles, even justified ones. We are joyous and give gratitude only for consolation and peace.

בַּזְּמַן הַזֶּה – *ba'zman hazeh*, **"at this time"** One understanding of this phrase is that we are simply thanking God for the miracles performed in the days of Chanukah – which happened "at this time" of year.

However, the phrase *ba'zman hazeh*, "at this time," can also be understood to mean that we are offering a double a measure of praise: not only for the miracles performed in ancient days, but also for the countless hidden miracles that are constantly performed every day to preserve life and health both for the individual and for the nation.

A deeper idea expressed by the kabbalists, the mystical masters, is that the phrase "at this time" means that there is particular significance in the date of the miracle because God visits the holy emanations of each miracle bestowed upon Israel annually, on the date it occurred.

כְּשֶׁעָמְדָה – *k'she'amdah*, **"[that] rose up"** Rabbi Joseph Soloveitchik points out that there are many terms that could have been used here. "Rose up" suggests determination. It was not just a decision. When one makes a *decision*, one may either carry it out or renege on it. However, "rose up" suggests that it was the major objective of the enemy. The Syrian Greeks were relentless in pursuing this goal. The wicked government in the days of Chanukah was determined to subjugate the spirit of the proud Judeans who refused to surrender to their culture. This was their goal, and it was central to their outlook. Rabbi Joseph Soloveitchik when teaching this insight pointed out that anti-Semitism is never marginal to anti-Semitic movements. It is central. This fierce hatred may be compared to Hitler's Nazi Germany; even when it was detrimental to their cause, the Nazis were determined to destroy the Jew.

לְהַשְׁכִּיחָם תּוֹרָתֶךָ – *l'hashkicham mi'Toratecha*, **"to make them forget your Torah"** The great contemporary Talmudist Rabbi Aharon Lichtenstein (1933–2015) explains this passage. There is a significant difference in tone between the two schemes of the Syrian-Greeks. On the one hand, וּלְהַעֲבִירָם מֵחֻקֵּי רְצוֹנֶךָ – to force them to transgress G-d's commandments – is clearly coercive, aggressive and threatening. The Jews had no choice but to transgress or die. In contrast לְהַשְׁכִּיחָם תּוֹרָתֶךָ – to make them forget God's Torah, is a more gentle approach, characterized by seduction and enticement. The Syrian-Greeks tried to entice us away from Torah, through their philosophy, their focus on physicality and living for the moment. Sadly they were quite successful.... For Jews living in modern Western society, לְהַשְׁכִּיחָם תּוֹרָתֶךָ, forgetting Torah, is the greatest threat. Western culture tempts us to glorify man over God, to invest our energies solely in the physical world and the whim of the moment; and to neglect our relationship to our Creator.

וּלְהַעֲבִירָם מֵחֻקֵּי רְצוֹנֶךָ – *u'l'ha'aviram me'chukei retzonecha*, **"Drive them away from the laws of Your will"** Since the Syrian Greeks sought to oppress the Jewish people by weakening their devotion to the Torah, "they desired to force them to transgress the *chukim*, the statutes of God." The *chukim* refer to the category of mitzvot that seemingly make no rational sense and are performed purely out of devotion to God.

Our oppressors thought that they could convince the Jewish people to first reject the mitzvot that have no logical foundation and then gradually induce them to reject the remainder.

וְאַתָּה – *V'Atah*, **"Then you"** Why is the name of God not mentioned in Al Hanisim? The Chassidic Rebbe Rabbi Yitzchak Vorker (1779–1848) pointed out that in the entire Al Hanisim prayer, God's name does not appear once. Rather, in its place, *Atah*, "You," is the way the prayer refers to God. The Rebbe suggested that we use this term because it reflects a personal and close relationship. The deep dedication to God that was reestablished through the miracles brought us closer to our Creator. Formal names are not necessary when there is such closeness and love.

גִּבּוֹרִים בְּיַד חַלָּשִׁים – *gibborim b'yad chalashim*, **"the strong into the hands of the weak"** Were the Maccabees really "weak"?

Rabbi Levi Yitzchak of Berditchev explains that the Maccabees were in fact very mighty. The Al Hanisim prayer describes them as *chalashim*, "weak ones," because the Maccabees considered themselves weak, insofar as they attributed their strength and might to God's assistance. They openly acknowledged that their victory came from God, and not from any skill or prowess on their part.

וּטְמֵאִים...וּרְשָׁעִים...וְזֵדִים – *u'tme'im... u'rsha'im... v'zedim*, **"impure... wicked... wanton"** Rabbi Soloveitchik suggests that the variety of terms describing the Maccabean victory, such as "the wicked into the hands of the righteous," does not merely reference the Jews' victory over the Syrian Greeks. Rather, it is intentionally ambiguous because, sadly, it also refers to the victory of the Jews over the Syrian Greek collaborators, the Jews who adopted the Hellenist lifestyle.

The "impure" were those Jews who preferred Grecian immorality to Jewish moral purity; the "wicked" and "wanton" ones refer to those Jews who aligned themselves with the prevailing culture and attempted to eradicate any loyalty to the study of Torah and observance of mitzvot.

וּטְמֵאִים בְּיַד טְהוֹרִים – *u'tme'im b'yad tehorim,* **"and the impure into the hands of the pure"** Who does "the impure" refer to?

Rabbi Joseph Soloveitchik taught that the Hasmoneans fought not only against enslavement to an imperial power, but also, and more to the point, against their own defilement, meaning for the purity of the soul of the entire Jewish people.

In those days so many Jews had chosen an "impure" path, contrary to the ethical and moral traditional Jewish life. The greatness of the miracle was not that the impure were not destroyed by the pure, but rather they were elevated and became pure. The Hellenized Jews were inspired and found their way back home. The "wicked one," the "wanton one," was not annihilated by the righteous, but he himself became holy.

וְאַחַר כֵּן בָּאוּ בָנֶיךָ לִדְבִיר בֵּיתֶךָ, וּפִנּוּ אֶת הֵיכָלֶךָ, וְטִהֲרוּ אֶת מִקְדָּשֶׁךָ, וְהִדְלִיקוּ נֵרוֹת בְּחַצְרוֹת קָדְשֶׁךָ, וְקָבְעוּ שְׁמוֹנַת יְמֵי חֲנֻכָּה אֵלּוּ, לְהוֹדוֹת וּלְהַלֵּל לְשִׁמְךָ הַגָּדוֹל. – *V'achar ken ba'u vanecha… v'kavu…,* **"And afterwards Your children came… and they established…"** The establishment of Chanukah is ascribed in this prayer to "children." Why?

The term *children* refers to the Jewish people as a whole; the Torah often calls the Jewish people Bnei Yisrael, "the children of Israel." There was a national transformation in which the newly united people reaffirmed their allegiance to God and the eternal significance of these days.

יְמֵי חֲנֻכָּה אֵלּוּ, לְהוֹדוֹת וּלְהַלֵּל – *yemei Chanukah eilu, l'hodot u'l'hallel,* **"these days of Chanukah to thank and to praise"** Rabbi Samson Raphael Hirsch taught as follows:

The Al Hanisim concludes with a clear statement of the essential act of the observance of Chanukah, which is, first and foremost, **לְהוֹדוֹת** – to give thanks. Rabbi Hirsch emphasizes that **הוֹדָיָה** (giving thanks) is much more than verbal acknowledgement. The root of **הוֹדָיָה** is **י-ד-ה** from which is also derived the word **יד** – hand. For a Jew, thanking God involves not only words but a "giving of one's hand," a dedication of all of one's actions, completely to God. As such, Chanukah is not only the time when the Temple was rededicated. On Chanukah, we are summoned to rededicate our entire lives to Torah and mitzvot.

וְעַל הַכֹּל יְיָ אֱלֹהֵינוּ אֲנַחְנוּ מוֹדִים לָךְ וּמְבָרְכִים אוֹתָךְ, יִתְבָּרַךְ שְׁמְךָ בְּפִי כָּל חַי תָּמִיד לְעוֹלָם וָעֶד. כַּכָּתוּב, וְאָכַלְתָּ וְשָׂבָעְתָּ וּבֵרַכְתָּ אֶת יְיָ אֱלֹהֶיךָ עַל הָאָרֶץ הַטֹּבָה אֲשֶׁר נָתַן לָךְ. בָּרוּךְ אַתָּה יְיָ, עַל הָאָרֶץ וְעַל הַמָּזוֹן.

So for everything, Lord our God, we thank You and bless You. May Your name be blessed in the speech of all living beings, constantly, for all time. For it is written: "And you shall eat, and be satisfied, and bless the Lord your God for the good land He gave you." Blessed are You, Lord, for the land and for the food.

The blessing for Jerusalem is the final blessing required by the Torah. It was composed in stages by Kings David and Solomon (Talmud, *Berachot* 48b).

רַחֵם נָא יְיָ אֱלֹהֵינוּ עַל יִשְׂרָאֵל עַמֶּךָ, וְעַל יְרוּשָׁלַיִם עִירֶךָ, וְעַל צִיּוֹן מִשְׁכַּן כְּבוֹדֶךָ, וְעַל מַלְכוּת בֵּית דָּוִד מְשִׁיחֶךָ, וְעַל הַבַּיִת הַגָּדוֹל וְהַקָּדוֹשׁ שֶׁנִּקְרָא שִׁמְךָ עָלָיו. אֱלֹהֵינוּ, אָבִינוּ, רְעֵנוּ, זוּנֵנוּ, פַּרְנְסֵנוּ, וְכַלְכְּלֵנוּ, וְהַרְוִיחֵנוּ, וְהַרְוַח לָנוּ יְיָ אֱלֹהֵינוּ מְהֵרָה מִכָּל צָרוֹתֵינוּ, וְנָא אַל תַּצְרִיכֵנוּ יְיָ אֱלֹהֵינוּ לֹא לִידֵי מַתְּנַת בָּשָׂר וָדָם וְלֹא לִידֵי הַלְוָאָתָם, כִּי אִם לְיָדְךָ הַמְּלֵאָה, הַפְּתוּחָה, הַקְּדוֹשָׁה וְהָרְחָבָה, שֶׁלֹּא נֵבוֹשׁ וְלֹא נִכָּלֵם לְעוֹלָם וָעֶד.

Have mercy, Lord our God, on Israel Your people, on Jerusalem Your city, on Zion the home of Your glory, on the kingdom of the house of David, Your anointed one, and on the great and holy house which is called by Your name. Our God, our Father, look after us and feed us, give us a livelihood and support us, and provide a respite for us — a respite for us, Lord our God, soon, from all our troubles. And please, let us not be dependent, Lord our God, neither on a gift, nor on a loan from a human being, but rather on Your full, open, holy, and generous hand, so that we should never feel embarrassed or ashamed.

לשבת: רְצֵה וְהַחֲלִיצֵנוּ יְיָ אֱלֹהֵינוּ בְּמִצְוֹתֶיךָ וּבְמִצְוַת יוֹם הַשְּׁבִיעִי הַשַּׁבָּת הַגָּדוֹל וְהַקָּדוֹשׁ הַזֶּה. כִּי יוֹם זֶה גָּדוֹל וְקָדוֹשׁ הוּא לְפָנֶיךָ, לִשְׁבָּת־ בּוֹ וְלָנוּחַ בּוֹ בְּאַהֲבָה כְּמִצְוַת רְצוֹנֶךָ וּבִרְצוֹנְךָ הָנִיחַ לָנוּ יְיָ אֱלֹהֵינוּ, שֶׁלֹּא תְהֵא צָרָה וְיָגוֹן וַאֲנָחָה בְּיוֹם מְנוּחָתֵנוּ. וְהַרְאֵנוּ יְיָ אֱלֹהֵינוּ בְּנֶחָמַת צִיּוֹן עִירֶךָ, וּבְבִנְיַן יְרוּשָׁלַיִם עִיר קָדְשֶׁךָ, כִּי אַתָּה הוּא בַּעַל הַיְשׁוּעוֹת וּבַעַל הַנֶּחָמוֹת.

Shabbat: Be pleased, Lord our God, to strengthen us through Your commandments, especially the commandment of the seventh day, this great and holy Shabbat. For this is indeed a great and holy day for You; to rest and be at ease, with loving concern for the command of Your will. So may it please You to grant us rest, Lord our God, with no trouble, or unhappiness, or weeping on our day of rest. And let us witness, Lord our God, the consolation of Zion, Your city, and the building up of Jerusalem, Your holy city, for You are the Lord of redemption, and the Lord of consolation.

בר״ח: אֱלֹהֵינוּ וֵאלֹהֵי אֲבוֹתֵינוּ, יַעֲלֶה וְיָבוֹא וְיַגִּיעַ, וְיֵרָאֶה וְיֵרָצֶה וְיִשָּׁמַע, וְיִפָּקֵד וְיִזָּכֵר זִכְרוֹנֵנוּ וּפִקְדוֹנֵנוּ, וְזִכְרוֹן אֲבוֹתֵינוּ, וְזִכְרוֹן מָשִׁיחַ בֶּן דָּוִד עַבְדֶּךָ, וְזִכְרוֹן יְרוּשָׁלַיִם עִיר קָדְשֶׁךָ, וְזִכְרוֹן כָּל עַמְּךָ בֵּית יִשְׂרָאֵל לְפָנֶיךָ, לִפְלֵיטָה לְטוֹבָה לְחֵן וּלְחֶסֶד וּלְרַחֲמִים, לְחַיִּים וּלְשָׁלוֹם בְּיוֹם רֹאשׁ הַחֹדֶשׁ הַזֶּה. זָכְרֵנוּ יְיָ אֱלֹהֵינוּ בּוֹ לְטוֹבָה, וּפָקְדֵנוּ בוֹ לִבְרָכָה, וְהוֹשִׁיעֵנוּ בוֹ לְחַיִּים. וּבִדְבַר יְשׁוּעָה וְרַחֲמִים, חוּס וְחָנֵּנוּ, וְרַחֵם עָלֵינוּ וְהוֹשִׁיעֵנוּ, כִּי אֵלֶיךָ עֵינֵינוּ, כִּי אֵל מֶלֶךְ חַנּוּן וְרַחוּם אָתָּה.

Rosh Chodesh: Our God and God of our fathers, may a reminder and a remembrance of us, and of our fathers, and of the Messiah the son of David Your servant, and of Jerusalem Your holy city, and of all Your people the house of Israel, ascend and arrive, reach and be noticed, and accepted, heard, noted, and remembered before You, for deliverance and well-being, for grace, kindness, and mercy, for life and peace on this day of the new month. Be mindful of us, Lord our God, on this day, for good, take note of us for blessing and preserve us in life. And with an act of redemption and mercy, have pity on us and be gracious to us, and be merciful to us and save us, for our eyes are directed toward You, for You are a gracious and merciful divine ruler.

וּבְנֵה יְרוּשָׁלַיִם עִיר הַקֹּדֶשׁ בִּמְהֵרָה בְיָמֵינוּ. בָּרוּךְ אַתָּה יְיָ, בּוֹנֵה בְּרַחֲמָיו יְרוּשָׁלָיִם. אָמֵן.

And may You rebuild Jerusalem, the holy city, speedily in our days. Blessed are You, Lord, Who in His mercy builds up Jerusalem. Amen.

וּבְנֵה יְרוּשָׁלַיִם עִיר הַקֹּדֶשׁ בִּמְהֵרָה בְיָמֵינוּ – *U'vneh Yerushalayim ir hakodesh bi'mherah v'yameinu,* "And may You rebuild Jerusalem, the holy city, speedily in our days" Reb Shlomo Carlebach shared the following story.

One night the holy Chassidic Rebbe Reb Elimelech of Lizhensk had a dream, in which he saw angels, all running quickly. Each one was carrying a brick and bringing it for the building of the Beit Hamikdash in Jerusalem. There were thousands of angels all bringing bricks for the building of our long-awaited Temple.

Reb Elimelech went over to one of the angels and asked him, "Why are there so many angels bringing bricks?" The angel turned to Reb Elimelech and said to him, "Don't you know? Each and every person needs to bring his own brick for the rebuilding of the Temple."

Rabbi Shlomo Carlebach taught that *each of us* needs to bring *our own* brick for the rebuilding of the Temple.

Most translate the phrase *bi'mherah v'yameinu*, "speedily and in our days," to mean that we are praying that Jerusalem and the Temple be rebuilt quickly so that we will be able to see it within our own lifetimes. Reb Shlomo taught that the phrase can also be understood to mean not "in our days," but "with our days." In other words, let us rebuild Jerusalem by the way we choose to live each day.

This is the meaning of the prayer: Each of us needs to contribute our part to the building of the Temple. Each one of us needs to bring our own brick so that the Temple will be rebuilt.

עִיר הַקֹּדֶשׁ – *Ir hakodesh*, **"The holy city."** Rabbi Shlomo Carlebach taught that the word 'ir' means city but the word 'ir' also means to wake up. "Jerusalem is called 'Ir Hakodesh', *the Holy City… but what it really means is that it is the city that wakes up all that is holy within us…. and we are just waiting for Jerusalem to wake up the world… let it be soon let it be now."*

בָּרוּךְ אַתָּה יְיָ אֱלֹהֵינוּ מֶלֶךְ הָעוֹלָם, הָאֵל אָבִינוּ, מַלְכֵּנוּ, אַדִּירֵנוּ בּוֹרְאֵנוּ, גּוֹאֲלֵנוּ, יוֹצְרֵנוּ, קְדוֹשֵׁנוּ קְדוֹשׁ יַעֲקֹב, רוֹעֵנוּ רוֹעֵה יִשְׂרָאֵל. הַמֶּלֶךְ הַטּוֹב, וְהַמֵּטִיב לַכֹּל, שֶׁבְּכָל יוֹם וָיוֹם הוּא הֵטִיב, הוּא מֵטִיב, הוּא יֵטִיב לָנוּ. הוּא גְמָלָנוּ, הוּא גוֹמְלֵנוּ, הוּא יִגְמְלֵנוּ לָעַד לְחֵן וּלְחֶסֶד וּלְרַחֲמִים וּלְרֶוַח הַצָּלָה וְהַצְלָחָה בְּרָכָה וִישׁוּעָה, נֶחָמָה, פַּרְנָסָה וְכַלְכָּלָה, וְרַחֲמִים וְחַיִּים וְשָׁלוֹם, וְכָל טוֹב, וּמִכָּל טוּב לְעוֹלָם אַל יְחַסְּרֵנוּ.

Blessed are You, Lord our God, King of the universe, the God Who is our Father, our King, our Mighty One, our Creator, our Redeemer, our Maker, our Holy One, the Holy One of Jacob, our Shepherd, the Shepherd of Israel, the King Who is good and does good to all, Who each and every day has been good, is good, and will be good to us. He gave, gives, and will always give us grace, kindness, and mercy, and respite, deliverance, and success, blessing and salvation, comfort, a livelihood and sustenance, and mercy and life and peace and everything that is good, and may He never let us lack anything that is good.

הָרַחֲמָן הוּא יִמְלֹךְ עָלֵינוּ לְעוֹלָם וָעֶד.

הָרַחֲמָן הוּא יִתְבָּרֵךְ בַּשָּׁמַיִם וּבָאָרֶץ.

הָרַחֲמָן הוּא יִשְׁתַּבַּח לְדוֹר דּוֹרִים, וְיִתְפָּאַר בָּנוּ לָעַד וּלְנֵצַח נְצָחִים, וְיִתְהַדַּר בָּנוּ לָעַד וּלְעוֹלְמֵי עוֹלָמִים.

הָרַחֲמָן הוּא יְפַרְנְסֵנוּ בְּכָבוֹד.

הָרַחֲמָן הוּא יִשְׁבֹּר עֻלֵּנוּ מֵעַל צַוָּארֵנוּ, וְהוּא יוֹלִיכֵנוּ קוֹמְמִיּוּת לְאַרְצֵנוּ.

הָרַחֲמָן הוּא יִשְׁלַח לָנוּ בְּרָכָה מְרֻבָּה בַּבַּיִת הַזֶּה וְעַל שֻׁלְחָן זֶה שֶׁאָכַלְנוּ עָלָיו.

הָרַחֲמָן הוּא יִשְׁלַח לָנוּ אֶת אֵלִיָּהוּ הַנָּבִיא זָכוּר לַטּוֹב, וִיבַשֶּׂר לָנוּ בְּשׂוֹרוֹת טוֹבוֹת יְשׁוּעוֹת וְנֶחָמוֹת.

May the Merciful One rule over us forever.

May the Merciful One be blessed in heaven and on earth.

May the Merciful One be praised for generation upon generation, and may He be glorified through us forever and ever, and may He be honored through us eternally.

May the Merciful One grant us an honorable livelihood.

May the Merciful One break the yoke from our neck and lead us upright to our land.

May the Merciful One send a plentiful blessing on this house and on this table at which we have eaten.

May the Merciful One send us Elijah the prophet, who is remembered for good and who will bring us good tidings of salvation and comfort.

בִּרְכַּת הָאוֹרֵחַ לְפִי הֲשַׁ"ע, עַל פִּי הַגְּמָרָא בִּבְרָכוֹת:

יְהִי רָצוֹן שֶׁלֹּא יֵבוֹשׁ בַּעַל הַבַּיִת בָּעוֹלָם הַזֶּה וְלֹא יִכָּלֵם לָעוֹלָם הַבָּא. וְיִצְלַח מְאֹד בְּכָל נְכָסָיו, וְיִהְיוּ נְכָסָיו (וּנְכָסֵינוּ) מֻצְלָחִים וּקְרוֹבִים לָעִיר, וְאַל יִשְׁלֹט שָׂטָן לֹא בְּמַעֲשֵׂה יָדָיו וְלֹא בְּמַעֲשֵׂה יָדֵינוּ. וְאַל יִזְדַּקֵּר לְפָנָיו וְלֹא לְפָנֵינוּ שׁוּם דְּבַר חֵטְא וַעֲבֵרָה וְעָוֹן מֵעַתָּה וְעַד עוֹלָם.

אִם סָמוּךְ עַל שֻׁלְחָן עַצְמוֹ:

הָרַחֲמָן הוּא יְבָרֵךְ אוֹתִי (וְאֶת אָבִי וְאֶת אִמִּי / וְאֶת אִשְׁתִּי / בַּעְלִי / וְאֶת זַרְעִי) וְאֶת כָּל אֲשֶׁר לִי,

אוֹרֵחַ אוֹמֵר:

הָרַחֲמָן הוּא יְבָרֵךְ אֶת (אָבִי מוֹרִי) בַּעַל הַבַּיִת הַזֶּה, וְאֶת (אִמִּי מוֹרָתִי) בַּעֲלַת הַבַּיִת הַזֶּה (אוֹתִי וְאֶת אִשְׁתִּי / בַּעְלִי / וְאֶת זַרְעִי וְאֶת כָּל אֲשֶׁר לִי) אוֹתָם וְאֶת בֵּיתָם וְאֶת זַרְעָם וְאֶת כָּל אֲשֶׁר לָהֶם,

May the Merciful One Bless:

At one's parents': my honored father, the man of this house, and my honored mother, the woman of this house — them, and their household, their children, and everything that is theirs...

For one's hosts: the man of this house, and the woman of this house — them, together with their household, their children, and everything that is theirs...

When eating at home: myself, my wife (or husband), and my children and everything that is mine...

(וְאֶת כָּל הַמְסֻבִּין כָּאן) אוֹתָנוּ וְאֶת כָּל אֲשֶׁר לָנוּ, כְּמוֹ שֶׁנִּתְבָּרְכוּ אֲבוֹתֵינוּ, אַבְרָהָם יִצְחָק וְיַעֲקֹב, בַּכֹּל, מִכֹּל, כֹּל, כֵּן יְבָרֵךְ אוֹתָנוּ כֻּלָּנוּ יַחַד בִּבְרָכָה שְׁלֵמָה, וְנֹאמַר אָמֵן.

…and all who are seated here, us, together with all that is ours, just as our fathers, Abraham, Isaac, and Jacob, were blessed totally, so may He bless us, all of us together, with a complete blessing, and let us say, Amen.

בְּכֹל מִכֹּל כֹּל – *ba'kol mi'kol kol*, "in everything, from everything, with everything" These three expressions, each indicating that no measure was lacking, are used respectively by the Torah referring to the patriarchs – Abraham, Isaac, and Jacob. The three verses are: "And God blessed Abraham *ba'kol*, in everything" (Genesis 24:1), "And I [Isaac] have partaken *mi'kol*, from everything" (Genesis 27:33), and "for God has been gracious to me [Jacob], and I have *kol*, everything" (Genesis 33:11).

Our patriarchs taught us the invaluable lesson that is a theme of the Grace after Meals: recognizing undeserved blessing and offering gratitude.

בַּמָּרוֹם יְלַמְּדוּ עֲלֵיהֶם וְעָלֵינוּ זְכוּת, שֶׁתְּהֵא לְמִשְׁמֶרֶת שָׁלוֹם, וְנִשָּׂא בְרָכָה מֵאֵת יְיָ וּצְדָקָה מֵאֱלֹהֵי יִשְׁעֵנוּ, וְנִמְצָא חֵן וְשֵׂכֶל טוֹב בְּעֵינֵי אֱלֹהִים וְאָדָם.

May a plea be heard on high, for them and for us, which will result in the security of peace. So may we receive a blessing from the Lord and righteousness from the God of our salvation. So may we find favor and understanding in the sight of God and man.

לשבת: הָרַחֲמָן הוּא יַנְחִילֵנוּ יוֹם שֶׁכֻּלּוֹ שַׁבָּת וּמְנוּחָה לְחַיֵּי הָעוֹלָמִים.

לר"ח: הָרַחֲמָן הוּא יְחַדֵּשׁ עָלֵינוּ אֶת הַחֹדֶשׁ הַזֶּה לְטוֹבָה וְלִבְרָכָה.

Shabbat: May the Merciful One bring us the day that will be totally Shabbat and rest in everlasting life.

Rosh Chodesh: May the Merciful One introduce this month to us with goodness and blessing.

הָרַחֲמָן הוּא יְזַכֵּנוּ לִימוֹת הַמָּשִׁיחַ וּלְחַיֵּי הָעוֹלָם הַבָּא, מִגְדּוֹל (בחול: מַגְדִּיל) יְשׁוּעוֹת מַלְכּוֹ וְעֹשֶׂה חֶסֶד לִמְשִׁיחוֹ לְדָוִד וּלְזַרְעוֹ עַד עוֹלָם. עֹשֶׂה שָׁלוֹם בִּמְרוֹמָיו, הוּא יַעֲשֶׂה שָׁלוֹם עָלֵינוּ וְעַל כָּל יִשְׂרָאֵל, וְאִמְרוּ אָמֵן.

May the Merciful One make us worthy of the days of the Messiah and the life of the world to come. He brings about great victories for His king and shows kindness to his anointed one to David and to his descendants forever. He who makes peace in His high places, may He bring about peace for us and for all Israel, and say, Amen.

יְראוּ אֶת יְיָ קְדֹשָׁיו כִּי אֵין מַחְסוֹר לִירֵאָיו. כְּפִירִים רָשׁוּ וְרָעֵבוּ וְדֹרְשֵׁי יְיָ לֹא יַחְסְרוּ כָל טוֹב. הוֹדוּ לַיְיָ כִּי טוֹב כִּי לְעוֹלָם חַסְדּוֹ. פּוֹתֵחַ אֶת יָדֶךָ וּמַשְׂבִּיעַ לְכָל חַי רָצוֹן. בָּרוּךְ הַגֶּבֶר אֲשֶׁר יִבְטַח בַּיְיָ וְהָיָה יְיָ מִבְטַחוֹ. נַעַר הָיִיתִי גַּם זָקַנְתִּי, וְלֹא רָאִיתִי צַדִּיק נֶעֱזָב וְזַרְעוֹ מְבַקֶּשׁ לָחֶם. יְיָ עֹז לְעַמּוֹ יִתֵּן, יְיָ יְבָרֵךְ אֶת עַמּוֹ בַשָּׁלוֹם.

Stand in awe of the Lord, you who are His holy ones, for there is nothing lacking to those who stand in awe of Him. Even young lions suffer want and hunger, but those who seek the Lord will not lack any good thing. Give thanks to the Lord, for He is good, for His kindness is everlasting. You open Your hand and satisfy the desire of all living. Blessed is the man who trusts in the Lord, and who makes the Lord the object of his trust. I was young and I have become old, and I have not seen a righteous man forsaken, and his children begging for bread. May the Lord give strength to His people. May the Lord bless His people with peace.

נַעַר הָיִיתִי – *Na'ar hayiti,* "I was young…" The standard translation of this verse is "I was young and have become old, and I have not seen a righteous man forsaken and his children begging for bread" (Psalm 37:5). This challenging verse has perplexed many over the years who have attempted to clarify its meaning.

Rabbi Joseph Soloveitchik offered a new meaning to this verse. The verb *ra'iti,* "seen," should be translated in the way in which it appears in the book of Esther. Esther pleads on behalf of the Jewish people saying, "For how can I watch (*ra'iti*) the evil that shall come unto my people? Or how can I watch (*ra'iti*) the destruction of my kindred?" (Esther 8:6).

The verb *lir'ot,* of which *ra'iti* is a conjugation, means here "stand as a passive witness to." This verse in Grace after Meals should thus be understood as "When the righteous were forsaken or his children forced to search for bread, *I never merely stood and watched.*"

This verse can be interpreted as a warning against being a mere bystander while other people suffer. As we conclude saying the Grace after Meals, we are called upon to engage in providing for those who are in need. We begin the Grace after Meals speaking of God's goodness in feeding the hungry, and we conclude with the injunction to do likewise ourselves.

אֶת עַמּוֹ בַשָּׁלוֹם – *et amo va'shalom,* "[God will bless] His people with peace" We conclude *Birkat Hamazon* with a prayer for peace. Rabbi Abraham Isaac Kook offered the following penetrating insight regarding peace:

According to the Sages: *Shalom,* "peace," is one of the sacred names of God; while *emet,* "truth," is His seal. What is the difference between "a name" and "a seal," such that one characterizes peace and the other truth? Rav Kook explains:

A name or signature is written letter by letter, until the whole name is completed. A seal, however, is imprinted, stamped, in one act. *Truth* is a seal – it is "all or nothing." Like a king's signet ring, it is dipped in molten wax and then stamped on a royal decree to authenticate it. If a signet is broken it cannot be used. Half a truth is a lie.

Peace, however, is like a name or a signature, and therefore can be attained only step by step, bit by bit. We must aspire to it piece by piece, and must not despair if we cannot achieve the prize of total peace all at once.

A FINAL TALE

The Milkman's Wife

IN A SMALL VILLAGE THERE LIVED TWO POOR FAMILIES. THEY WERE NEIGHBORS. The milkman's family and the shoemaker's family.

The milkman would wake up with the rising of the sun, he would milk his cow and then would make his way through town carrying his heavy milk crates. He would go house to house selling his milk. The milkman's wife also worked each day. From the remaining milk she would prepare butter and cheese and she would stand in the market to sell her items.

Each evening at the end of a long day of work the milkman's family would sit down to dinner. They appreciated the quiet time together before they would lie their tired heads on their pillows for the night.

The shoemaker also worked hard to support his family. But the opportunity to fix shoes was more sparse and making a living was more challenging. In this poor village those that had shoes would often go for months, maybe even years, without fixing their shoes. There were even some residents, the poorest of the village, who would walk around without shoes. Therefore, making an ample living to support his family often did not come easily to the shoemaker.

The shoemaker's wife was not well. She did all she could to care for her children and was unable to devote any other time towards a profession that would generate income.

The milkman and his wife had compassion for the shoemaker's family. Often they approached their home offering them milk or cheese. However, the shoemaker, who would always warmly greet them would proudly say, "Thank you so much for your offer, but we have all that we need, we are fine."

With the holiday of Chanukah soon to arrive, there was a palpable feeling of joy throughout the village. Menorahs were polished and placed in the windows. Potatoes were purchased in large quantities in the marketplace to be used for fried *latkes*. Every child was cheerful as they anticipated playing dreidel and receiving Chanukah *gelt* in honor of the celebration.

The joy of the festival was felt in every Jewish home. Although, sadly, in one home, the home of the shoemaker, there was no menorah to be found sitting at the window. Their home looked dark. When the first night of Chanukah arrived not even one candle was lit. Unfortunately, the shoemaker did not have the means to purchase the provisions needed to celebrate.

Looking across the way to the shoemaker's window, the milkman's wife felt so sad. She couldn't bear to look. She lowered her eyes to the floor when suddenly she noticed one of her husband's boots. One of her husband's boots had a small tear.

"Just a minute," she blurted out in a loud voice, "come my children, Daddy's shoes need to be fixed…right away! It's not right to light Chanukah candles with ripped shoes!"

"My dear wife, it is a very small tear, barely noticable, is it really necessary to fix them right now?" asked the milkman.

"If not now when?" answered his wife. Without waiting another second she grabbed a bottle of oil from the kitchen, instructed her husband to pick up a pile of wood that sat by their fireplace, and handed their children a large bowl of potatoes. The milkman's family quickly walked across the way to their neighbors, the shoemaker's family.

The wife of the milkman knocked on the door. "My husband's shoes need fixing", she said to the shoemaker who was quite surprised to find a customer standing at the door at this late hour. "We are not able to pay for the repair, however, we brought some wood for a fire, some oil, and a few potatoes. Hopefully these can cover the cost…and being that we need the shoes fixed right away we are happy to stay here and wait…and maybe we can join you for the Chanukah lighting?"

The shoemaker looked at the shoes and was a bit confused as to the urgency to have them fixed. His wife stepped forward and quickly brought them in from the cold wind outside.

They placed the wood in the fireplace and the house quickly began to warm up. The shoemaker's wife went to the kitchen and carefully removed the menorah that had been sitting alone on a high shelf in the cupboard. She lovingly began to dust off the menorah that had not been used since last year. While everyone was joyfully preparing for the kindling of the Chanukah menorah, the shoemaker quietly sat by the light of the fireplace and began fixing the milkman's shoe.

Both families then gathered as one to light the menorah.

The milkman's wife whispered to her children, "One candle lights another candle . . . and the light is not diminished . . . it grows even stronger."

Indeed it was a night of great happiness and warmth. Together both families chanted the blessings and lovingly lifted their voices in harmony singing the songs of Chanukah. The *latkes* tasted more delicious than ever. Not only the children, but everyone sat on the floor playing dreidel until the flames of the menorah were close to burning out.

The hour was late and the milkman's family said farewell and returned home. They carried their sleeping children in their arms and gently placed them under their blankets in their warm beds. The milkman and his wife then stood together by their window and looked across the way at the window of the shoemaker's home. They both gazed at the humble menorah that was still lit, spreading a great light.

✡ ✡ ✡

This heartwarming story reminds us of how beautiful it is to share our holiday with others.

When we make a special effort to assist those who may be struggling or those who may feel alienated we increase their joy - and ours as well.

Our mitzvah of lighting is incomplete as long as there are those in need of companionship and a warm embrace on these eight nights. The light of the candles burns brightest when we uplift others. Rabbi Shlomo Carlebach once said, "If you want to feel the real the joy of Shabbat and the Holidays - give it to someone else."

May we reach out during these eight days, and beyond, to all those in our lives; to our children, grandchildren, to our extended family and friends… and to those who may need a friend.

The Sages teach that the ideal place to light the menorah is in the doorway opposite the mezuza. What is the significance of this custom? The chassidic master, the Sfat Emet explains that just as the mezuza is always affixed to the house, we pray that the impact of the Chanukah lights stay with us year round (Sfat Emet Chanukah 5634).

Our courageous forefathers from long ago, the Chashmonaim, searched and found one last jug of pure oil. The chassidic master, the Sfat Emet, writes that this jug of pure oil symbolizes the *nekuda hatemuna*, the hidden spark, the hidden point of purity found in every Jew (Sfat Emet Chanukah 5632).

During this holiday of miracles may our inner spark be ignited and transformed into a great flame that we lovingly share with every brother and sister.

Chanukah Sameach!

BIOGRAPHICAL SKETCHES

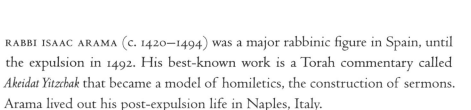

RABBI ISAAC ARAMA (c. 1420–1494) was a major rabbinic figure in Spain, until the expulsion in 1492. His best-known work is a Torah commentary called *Akeidat Yitzchak* that became a model of homiletics, the construction of sermons. Arama lived out his post-expulsion life in Naples, Italy.

RABBI SHLOMO ZALMAN AUERBACH (1910–1995) was one of the most prominent rabbinic figures of the twentieth century. A child prodigy, he grew up to become head of the Kol Torah Yeshiva in his native Jerusalem. His halachic decisions were influential worldwide.

RABBI AVRAHAM DOV OF AVRITCH (1765–1840) was a student of Rabbi Levi Yitzchak of Berdichev. After serving as a Rebbe in the Ukraine, at the age of sixty-five he made aliyah to Tzfat, in whose Old Cemetery he is buried. He is famous for his book on Chassidism, *Bat Ayin*. The synagogue where he served as the rabbi in Tzfat is still in use today and bears his name: the Avritcher Shul.

BAAL SHEM TOV, RABBI YISRAEL BEN ELIEZER (c. 1700–1760), brought a new spirit to downtrodden Jewry during difficult days of pogroms and economic hardship in Europe. The approach he initiated, Chassidism, emphasized an intense personal relationship with God no matter one's level of Torah scholarship.

RABBI LEVI YITZCHAK OF BERDITCHEV, THE BERDITCHEVER REBBE (c. 1740–1810), was a Chassidic Rebbe from the third generation of Chassidism who emphasized the importance of spiritual joy and enthusiastic prayer. He was known as an enthusiastic advocate, always finding a reason to judge a fellow Jew favorably.

RABBI SHALOM NOACH BEREZOVSKY, REBBE OF SLONIM (1911–2000), became the Slonimer Rebbe in 1981. He previously had founded the Slonimer Yeshiva in Jerusalem, from which the Chassidut was rebuilt after the devastation of the

Holocaust. His work the *Netivot Shalom* is widely known and studied today by Chassidim as well as non-Chassidim.

RABBI SHMUEL BORNSTEIN, REBBE OF SOCHATCHOV (1856–1926), is called the Shem Mishmuel after his major work of the same name. A grandson of the Kotzker Rebbe, he was a prominent rabbinical figure in Poland.

RABBI NACHMAN OF BRESLOV (1772–1811), the great-grandson of the Baal Shem Tov, was a Chassidic Rebbe whose complex theological teachings and popular allegorical Chassidic stories focus on the worship of God with intense spiritual joy. His main works include *Likutei Moharan, Sippurei Ma'asiyot* and *Sefer Tikkun Haklali*. Today's Breslov Chassidic movement includes descendants of the original followers of Rabbi Nachman as well as many Jews who have been inspired to Jewish observance by Rabbi Nachman's teachings.

RABBI NOSSON OF BRESLOV (1780–1844) was the foremost disciple of Rebbe Nachman of Breslov and the torchbearer of his Rebbe's teachings, committing them to memory and preserving them in written form for future generations. His major works *Likutei Halachot* and *Likutei Tefilot* are both based on the writings and teachings of his master, Rebbe Nachman. No successor to Rabbi Nachman was named upon his death, but Rabbi Nosson's work helped keep the Breslov Chassidut alive.

RABBI SHLOMO CARLEBACH (1926–1994) was a modern-day Chassidic Rebbe. With his music and teachings he spread a message of traditional Judaism and loving-kindness throughout the world by way of his guitar, voice, and overflowing loving heart. Many of his original musical compositions are used during synagogue services by congregations worldwide.

RABBI YOSEF CARO (1488–1575), also called the Beit Yosef for his work of the same name, is best known for his later compendium of Jewish law, the *Shulchan Aruch*. This code of law, first printed in 1565, would become broadly recognized as authoritative by world Jewry. Born in Toledo, Rabbi Caro was forced to flee Spain in 1492; he eventually made his way to Tzfat, where he lived most of his life.

RABBI ISRAEL MEIR OF RADIN, THE CHAFETZ CHAIM (1839–1933), was a beloved leader, ethicist, and halachist, recognized for his extremely righteous, humble, and pious conduct. In addition to his eponymous work on the laws of proper speech, he wrote the *Mishnah Berurah*, an important modern halachic work.

RABBI YOSEF SHALOM ELYASHIV (1910–2012) was known as the premier halachic authority during his lifetime. Born in Lithuania, he came to the Land of Israel as a boy and lived a quiet life of study in the Meah Shearim neighborhood of Jerusalem. He was a revered decisor of Jewish law, and when he died at the age of 102, half a million people poured into the streets of Jerusalem to accompany him to his final rest.

RABBI YECHIEL MICHEL EPSTEIN (1829–1908), the rabbi of Novardok, Lithuania, for over thirty years, is known as the Aruch Hashulchan for his halachic compendium of that name. A luminary in the Lithuanian Torah world, he was related by marriage to the Netziv of Volozhin.

RABBI ZVI PESACH FRANK (1873–1960), born in Kovno, Lithuania, came to the Land of Israel as a child and became a fixture in Jerusalem. He was the chief rabbi of Jerusalem and head of Jerusalem's rabbinical court. Rabbi Frank played a role in creating Israel's Chief Rabbinate and supported Rabbi Abraham Isaac Kook as the first holder of that office.

RABBI YEHUDAH LEIB ALTER OF GER, THE SFAT EMET (1847–1905), was a Polish Chassidic Rebbe from the Ger dynasty. His collected teachings on the Torah and festivals were published in his beloved work *Sfat Emet*, the name by which he is widely known.

RABBI SAMSON RAPHAEL HIRSCH (1808–1888) was a German rabbinical leader and creator of the *Torah-im-derech-eretz* (Torah together with the ways of the world) synthesis by which he successfully defended traditional Judaism. He revived Orthodox Jewish life in Germany in the nineteenth century and in particular the community of which he became rabbi, Frankfurt am Main.

AVRAHAM IBN EZRA (1089–1167) was a great Spanish rabbi, philosopher, poet, and astronomer who led a somewhat nomadic life after persecution drove him from Spain. His commentary on the Tanach remains widely popular. He also wrote beautiful *zemirot*, songs for the Sabbath, some of which are among the standards sung today.

RABBI ABRAHAM ISAAC HAKOHEN KOOK (1865–1935) was the first Ashkenazic chief rabbi in pre-state Israel. He devoted himself to rebuilding the Holy Land and teaching that the central mitzvah of Judaism is the return of the Jew to the Land of Israel. The national religious yeshiva he founded in Jerusalem, Mercaz HaRav, remains an important institution in Israeli society.

RABBI MORDECHAI LEINER, THE ISHBITZER REBBE (1801–1854), was a disciple of Rabbi Simcha Bunim of Peshischa and Rabbi Menachem Mendel of Kotzk. He founded the Ishbitz/Radzyn dynasty in 1839. The work *Mei Shiloach*, compiled by his grandson, details his strikingly original Chassidic teachings. Rabbi Shlomo Carlebach led the modern popularization of the Ishbitzer's thought.

RABBI MENACHEM MENDEL MORGENSTERN, THE KOTZKER REBBE (1787–1859), was a fiery Polish Chassidic Rebbe whose hallmark was radical (and sometimes brutal) honesty. One of his prominent disciples was Rabbi Yitzchak Meir Alter, the first Gerrer Rebbe (known as the Chidushei Harim), and the Chassidut of Ger is said to have its spiritual roots in the Kotzker's starkly truth-seeking path.

RABBI ARYEH LEVIN (1885–1969) was affectionately called the *tzaddik* or righteous one of Jerusalem for his extraordinary kindness to all, and especially to disadvantaged people. His particular devotion to Jewish prisoners was legendary, and Rabbi Kook officially named him Jewish Prison Chaplain during the years of the British Mandate.

RABBI AHARON LICHTENSTEIN (1933–2015), born in Paris, was raised in the United States, where he was an important student and eventually son-in-law to Rabbi Joseph B. Soloveitchik. A prominent centrist Orthodox rabbi, he was a leading

Rosh Yeshiva at Yeshiva University before moving to Israel and serving as head of Yeshivat Har Etzion as well as Yeshiva University's Gruss Kollel.

RABBI JUDAH LOEW, THE MAHARAL (c. 1525–1609), is most closely associated with the city of Prague, where he served as rabbi for a number of years. His supercommentary on Rashi, called *Gur Aryeh al haTorah*, is a classic of Judaic scholarship. He is also widely known as the reputed fashioner of the mystical golem, a legendary creature made from inanimate material and brought to life.

RABBI SIMCHA BUNIM OF PESHISCHA (1765–1827), a disciple of the Maggid of Kozhnitz, became a prominent leader in the Polish Chassidic world in his own right. He left no written works, but his influence can be inferred from the list of his students, who included the Kotzker Rebbe, the Vorker Rebbe, the Ishbitzer Rebbe, and the Chidushei Harim.

RAMBAM, RABBI MOSES BEN MAIMON OR MAIMONIDES (1135–1204), is one of the best-known rabbinical figures in history. Born in Cordoba, Spain, he fled to Egypt with his family to escape religious persecution. Like many Sephardic rabbis, he was a physician, but he is remembered for his prolific corpus of Judaic writings. He is perhaps best known for his halachic compendiums the *Mishneh Torah* and *Sefer Hamitzvot* and for his philosophical work *Guide for the Perplexed*.

RAMBAN, RABBI MOSHE BEN NACHMAN OR NACHMANIDES (1194–1270), was a prominent Sephardic scholar who, like Rambam before him, also practiced as a physician. His writings are marked by a tenacious respect for tradition. He wrote extensive commentary on the Talmud as well as Torah commentary and philosophical works. After being forced to defend Jewish belief in the Disputation of Barcelona, he was exiled from Spain and spent the end of his life in the Land of Israel.

RABBENU NISSIM, RAN (1320–1376), was a scholar and physician in Spain. He was recognized as a halachic authority in his lifetime. He wrote Talmudic commentary and among other works left a collection of sermons called *Derashot Haran*.

RASHI, RABBI SHLOMO YITZCHAKI (1040–1104), lived in medieval France and often used the French language in his scholarly writings. Rashi wrote startlingly prolific commentaries on the Torah text and Talmud. Rashi's work focuses on explaining the meaning of the words and hence is considered an indispensable aid to study of the canonical works of Jewish religious literature.

RABBI ISAAC JACOB REINES (1839–1915), born in Belarus and educated at the Volozhin Yeshiva in the Lithuanian tradition, founded the Mizrachi Religious Zionist movement. He worked tirelessly on behalf of Zionist causes but never himself merited to live in the Land of Israel.

RABBI YISRAEL BEN ZE'EV WOLF LIPKIN, YISRAEL SALANTER (1809–1883), born in Zagare, Lithuania, was an extremely learned scholar whose emphasis on scrupulous observance of laws of interpersonal behavior led him to found the *mussar* movement of religious self-improvement and self-mastery. His ethical system remains a pillar in today's religious world.

RABBI MENACHEM MENDEL SCHNEERSON, THE LUBAVITCHER REBBE (1902–1994), born in the Ukraine, worked tirelessly on behalf of European Jewry in Berlin and later Paris, where he tried to save Jews from the Holocaust until he and his wife escaped Europe and settled in the United States. In New York he succeeded his father-in-law as the fifth Lubavitcher Rebbe, a post he invested with an unusual degree of concern for world Jewry. His students and emissaries have impacted the Jewish community the world over.

RABBI MOSES SCHREIBER, THE CHATAM SOFER (1762–1839), author of a work by that name, was the communal rabbi in Pressburg, Germany. Vastly erudite both in Talmudic studies and various secular subjects, he nevertheless was uncompromising in upholding traditional methods of study and maintained a fierce loyalty to the letter of the law.

RABBI CHAIM LEIB SHMUELEVITZ (1902–1979), born in Kovno, Lithuania, taught in the Mir Yeshiva in Poland, serving as head of the yeshiva for five years when its members sought refuge from the Holocaust in Shanghai. After the yeshiva was able to relocate to the United States, he joined its branch in Jerusalem, where he stayed for the rest of his life, leaving his mark as a phenomenal and inspirational educator.

RABBI CHAIM SOLOVEITCHIK, REB CHAIM BRISKER (1853–1918), was born in Volozhin to his father Rabbi Yosef Dov Soloveitchik. He served as a rabbi in Belarus and was a brilliant and innovative teacher. His son Rabbi Yitzchak Zev Halevi Soloveitchik, who lived in Jerusalem, was also known as the Brisker Rav; his son Rabbi Moshe Soloveitchik and grandson Rabbi Joseph B. Soloveitchik each served in turn as head of Yeshiva University's rabbinical school in New York.

RABBI JOSEPH B. SOLOVEITCHIK (1903–1993) was the leader of the Modern Orthodox rabbinate in the United States and became the spiritual mentor to a generation of Orthodox Jews due to his mastery of *halachah*, his intellectual sophistication, and his interest in the philosophical and practical concerns of modern Jewry.

RABBI TZVI ELIMELECH SPIRA, REBBE OF DINOV (1783–1841), was a student of the Seer of Lublin. Known for his humility and great love for the Jewish people, he promoted the study of Kabbalah, Jewish mysticism. Rebbe Tzvi Elimelech was a prolific writer; the most familiar of his twenty-nine volumes of Torah teachings is the *Bnei Yissaschar.*

AVRAHAM TWERSKY OR REB AVREM'L, THE TRISKER MAGGID (1806–1889), was one of the eight sons of the Rebbe of Chernobyl, a prominent Chassidic dynasty. He was known for his ascetic practices and for the blessings and guidance he dispensed. His book *Magen Avraham*, published in his old age, is a collection of his words of Torah.

RABBI CHAIM OF VOLOZHIN (1749–1821) was the main student of Lithuania's greatest scholar, the Vilna Gaon. Reb Chaim founded the Volozhin Yeshiva and taught there using the method of the Vilna Gaon, which became the standard model for yeshiva learning. His book *Nefesh Hachaim* lays out his philosophy, which was fiercely opposed to the Chassidic approach.

RABBI MENACHEM MENDEL KALISH, THE VORKER REBBE (1819–1868), was the son of the famed Reb Yitzchak Vorker (1779–1848). Rebbe Menachem Mendel was a tremendous advocate of the spiritual power of silence. He felt that one should exercise silence among other people, not in solitude where the urge to gab is never tested. As a result of his extreme verbal restraint, very few of his teachings were passed on.

RABBI SHIMON BAR YOCHAI, RASHBI (C. 70 CE), was a tannaitic sage of the Mishnaic era who studied with the famed Rabbi Akiva. After Rabbi Akiva was put to a martyr's death by the Roman emperor Hadrian as part of a crackdown following the Bar Kochba revolt, Rabbi Shimon bar Yochai was forced to hide in a cave with his son for thirteen years to avoid arrest. During that time he is said to have written the *Zohar*, the principle Kabbalah text. Rabbi Shimon's yahrzeit is joyfully observed each spring on the holiday of Lag B'Omer at his tomb in Meron in the north of Israel.

RABBI SHLOMO YOSEF ZEVIN (1888–1978), born in Minsk, experienced persecution at the hands of Soviet Communists for teaching Torah. In 1935 he was able to make aliyah to the Land of Israel, where he became a prominent Religious Zionist. He wrote many works but is particularly known for the *Encyclopedia Talmudit*, which he founded.

ACKNOWLEDGMENTS

THE DAYS OF CHANUKAH ARE DESIGNATED AS A TIME *L'HODOT U'L'HALLEL*, "TO give thanks and praise."

It is my great pleasure to offer my personal thanks and praise to those who have helped bring this book to life.

First to the Holy One blessed be He, for all the blessing bestowed upon me and my family, *Hashem ori v'yishi... Hashem ma'oz chayai* (ה׳ אוֹרִי וְיִשְׁעִי... ה׳ מָעוֹז־חַיַּי), "Hashem is my light and my salvation, Hashem is the stronghold of my life" (Tehillim 27:1).

To my beloved parents Rabbi Harvey, *z"l*, and *tibadel l'chaim*, Judy Goldscheider, for their love and warmth. They instilled within me love for Torah and faith in God. My father and mother's devotion to Judaism and their dedication to serving Klal Yisrael made an indelible imprint on my own life. This book is a fruit of their labor. Thinking back on my childhood, I can still picture those cold New York Decembers and can still feel the warmth and joy of those nights of Chanukah. Gathering as a family at the windowsill for the menorah lighting, excitedly receiving gifts, and enjoying my mother's homemade sweet latkes will always remain etched in my mind and heart.

To my in-laws, Arthur and Judi Goldberg, I owe a special debt of gratitude. They were instrumental in providing me with the opportunity to devote time to the writing of this book. Their constant showering of love and support is remarkable. Our family feels blessed and cherishes the close relationship we share together. My mother-in-law Judi Goldberg also dedicated many hours reading and editing the material for this book. I thank you.

To my "editor in chief" in this work and in my life, my beloved *eishet chayil* Karen: words are not sufficient to express my thanks. This book is a partnership. I could not have written it without you. You devoted so much time assisting me every step of the way. To you I express my appreciation, gratitude, and admiration. May the words of Torah that we share with others through the teachings of this book bring light and blessing into our own home. Together may we merit the blessing:

וזכני לגדל בנים ובני בנים

חכמים ונבונים

אוהבי ה' יראי אלוקים אנשי אמת

זרע קודש בה' דבקים

(*Yehi Ratzon said over the Shabbat candles*)

This Chanukah book was written with the hope that many Jews will enjoy and be inspired by its content. However, this volume, at its heart, is a gift to my children. May they lovingly receive these Torah insights and inculcate them in their own lives. To Shalom Mordechai, Yonah Michael, Shira Ariella, Yakir Yisrael, Ora Yaffa, Tehila Moriya, Elisha Chanina *z"l*, Zvi Aryeh, Elisheva Bracha, Sara Rachel, and Eden Menucha: May these teachings find a place in your hearts and in your souls.

I dedicate this work in memory of our beloved son Elisha Chanina, *z"l*. Lishi brought endless light to our lives each day. *Ner Hashem nishmat adam* נֵר ה' נִשְׁמַת אָדָם, "The soul of a person is God's candle" (Proverbs 20:27). Lishi's candle continues to shine. The Chanukah flames instill within us the faith that the soul of the individual lives on, and that we will once again be reunited with our beautiful son, on the great day of redemption, which we pray will speedily come.

The reader will notice three major personalities quoted throughout this volume: Rabbi Abraham Isaac Kook (1865–1935), Rabbi Joseph B. Soloveitchik (1903–1993), and Rabbi Shlomo Carlebach (1925–1994). They played an extraordinary role in shaping Jewish life in contemporary times and have greatly influenced my own path as a Jew.

I express my profound thanks and gratitude to our dear friends David and Cindy Pitkoff.

Our tradition emphasizes the indispensability of close friendships: *Kenei lecha chaver*, "Acquire a friend for yourself" (*Pirkei Avot* 1:6). The Pitkoff family hold this most honored place in our lives as beloved *chaveirim*. They have been with us every step of the way, during our time together in New York and beyond. They remain our precious friends, although we now live many miles apart. David and Cindy together with their children Joshua, Danielle, and Andrew, are people of exceptional kindness, sensitivity, and idealism. They are admired role models to so many of us who learn from their leadership, *chesed*, and *ma'asim tovim*. The Pitkoffs have honored their beloved parents by so generously contributing to the publication of this volume. I am touched that the Pitkoff family has partnered with me in this special endeavor to share Torah teachings and reach Jews around the world. In the spirit of Chanukah, I pray that Bernard and Rita's light continues to shine for years and years to come. May God bless you and your entire family with continued good health and joy, and may you have great *nachas* from your children and grandchildren always.

Special thank you and gratitude to Rabbi Menachem Genack for welcoming this compendium of Chanukah teachings to his remarkable collection of OU Press publications. I am most honored and humbled to have his words of Torah serve as a beautiful preface which opens this book. My close relationship with the OU goes back many years. From my early involvement with NCSY to serving as a rabbi in OU member shuls, and today teaching at the OU Center in Israel. I feel blessed to partner with the OU by publishing a book in partnership with them with the goal of enhancing Torah knowledge and mitzvah observance across the Jewish world.

I sincerely thank Rabbi Simon Posner for overseeing every aspect of this publication and for his professionalism. I thank him for expertly coordinating the multifaceted process of publication with patience and perseverance.

I am also indebted to Rabbi Gad Buchbinder for his expert eye and skill in editing the text.

I have great appreciation for those who worked on this project.

First, I thank Aitana Perlmutter, an exceptionally creative and gifted artist and close friend. This is the second project that we have collaborated on, and I feel blessed to partner together to share the beauty of Judaism with our brothers and sisters. The original art pieces that adorn the cover and the eight sections of this volume not only enhance and bring vitality to this book but are a beautiful contribution to contemporary Jewish art. The rendition of nine menorahs that were uniquely created for this volume reveal the joy and celebration found in the festival of Chanukah. Her contribution to this book was carried out as a labor of love, or as our tradition terms it, *l'shem Shamayim*, as an act done "for the sake of heaven." To Aitana, may you continue to be blessed to inspire others with the beauty and light that shines through your creativity and art.

I feel most fortunate to have worked together with a close friend as my chief editor on this book. How often does one find a pulpit rabbi and his synagogue president remaining the closest of friends? Douglas Altabef served as president of Mount Kisco Hebrew Congregation during my tenure there as rabbi. We both made aliyah to Israel within a couple of years of one another. He and his wife Linda were remarkable role models of kindness and commitment in our community in New York and continue to be here in the Holy Land. Doug's devotion to this book is an extension of his vision and efforts to ensure that the wisdom of Judaism be promulgated among the Jewish people. His skillful editing, keen insight and advice, and tremendous talent have greatly enhanced each and every page of this book.

I am most grateful to my dear friend and *chavrusa* Mark Bilski for his friendship. His close reading, wisdom, and insightful comments have helped to enrich this volume.

Special thanks to our close family friend Joanne Dresner for reviewing and expertly editing the manuscript.

Thank you to Raphaël Freeman for typesetting the book. A very special thank-you to Natalie Friedemann-Weinberg for her amazing graphic design. It was a great pleasure to work with such an immensely talented and remarkably creative person. Thank you to Kezia Raffel Pride for her help in copyediting the text.

Acknowledgments to Rabbi Aryeh Pinchas Strickoff, who graciously granted permission to include his unique explanatory commentary of Maoz Tzur from his work *Inside Chanukah*. His book is a remarkable resource that I greatly benefited from in my preparation of this book.

And to my dear friend and trailblazing teacher and publisher of Breslov Chassidut, Rabbi Chaim Kramer, founder and head of the Breslov Research Institute, for permission to include in the lighting section a Chanukah prayer from Reb Nosson, taken from the book *The Fiftieth Gate*.

I would like to thank my dear friend Rav Simcha Hochbaum for allowing me to share, for the first time in writing, the remarkable story of his son Yedidya. Rav Simcha is one of the contemporary heroes of Israel. Making aliyah from New York to Chevron with his family, he inspires thousands each year in the holy city with his teachings and his unique spirituality.

SOURCES

Introduction

Based on story told by Rabbi Shlomo Carlebach, cited in *Time for My Soul: A Treasury of Jewish Stories for Our Holy Days,* by Annette Labovitz and Eugene Labovitz (Northvale, NJ: Jason Aaronson, 1996), xix–xx. Used by permission.

TRANSFORMING YOUR MENORAH LIGHTING

Rabbi Alexander Ziskind, *Yesod V'Shoresh Ha'avodah, sha'ar* 12, ch. 1; Rabbi Yair Chaim Bachrach (1639–1702), *Mekor Chaim, Hilchot Chanukah, Orach Chaim* 672:2; Rabbi Levi Yitzchak of Berditchev, *Kedushat Levi, Derushim L'Chanukah*; Rabbi Joseph B. Soloveitchik, *Days of Deliverance: Essays on Purim and Hanukkah,* ed. Eli D. Clark, Joe B. Wolowelsky, and Reuven Ziegler (Jersey City, NJ: Ktav, 2007), 131, 169. "Fulfilling the essence of the mitzvah of lighting the Chanukah menorah can be deduced from the Rambam, where he writes: 'On each of the eight nights, candles are lit in the evening...in order to publicize and *reveal* the miracle' (Laws of Chanukah 3:3). Based on this passage Rabbi Soloveitchik felt that the Rambam believed that the precept of lighting the Chanukah candles requires more than merely lighting the menorah. It consists in sharing its meaning and internalizing its message."

TURNING OUR CHILDREN INTO GREAT LIGHTS

Based on Aharon Ziegler, *Halakhic Positions of Rabbi Soloveitchik,* vol. 2 (Northvale, NJ: Jason Aaronson, 1998), 151–52. Used by permission.

CHANUKAH: A FRAMEWORK FOR OUR FUTURE

Based on Joseph Epstein, ed., *Shiurei HaRav: A Conspectus of the Public Lectures of Rabbi Joseph B. Soloveitchik* (Jersey City, NJ: Ktav, 1994).

THE MENORAH WILL BE LIT AGAIN: A PRAYER

Yechiel Spero, *Touched by Their Tears: A Kinnos Companion* (New York: ArtScroll Mesorah), 284. Used by permission.

Part 1: Lighting the Menorah

Preparing to Light

PRAYERS BEFORE LIGHTING

Mishnah Berurah 627:1:10, *Chayei Adam* 154:20, and *Magen Avraham* 672:5.
Reb Nosson's prayer from Yaacov Dovid Shulman, trans., *The Fiftieth Gate: Likutey Tefilot; Reb Noson's Prayers*, vol. 5 (Jerusalem: Breslov Research Institute, 2014). Used by permission.

The Menorah Lighting

THE PROCEDURE AND BLESSINGS FOR LIGHTING

Mishnah Berurah 676:4:8.

§ *Baruch*

Based on Rabbi Immanuel Bernstein, *Aggadah: Sages, Stories and Secrets* (Monsey, NY: Mosaica, 2015), 227.

§ *Baruch Atah*

Based on Rabbi Joseph B. Soloveitchik, *The Koren Mesorat HaRav Siddur: A Hebrew/English Prayer Book with Commentary* (Jerusalem: Koren, 2011), 1006.

§ *Ado-nai*

Based on Arnold Lustiger, ed., *Chumash Mesoras Harav Sefer Bereishis: Chumash with*

Commentary Based on the Teachings of Rabbi Joseph B. Soloveitchik (New York: OU Press and Ohr Publishing, 2013), 95.

ॐ *Melech ha'olam*

Based on Arnold Lustiger, ed., *Chumash Mesoras Harav Sefer Vayikra: Chumash with Commentary Based on the Teachings of Rabbi Joseph B. Soloveitchik* (Edison, NJ: Ohr Publishing, 2016), 211.

ॐ *l'hadlik ner shel Chanukah*

Sefer Kedushat Levi, Chanukah; Rabbi Shlomo Carlebach, "Chanukah Gems from Reb Shlomo," collected by Reb Sholom Brodt, *Torah Circle Blog*, August 15, 2010.

ॐ *She'asah nisim la'avoteinu*

Based on Ziegler, *Halakhic Positions of Rabbi Soloveitchik*, vol. 2, 45. Used by permission.

After the Kindling

HANEROT HALALU: *KODESH HEM*

Based on Rav Moshe Zvi Neria, *Moadei Haraya* (Kfar Darom: Machon HaTorah V'Haaretz, 2014), 163.

ॐ *Ela lirotam bilvad*

Shabbat 9a, HaRan, *b'dapei HaRif.*

MAOZ TZUR

Based on Rabbi Aryeh Pinchas Strickoff, *Inside Chanukah* (Spring Valley, NY: Feldheim, 2012). Used by permission.

"Concerning the Jews," *Harper's Magazine* 99, no. 592 (September 1899): 535.

🎵 *Maoz Tzur yeshuati*

Based on Nosson Sherman, Hirsch Goldwurm, Meir Zlotowitz, *Chanukah: Its History, Observance and Significance; A Presentation Based on Talmudic and Traditional Sources* (New York: ArtScroll Mesorah, 1986), 130.

🎵 *u'fartzu chomot migdalai*

Based on Rabbi Abraham Isaac Kook, *Ein Aya, Shabbat* 21a.

🎵 *u'minotar kankanim*

Based on Katz, *The Soul of Chanukah*, 34.

PSALMS

🎵 *Psalm 90:17: Vihi noam*

Based on Harris L. Selig, *Links to Eternity: Jewish Holidays and Festivals; Homiletical Essays* (New York: Bloch, 1957), 194.

🎵 *Psalm 67*

Commentary of Abudarham (fourteenth century).

🎵 *Psalm 30: Mizmor shir*

Rabbi Abraham Isaac Kook, *Siddur Olat Rayah.*

The Deeper Meaning

EIGHT MEDITATIONS WHEN LIGHTING FROM RABBI SHLOMO CARLEBACH

Based on Shlomo Katz, *The Soul of Chanukah: Teachings of Rabbi Shlomo Carlebach* (Monsey, NY: Mosaica, 2013), and oral transmissions.

WHY DO WE LIGHT WITH OLIVE OIL?

Based on Rav Matis Weinberg, *Patterns in Time*, vol. 8, *Chanukah* (Spring Valley, NY: Feldheim, 1988), 236.

Torah sources on olive oil based on Sholom Brodt, *Exodus: The Model of Personal Liberation* (Jerusalem: Yeshivat Simchat Shlomo, 2013), 93. Used by permission.

Story about olive trees heard from Doug Altabef from his personal experience.

Based on Rebbe Tzvi Elimelech of Dinov, *Bnei Yissaschar, Ma'amarei Chodesh Kislev–Tevet* 2:8, 2:9, 3:49.

A KABBALISTIC PERSPECTIVE ON THE THIRTY-SIX CANDLES OF CHANUKAH

Shlomo Carlebach teaching heard from R. Simcha Hochbaum, a *musmach* of R. Shlomo.

Thoughts on the word *tov* based on Strickoff, *Inside Chanukah*, 405. Used by permission.

Part 2: A Teaching for Each Candle

The First Night: Peace

FIRE OR LIGHT? THE GREAT CHANUKAH DEBATE

Based on Rav Shlomo Yosef Zevin, *Hamoadim B'Halacha* (Mevaseret Zion: Kol Mevaser).

Simon Jacobson, *Toward a Meaningful Life: The Wisdom of the Rebbe Menachem Mendel Schneerson* (New York: William Morrow, 2004), 133. Used by permission.

The Second Night: Love

BE A LAMPLIGHTER

Based on "Be a Lamplighter," chabad.org, http://www.chabad.org/therebbe /livingtorah/player_cdo/aid/2755532/jewish/Be-a-Lamplighter.htm. Mendel Kalmenson, *Seeds of Wisdom: Based on Personal Encounters with the Rebbe, Rabbi Menachem M. Schneerson, of Righteous Memory* (New York: Jewish Educational Media, 2013), 97.

TURNING SPEARS INTO PLOUGHSHARES

Simcha Raz, *The Sayings of Menahem Mendel of Kotsk*, trans. Edward Levin (Northvale, NJ: Jason Aronson, 1995), 48. Used by permission.

The Third Night: Family

SHALOM BAYIT: THE TEACHING OF A SINGLE CANDLE

Based on Rabbi Paysach J. Krohn, *Around the Maggid's Table: More Classic Stories and Parables from the Great Teachers of Israel* (New York: ArtScroll Mesorah, 1989). Used by permission.

BUILDING A HOLY HOME

Based on Lustiger, *Chumash Mesoras Harav Sefer Bereishis*, 247.

Baal Shem Tov story based on Rabbi Dr. Abraham J. Twerski, *Twerski on Chumash* (New York: ArtScroll Mesorah, 2003), 161. Used by permission.

THE TREASURE OF CHANUKAH

David Asher Brook, "The Story of Isaac Ben Yakil," http://www.chabad.org /blogs/blog_cdo/aid/2166670/jewish/The-Story-of-Isaac-Ben-Yakil.htm. Used by permission from Chabad.org.

Based on Reb Simcha Bunim of Peshischa, *Sefer Simchat Yisrael*.

Chafetz Chaim story based on Twerski, *Twerski on Chumash*, 248. Used by permission.

The Fourth Night: Heroism

THE GREAT HEROINES

Judith's story based on *Kol Bo, siman 44*.

Discussion of mothers and the struggle over circumcision based on Yaakov Medan, "They, Too, Were Part of the Miracle," Yeshivat Har Etzion Virtual Beit Midrash, http://billings.vbm-torah.org/en/they-too-were-part-miracle. Lubavitcher Rebbe anecdote based on Jacobson, *Toward a Meaningful Life*, 179. Used by permission.

WHO WAS THE TRUE HERO OF CHANUKAH?

Heard from Rabbi Dovid Gottlieb.

Kotzker Rebbe anecdote based on Raz, *The Sayings of Menahem Mendel of Kotsk*, 117. Used by permission.

NOAM'S ETERNAL FLAME

Based on Aharon Ha'Tell and Yaniv Ben Or, *Lighting the Way to Freedom: Treasured Hanukkah Menorahs of Early Israel* (Jerusalem: Devora, 2006), 34.

Rabbi Aharon Lichtenstein anecdote based on Rabbi Eliyahu Safran, "Holy Garments: Reflections on the IDF Uniform," *The Jewish Press*, July 3, 2013. Used by permission.

WHAT DOES THE WORD CHANUKAH MEAN?

Based on Rabbeinu Nissim, *Ran*; *Kitzur Shulchan Aruch, Laws of Chanukah*; Avraham Yisrael Rosenthal, *K'Motzei Shallal Rav* (Jerusalem: Machon Harav Frank, 2006), 43; Yaakov Yisrael Posen, *Adaraba* (Jerusalem: Irgun Shalom Al Yisrael, 2015), p. 745.

The Fifth Night: Miracles

QUALITY OVER QUANTITY

Based on Shlomo Zevin, *Hamoadim B'Halacha*, vol. 2, 57.

MAKING A MIRACLE GREAT

Based on David Holzer, *The Rav Thinking Aloud on the Parsha Sefer Shemos: Transcripts of Shiurim from Rabbi Joseph B. Soloveitchik* (New York: J Levine/Millennium, 2011), 22–23. Also based on Rabbi Joseph B. Soloveitchik, *Vision and Leadership: Reflections on Joseph and Moses*, ed. David Shatz, Joel B. Wolowelsky, and Reuven Ziegler (Jersey City, NJ: Ktav, 2012), 88.

YEDIDYA'S LIGHT

Told to me firsthand by Yedidya's father, Rabbi Simcha Hochbaum.

Lubavitcher Rebbe quote based on Jacobson, *Toward a Meaningful Life*, 21. Used by permission.

SEEING WITH CHANUKAH EYES

Based on Tzlotana Barbara Midlo, *Lamed Vav: A Collection of the Favorite Stories of Rabbi Shlomo Carlebach* (Lakewood, NJ: Israel Book Shop, 2004), 79; and also on Shlomo Carlebach, audio recording.

Kotzker Rebbe anecdote from Raz, *The Sayings of Menahem Mendel of Kotsk*, 5. Used by permission.

The Sixth Night: Hope

IN PRAISE OF THE ROOSTER

Based on Rabbi Shimon Schwab, *Rav Schwab on Iyov: The Teachings of Rabbi Shimon Schwab on the Book of Job* (New York: ArtScroll Mesorah, 2005), 406.

Lubavitcher Rebbe teaching based on Jacobson, *Toward a Meaningful Life*, 19. Used by permission.

CHANUKAH: A NEW BEGINNING

Based on Rabbi Shmuel Bornstein, *Shem Mishmuel on Chanukah*; Shlomo Carlebach recording, Lag B'Omer, May 22, 1989, at Young Israel of Santa Monica, available at https://www.youtube.com/watch?v=XhuCWboTV9U, 34:00.

WHY WE LIGHT AT NIGHT

Based on Rabbi Eliezer Melamed, *Peninei Halakha: Laws of Shabbat*, vol. 1 (Jerusalem: Maggid, 2016). Based on Rabbi Jonathan Sacks, http://www.rabbisacks.org/8-thoughts-8-nights/. Used by permission.

Parable heard from Rav Doni Marcus, Chanukah *shiur*.

THE ARCH OF TITUS: FROM SPLENDOR TO DEGRADATION AND BACK AGAIN

Based on Steven Fine, "Hanukkah at the Arch of Titus," YU News, December 15, 2015.

BEAUTIFYING OUR *TZEDAKAH*

Carlebach anecdote based on Yitta Halberstam, *Holy Brother: Inspiring Stories and Enchanted Tales about Rabbi Shlomo Carlebach* (Northvale, NJ: Jason Aronson, 2002), 87. Used by permission.

Sanzer Rav anecdote based on Twerski, *Twerski on Chumash*, 180. Used by permission.

THE CANDLE THAT WOULD NOT BE EXTINGUISHED

Based on Eliezer Shore, "The Penny Candle," as heard from R. Shlomo Carlebach, http://www.shemayisrael.co.il/publicat/bas_ayin/archives/kislev/story.htm. Used by permission.

Sfat Emet teaching from Rabbi Yehuda Leib Alter, *Sfat Emet on Chanukah*.

The Seventh Night: Unity

MENDING FENCES ON CHANUKAH

Based on Eliyahu Kitov, *The Book of Our Heritage*, vol. 1, Tishrey–Shevat (Spring Valley, NY: Feldheim, 1973), 282.

Rabbi Shlomo Zalman Auerbach anecdote based on Yaakov Yisrael Posen, *Adaraba*, 294.

JOSEPH AND CHANUKAH

Based on Zev Eleff, ed., *Mentor of Generations: Reflections on Rabbi Joseph B. Soloveitchik* (Jersey City, NJ: Ktav, 2008), 197.

Rabbi Kook anecdote based on James David Weiss, *Vintage Wein: The Collected Wit and Wisdom, the Choicest Anecdotes and Vignettes of Rabbi Berel Wein* (New York: Shaar, 1992), 231.

WHERE TO PLACE THE MENORAH

Based on Rambam, Laws of Chanukah 4:7; Avraham Yisrael Rosenthal, *K'motzei Shalal Rav*, 126.

Lubavitcher Rebbe anecdote based on oral transmission.

THE WINDOW SHUTTERS OF CHELM

Based on a story heard in a lecture by Yitzchak Breitowitz, Jerusalem 2016.

Karliner Rebbe anecdote based on Rabbi Shlomo Yosef Zevin, *A Treasury of Chassidic Tales on the Festivals* (New York: ArtScroll/Mesorah, 1982), 281.

GIVING THE GIFT OF LIGHT

Based on Jonathan Sacks, "8 Short Thoughts for 8 Chanukah Nights," November 25, 2013, http://www.rabbisacks.org/8-thoughts-8-nights/. Used by permission.

A tzaddik in peltz anecdote based on Shoshannah Brombacher, "A Tzaddik in a Fur Coat," http://www.chabad.org/library/article_cdo/aid/258534/jewish/A-Tzaddik-in-a-Fur-Coat.htm.

BLACK FIRE ON WHITE FIRE

Based on "Empty Spaces & Rav Mendele Vorker's Letter," *Dixie Yid*, March 15, 2010, http://dixieyid.blogspot.co.il/2010/03/empty-spaces-rav-yitzchak-vorkers.html. Used by permission.

Ruzhiner Rebbe anecdote based on Twerski, *Twerski on Chumash*, 240. Used by permission.

BELLS AND POMEGRANATES

Based on Bernstein, *Aggadah*, 89.

Rabbi Samson Raphael Hirsch teaching based on Samson Raphael Hirsch's *Commentary on the Torah*, Parshat Tetzave (Exodus 28:31).

The Eighth Night: Holiness

WHY EIGHT?

Maharal of Prague, *Ner Mitzvah*.

Rabbi Chaim of Volozhin anecdote based on Rabbi Chaim of Volozhin, *Nefesh Hachaim* 1:4.

Based on Rabbi Samson Raphael Hirsch, *Collected Writings of Rabbi Samson Raphael Hirsch* (Spring Valley, NY: Feldheim, 1996), 209.

A TREE OF LIGHT

Based on Shlomo Carlebach, "The Texas Mikveh," https://www.youtube.com/watch?v=ONC2P75dK5c.

THE PURITY OF CHANUKAH

Rabbi Levi Yitzchak of Berditchev anecdote based on Rabbi Dr. Abraham J. Twerski, *Ten Steps to Being Your Best: A Practical Handbook to Enhance Your Life in Every Way* (New York: ArtScroll Shaar Press, 2004), 84. Used by permission.

BEING A CHILD ON CHANUKAH

Based on Joseph Epstein, ed., *Shiurei HaRav*, 122.

Rabbi Aaron Soloveitchik anecdote based on Rabbi Paysach J. Krohn, *Reflections of the Maggid: Inspirational Stories from around the Globe and around the Corner* (New York: ArtScroll Mesorah, 2002), 247. Used by permission.

HOW LONG MUST THE LIGHT LAST?

Bat Ayin, Chanukah; *Kedushat Levi*, Chanukah, section 5.

Rebbe Avraham Dov of Avritch anecdote from Avraham Dov of Avritch, *"Drushim L'Chanukah."*

Lubavitcher Rebbe anecdote based on "The Diamond Collector," http://www.chabad.org/library/article_cdo/aid/1200/jewish/The-Diamond-Collector.htm.

A KISS FROM ABOVE

Shulchan Aruch, Orach Chaim 671:1; Rabbi Sholom Noach Berezovsky, *Netivot Shalom* (Jerusalem: Machon Emunah V'Daat, 2001), Ma'amarei Chanukah, 65.

Rabbi Chaim Shmuelevitz teaching based on Rosenthal, *K'Motzei Shallal Rav*, 64.

CELEBRATING THE UNIQUENESS OF EACH OF US

Based on R. Mordechai Yosef M'Ishbitz, *Mei Hashiloach*, Tractate *Shabbat*, s.v. *Hadlakah oseh mitzvah*.

Rabbi Jonathan Sacks anecdote from Rabbi Jonathan Sacks, "Transcript: Chief Rabbi Sacks Highlights Rebbe's Inspiring Charge," November 20, 2011, http://www.chabad.org/news/article_cdo/aid/1691120/jewish/Transcript-Chief-Rabbi-Sacks-Highlights-Rebbes-Inspiring-Charge.htm. Used by permission.

WINGS TO FLY

Based on Bernstein, *Aggadah*, 217; Scherman, et al., *Chanukah*, 106.

Part 3: Customs & Birkat Hamazon, Grace after Meals

Customs of Chanukah – Deeper Insights

PLACEMENT OF THE MENORAH

Yerachmiel Tilles, "Bend Down Low," in *Festivals of the Full Moon*, available at http://www.kabbalaonline.org/kabbalah/article_cdo/aid/379333/jewish/Bend-Down-Low.htm. Used by permission.

SUFGANIYOT, DONUTS, ON CHANUKAH: A THOUSAND-YEAR-OLD CUSTOM

Rav David Brofsky, "Shiur # 45: Sufganiot," The Israel Koschitzky Virtual Beit Midrash, Yeshivat Har Etzion, http://etzion.org.il/en/shiur-45-sufganiot. Used by permission.

❧ *Symbol of an Overt Miracle*

Rabbi Gabe Greenberg, "Mikeitz – Chanukah and the Dreidl," Congregation Beth Israel, December 21, 2014, http://bethisraelnola.com/mikeitz-chanukah-and-the-dreidl/. Used by permission.

❧ *A Lesson from the Dreidel*

Vizhnitzer Rebbe, *Damesek Eliezer*.

WHY WE GIVE CHANUKAH *GELT*

❧ *What Gift to Give*

Based on Rabbi Mendel Weinbach, "In Place of a Gift," Ohr Somayach, http://ohr.edu/4231.

Birkat Hamazon – Grace after Meals

INTRODUCTION

Shulchan Aruch: Rema, Ben Ish Chai: Parshat Vayeshev 28, *Chazon Ovadia*, 18. Maharshal, *She'elot U'teshuvot Maharshal* 65.
The *Yam Shel Shlomo* 7:30 writes that the Rambam (Laws of Chanukah 3:3) holds that the meals of Chanukah are a mitzvah and not voluntary.

A STORY

Based on Yitzhak Buxbaum, *The Light and Fire of the Baal Shem Tov* (New York: Bloomsbury Academic, 2006).

SHIR HAMA'ALOT

§ *Hazorim b'dimah b'rinah yiktzoru*
Rabbi Samson Raphael Hirsch.

SECOND PARAGRAPH OF BIRKAT HAMAZON

§ *Nodeh Lecha…*
Based on Rabbi Yitzchak Hutner, *Pachad Yitzchak*, Chanukah, as interpreted and adapted by Rabbi Pinchas Stolper, *Chanukah in a New Light: Grandeur, Heroism and Depth* (Lakewood, NJ: Israel Book Shop, 2005), 28.

AL HANISIM

§ *ke'she'amdah*
Based on Rabbi Aaron Rakeffet-Rothkoff, *The Rav: The World of Rabbi Joseph B. Soloveitchik*, vol. 2 (Jersey City, NJ: Ktav, 1999), 154.

§ *v'al hamilchamot*
Based on *Likutei Hamahariach*, vol. 3, "Seder Dinei U'Minhagei Chanukah," cited in Strickoff, *Inside Chanukah*, 118.

§ *l'hashkicham mi'Toratecha*
Dr. Dodi Fishman Tobin, "Al Hanisim," Matan Online, https://www.matan .org.il/eng/show.asp?id=71056. Used by permission.

§ *u'l'ha'aviram me'chukei retzonecha*
Bnei Yissaschar, Ma'amerei Chodesh Kislev–Tevet 4:61.

§ *gibborim b'yad chalashim*

Kedushat Levi, Derushim L'Chanukah

❧ *u'tme'im...u'rsha'im...v'zedim*

Based on Soloveitchik, *Days of Deliverance*, ed. Clark et al.

❧ *u'tme'im b'yad tehorim*

Based on Soloveitchik, *Days of Deliverance*, ed. Clark et al., 154.

❧ *V'achar ken ba'u vanecha...v'kavu...*

Based on Rabbi Yitzchak Hutner, *Pachad Yitzchok*, Chanukah, as interpreted and adapted by Stolper, *Chanukah in a New Light*, 178.

❧ *yemei Chanukah eilu l'hodot u'l'hallel*

Tobin, "Al Hanisim," Matan Online, https://www.matan.org.il/eng/show.asp?id=71056. Used by permission.

In memory of our beloved son Elisha Chanina Goldscheider, *z"l*

אלישע חנינא ז״ל בן הרב אהרן אברהם וחנה מינדל

Lishi brought endless light to our lives each day. *Ner Hashem nishmat adam* נֵר יְהֹוָה, נִשְׁמַת אָדָם, "The soul of a person is God's candle" (Proverbs 20:27).

Lishi's candle continues to shine. The Chanukah flames instill within us the faith that the soul of the individual lives on, and that we will once again be reunited with our beautiful son, on the great day of redemption, that we pray will speedily come.

I would like to dedicate my work in this project to my mother, Esther Malka Meyerfeld, *z"l*

The wisdom, strength, and beauty of Judaism as illuminated in this book encompass the very essence of who she was and what she held dear and near to her heart.

Aitana Perlmutter

Chanukah is the Festival of Lights.
We dedicate the "blessings" section of this book
to our children and grandchildren
who are the lights of our lives.

Judi and Arthur Goldberg

8 NIGHTS

Dedicated to the Lights in My Life

DAY ONE: In memory of my beloved husband
Rabbi Harvey Goldscheider, *z"l*

DAY TWO: In memory of my beloved parents
Max and Evelyn Brickner, *z"l*

DAY THREE: In memory of my beloved in-laws
Albert and Minnie Goldscheider, *z"l*

DAY FOUR: In honor of my children and grandchildren
Elana Goldscheider and Kenny Fisher,
Avital, Yakira, and Zvi

DAY FIVE: In honor of my children and grandchildren
Karen and Aaron Goldscheider, Shalom, Yonah, Shira,
Yakir, Ora, Tehila, Elisha *z"l*, Zvi, Elisheva, Sara, and Eden

DAY SIX: In honor of my children and grandchildren
Amy and Jeremy Goldscheider, Arielle and Ezra

DAY SEVEN: In honor of my children, grandchildren, and great-grandchild
Lori and Hillel Goldscheider, Atara, Aliza, Shlomo, and Yaffa
Meira and Yitzi Smith and Zvi Aryeh

DAY EIGHT: In memory of my precious grandson
Elisha Chanina Goldscheider, *z"l*

Judy Goldscheider